Rationalities in History

In *Rationalities in History* the distinguished historian David d'Avray writes a new comparative history in the spirit of Max Weber. D'Avray provides a strikingly original reassessment of seminal Weberian ideas, applying a theory of social theory to the comparative history of religion and the philosophy of law. Integrating theories of rational choice, anthropological reflections on relativism, and recent philosophy of rationality with Weber's conceptual framework, d'Avray seeks to disengage the idea of 'rationalisation' from its enduring association with Western 'Modernity'. To demonstrate the ways in which concepts of rationality can be utilised by historians, d'Avray takes the examples of Buddhism, Imperial China and early-modern Catholicism – in the latter case building upon hitherto unpublished archival research. This ambitious synthesis of social theory and comparative history will engage both social scientists and historians from advanced undergraduate level upwards, stimulating interdisciplinary discourse, and making a significant contribution to the methodology of history. D'Avray explores the potential of this new Weberian analysis further in his companion volume, *Medieval Religious Rationalities*.

D. L. D'AVRAY is Professor of History at University College London. A fellow of the British Academy since 2005, d'Avray has published widely on his research interests in medieval history.

Rationalities in History

A Weberian Essay in Comparison

D. L. d'Avray

CAMBRIDGE
UNIVERSITY PRESS

CAMBRIDGE UNIVERSITY PRESS
Cambridge, New York, Melbourne, Madrid, Cape Town, Singapore,
São Paulo, Delhi, Dubai, Tokyo, Mexico City

Cambridge University Press
The Edinburgh Building, Cambridge CB2 8RU, UK

Published in the United States of America by Cambridge University Press,
New York

www.cambridge.org
Information on this title: www.cambridge.org/9780521128087

First published 2010

Printed in the United Kingdom at the University Press, Cambridge

A catalogue record for this publication is available from the British Library

Library of Congress Cataloguing in Publication data
D'Avray, D. L.
Rationalities in history : a Weberian essay in comparison / D. L. d'Avray.
    p.   cm.
Includes bibliographical references and index.
ISBN 978-0-521-19920-9 (hbk.) – ISBN 978-0-521-12808-7 (pbk.)
1. Religions – Philosophy.   2. Law – Philosophy.   3. Religions – History.
4. Weber, Max, 1864–1920 – Political and social views.   5. Weber, Max,
1864–1920 – Influence.   6. Rationalism – Philosophy.   7. Rational choice
theory.   8. Relativity.   9. Values.   10. Modernism (Aesthetics)   I. Title.
BL51.D367   2010
302′.1309 – dc22   2010015494

ISBN 978-0-521-19920-9 Hardback
ISBN 978-0-521-12808-7 Paperback

To Julia

Contents

Preface and acknowledgements

A series of courses at UCL lie behind this book: a course consisting mostly of social theory which kind colleagues allowed me to teach to MA students in the mid-nineties, during which I became convinced by Max Weber's approach, another on 'Weber for historians', and above all the 'History and Sociology of Rationality', for undergraduates. The capacity of the latter to understand and criticise constructively suggests that a book that came out of that course could be comprehensible even to students and scholars normally allergic to social theory. More theoretically inclined colleagues may actually find the book harder, if they try to force it into familiar schemata. The best way to read *Rationalities in History* would in fact be to approach it with a clever undergraduate's open-mindedness.

For anyone who ends up in sympathy with the approach, a natural sequel is the sister volume, *Medieval Religious Rationalities*, in which the sociology of rationality is applied in a more concentrated form to a particular field. The two books are closely linked. The present volume outlines the general social forms explored for a specific period in *Medieval Religious Rationalities*. Astute readers will observe that the books have parallel structures.

The present, more general, volume is even more indebted than usual to the kindness of colleagues because it ranges so far from the author's research base. The following list surely omits some of the many who have helped. I must thank Martin Daunton and John North for trusting me to teach MA Modern History students. A British Academy Research Readership gave me time to work my way into new fields while continuing work in my old areas of expertise. Ken Binmore coached me in Rational Choice Theory. John Bell, Julian Hoppit, Charles Stewart and Rebecca Spang gave me bibliographical leads. Caroline Humfress read and commented on passages about Roman law, and argued with me, as did Werner Menski, Lynn Welchman, Andrew Lewis, Effa Okupa, Sami Zubaida and Yossi Rapaport, through meetings of the Bloomsbury Sacred Law Group. The archival work on the body that had the task of implementing the Council of Trent was assisted by Benedetta Albani and Marc Smith. Diarmaid McCullough read a section on the Protestant Reformation. Richard Gombrich gave advice on Buddhist monasticism. The Alexander von Humboldt Stiftung funded crucial research visits to Munich through its programme for former fellows. Richard Kieckhefer, Bonnie Blackburn and Julia Walworth helped with the whole project. The students on the 'History and Sociology of Rationality Course' made the book what it is: I wish I could list the many individuals who gave me ideas. John Sabapathy taught some of them with me and read the whole book, to its great profit. The publishers' anonymous readers were nearly always right. The staff of Cambridge University Press were more than helpful throughout.

Introduction

Scope of the book

The aim of the present work is to develop a concept of value rationality that helps explain why people hold on doggedly to their convictions; to balance this with observations on how values nonetheless do change; to bring out the interdependence of instrumental and value rationality; to discredit special association of formal rationality with 'modernity'; and to show how value-driven instrumental reasoning draws lines between formal and substantive legal rationality. These concepts of rationality represent ways of thinking which are virtually never found in a 'pure' form in history but which one may distinguish analytically, not for the sake of classification as an end in itself, but to explain their mutual relations.

The book is aimed at both social scientists and historians, from intellectually ambitious undergraduates upwards. Historians may wonder if they need so much social theory. Those historians who persevere into the second third of the book should find that the theory pulls its empirical weight; and in some parts of the last third of the book the concepts are put to work on unpublished and unstudied documents generated by the institution established to implement the Council of Trent. Gluttons for punishment with an appetite for more concentrated applications of the concepts may turn to the sister volume on the rationalities of medieval religion.[1] The medieval volume should be seen in the comparative perspective that the present book tries to provide.

Here the starting point will be a brief explanation of the kind of Weberian sociology or comparative history which will serve as a method. The form of Weberian thought permeating the current investigations will be distinguished from others, especially from the 'developmental' reading of Weber which concentrates on the origins of 'modernity'. Along the way, working definitions of rationality and irrationality[2] are sketched out. After

---

[1] d'Avray, *Medieval Religious Rationalities*.
[2] For a fuller though still inadequate treatment of irrationality, or rather 'diminished rationality', see *ibid.*, ch. 1(a).

this introduction to the key concepts, the approach adopted is situated within the spectrum of theories about rationality, starting with Rational Choice Theory or 'RCT', hugely influential in the social sciences though hardly at all on historians, who ought to substitute informed reservations for blissful ignorance. This section may be useful in a subsidiary way as a rapid 'Teach Yourself RCT'. But RCT is important as a limiting case: it concentrates almost exclusively on instrumental rationality and conceals value rationality in a box marked 'preferences'. The rest of the book shows how instrumental rationality is transformed by being filtered through value systems. RCT and some other theories of universal rationality are then contrasted with the other end of the spectrum, the theories of some anthropologists and philosophers that there is no universal human rationality at all.

After surveying the theoretical fields the argument proper begins. The symbiosis of instrumental and value rationality is the key component of it. Instrumental reasoning is a human universal, but this is not obvious to careful students of societies distant in time or culturally because it tends to take its first principles from value rationalities, which are exceedingly diverse. These value rationalities are the plural sort that anthropologists call 'cultures', though subcultures and individuals have them too. Their ability to shrug off intellectual objections is remarkable, and often mistaken for pig-headed resistance to the truth or plain stupidity. Such immunity to empirical falsification transcends secular–religious[3] and the dubious 'primitive'–'modern' divides. There are at least two (complementary) explanations. Firstly, value rationalities consist of many convictions each of which is antecedently probable, granted the rest. Refutation of any one conviction has to surmount this high probability bar; yet to attack all of them simultaneously presents practical difficulties, running counter to the normal method of focusing on one point of dispute at a time. Secondly, value systems are cemented by experience or simulacra thereof. This makes them more tenacious than purely abstract and verbal convictions. Still they do sometimes change, and the book examines the 'dynamics' of value systems: the factors explaining their advances and retreats. In this ebb and flow, value and instrumental rationality constantly interact, as they do with formal and substantive rationality. Formal rationality (e.g., in the USA, 'evidence illegally obtained is inadmissible in court') and substantive rationality (e.g., also in the USA,

---

[3] As starkly argued by Gray, *Black Mass*. Cf. Cohen's 'Paradoxes of Conviction', in *If You're an Egalitarian*, 7; note also 16–18, his thought-provoking extension of the argument to convictions neither religious nor political, such as the philosophical distinction between 'analytical' and 'synthetic' propositions.

Michigan judges refusing to give a 20-year sentence for selling a reefer, or an English jury acquitting Clive Ponting) are then drawn into the argument. This pair of concepts is sometimes lined up with instrumental and value rationality respectively, so as to equate substantive reasoning with value rationality and formal rationality with instrumentality. Any such alignment is a source of confusion: e.g. the substantive reasons for cutting through formal rules can be purely instrumental (political, for example: cash for honours). The instrumental–value and formal–substantive distinctions are most usefully treated as cross-cutting. The most helpful ideal-type is that values guide instrumental decisions about when to do things by the book, and when to suspend the formal rules. The archive of the 'Congregation of the Council' (of Trent) is mined for material illustrating this process, the reasoning behind the dissolution of marriages unconsummated for reasons other than impotence being very apposite. These are the main theses of the book, highly compressed.

This is an 'essay' rather than a survey. The number of publications dealing with rationality in one way or another is extraordinary.[4] People interested in rationality come to the topic from a variety of different directions and with quite different quiverfuls of bibliographical expertise. Any claim to have surveyed all the literature, even in a decade of research, would be spurious and I apologise in advance to all the scholars whose favourite book or article I have failed to cite. On the other hand, the essay tries to make connections between different sectors of modern academic 'rationality' research which seem hardly to communicate with each other. Its framework is designed to bring together research from different disciplines; if it succeeds, the credit should go to some seminal ideas of Max Weber.

The essay is 'Weberian' in that his ideal-types of rationality were the starting point, but some disclaimers must be made from the start. The book is not an explication of Weber's texts. In particular, the key concept of 'value rationality' is defined in a way which might or might not have met his approval. Weber discusses 'values' (*Werte*) in two different kinds

---

[4] A search on 17 March 2006 in JSTOR, the electronic database containing many English-language academic journals, yielded 58,147 hits for 'rationality'. A search on the same date in the British Library online catalogue flushed out 859 titles with 'rationality' (in the nature of the catalogue these must be predominantly whole monographs). In consequence, almost anyone interested in rationality will find that I have neglected a publication that they consider fundamental. By way of introductions: Wilson, *Rationality* and Hollis and Lukes, *Rationality and Relativism* are major collections of essays on the side of the spectrum nearer to cultural relativism; Tambiah, *Magic, Science, Religion, and the Scope of Rationality*, Chapter 6, gives an account of the rationality debate. Coleman, *Foundations of Social Theory*, is a sociologist's *summa* of rationality theory situated on the rational choice, universal reason, end of the spectrum.

of contexts: (i) as a rational force in history,[5] and (ii) in connection with scholarly method and the possibility of 'value freedom',[6] but in neither context does he spell out very explicitly what he means by the word. I go beyond him in what I think is his spirit, but if I am wrong in tracing my thoughts back to a Weberian source, all that follows is that I am more independent than I think I am. The book's core arguments would be unaffected. Similarly the discussion of 'formal' and 'substantive' (or 'material') rationality draws proximately on a later clearer study, in a Weberian tradition though not consciously so, it would seem.[7]

Again, Weber's ideal-types are applied here to fresh historical material. His ideal-types are clear-cut concepts and causal schemata designed to facilitate investigation of the infinite complexity of the past;[8] one could think of them as a questionnaire, one to which simple 'yes/no' answers should never be expected. Precisely formulated concepts are needed for these questions because the meanings and concepts at work in history (History as lived, the History historians study as opposed to their own writings) are often confused, imprecise, inconsistent and socially constructed[9] in different ways – so that we cannot restrict ourselves to 'the concepts of the time' when formulating research questions, though the research questions, concepts and explanatory schemata will have been formulated to fit and make sense of the 'concepts of the time'. Weber tried to form clear, custom-built scholarly concepts to get a grip on the messy, tangled concepts at work in social life. His ideal-types were like a vast set of made-to-measure suits: the wide range increased the chance of a good fit to the individual case but even so he knew that alterations

[5] See below p. 61 at n. 84.
[6] See d'Avray, *Medieval Religious Rationalities*, index, *s.v.* 'value-freedom'.
[7] Atiyah and Summers, *Form and Substance in Anglo-American Law*.
[8] 'The ideal-type is a mental construct, which is not to be identified with historical reality, let alone with the "essence" of reality and whose purpose is still less to serve as a framework to which reality should be orientated as to an ideal, but whose meaning is that of a purely theoretical limiting case against which reality is measured, or with which it is compared, to clarify certain important components of its empirical content.' (Passage beginning 'ist ein Gedankenbild' and ending 'mit dem sie verglichen wird' in Weber, 'Die "Objektifität sozialwissenschaftlicher und sozialpolitischer Erkenntnis', in *Gesammelte Aufsätze zur Wissenschaftslehre*, 194.) The reference to the 'essence' of reality may be an allusion to Hegelianism. Some other phrases could be read differently but I interpret in the light of Weber's thought generally. Cf. the passage beginning 'Nichts aber ist allerdings gefährlicher' and ending 'oder daß man sie als ein Prokrustesbett benutzt' (*ibid.*, 195).
[9] For an example of an intelligent 'social constructionist' approach to religion see Beckford, *Social Theory and Religion*, e.g. 100–1 on 'pluralism': a muddy concept which needs to be analysed in terms of the much clearer concepts he formulates. An example (not from Beckford): 'continents' can be called social constructs because they are a living force as concepts without corresponding to anything that can be defined exactly by geologists, which does not mean that 'continents' are 'just discourse' or have no relation to reality.

would normally be required. These ideal-types or questions were distilled in a pragmatic way from his own vast knowledge of world history and were intended to be applied back to history to increase empirical understanding – a helical process rather than a circular one.

Varieties of comparative history

Comparative history in a specifically Weberian sense is the empirical work to which these ideal-types are set here. In comparative history[10] there are often only two comparanda, often social systems contemporary with one another, say religious life in England and Italy in the same century;[11] sometimes of a specific and precisely delimited phenomenon, such as funeral preaching in two different periods,[12] and sometimes of two larger constructs, such as medieval and Buddhist monasticism.[13] This two-term type of comparison works in various ways but one of the most effective is the simplest: each side of the comparison generates questions about the other, and draws attention to significant absences in the other that might otherwise have gone unnoticed. The historian or social scientist may then go on to suggest explanations for the differences, which of course presuppose a good deal of underlying similarity. A more ambitious kind of comparative history may take a larger number of regions from the same period, as with Chris Wickham's study of the early medieval West.[14] Weber's most distinctive style of comparative history is more ambitious still, however: his opus magnum, *Wirtschaft und Gesellschaft*, is in effect a world history on analytical principles.

Max Weber and analytical world history

Analytical history is taken for granted within the framework of individual periods; it became so dominant that in the 1970s narrative history could be presented as a justified revisionist reaction against a dominant trend.[15] World history is a different matter; on this scale an overall analytical structure has seldom been chosen. The overarching principle of organisation remains narrative with allowance for regional differences. Thus in the remarkable volume by John Roberts chronology and geography, time and place, are interwoven to tell a coherent story from pre-history to

[10] For a thoughtful recent discussion, see Wickham, *Problems in Doing Comparative History*; for the practice of it on a massive scale, his *Framing the Middle Ages*.
[11] Brentano, *Two Churches*.
[12] e.g. d'Avray, 'Comparative History of Memorial Preaching'.
[13] Friedrich-Silber, *Virtuosity, Charisma, and Social Order*.
[14] Wickham, *Framing*.   [15] Stone, 'The Revival of Narrative'.

the present.[16] Or again, to quote the 'manifesto' article of the recently founded *Journal of Global History*, 'the needs of a globalizing world' are leading to

> a reordering of classical and established historiographies from all cultures to make space for histories that are attempting to disengage from national, regional, ethnic and religious traditions. Such histories would become involved with the construction of meta-narratives that might, at one and the same time, deepen our understanding of diversities and scale up our consciousness of a human condition that has for millennia included global influences, and intermingled with local elements in all its essential dimensions.[17]

This is a crucially important emphasis; and of course a central meta-narrative is the story of how the West subsequently came to dominate the rest.

Meta-narrative can nonetheless be complemented by meta-analysis. In the latter world history is treated thematically rather than chronologically – just as historians are used to doing within particular periods, but on a larger scale. To the objection that this is impossibly ambitious, the answer is that, if so, global history is presumably impossible also in a meta-narrative form. Either the canvas is too large or it is not. If it is not, a grand narrative is not the only thing one can paint on it.

Many people think of Weber as presenting a grand narrative of the rise to domination of Western rationality, but this is to miss two features of his oeuvre. First, he clearly came to find other civilisations interesting and important in their own right. Probably his work on China and India was originally inspired by a desire to explain why industrial capitalism developed in the West only, but his investigations clearly took on a life of their own. Secondly, the mature form in which he presented his results was not narrative but analytical. His opus magnum, *Wirtschaft und Gesellschaft*, is structured not by chronology and periodisation, but by themes or topics.

Weber's *Wirtschaft und Gesellschaft* must stand almost alone as an example of analytical world history. His original intention was probably more modest: to provide ideal-types for historians working on more specific periods.[18] Possibly that remained his formal remit in his own mind. It

---

16 Roberts, *The New Penguin History of the World*.
17 O'Brien, 'Historiographical Traditions and Modern Imperatives', 38.
18 'We have already in several places taken it for granted as self-evident that sociology constructs concepts representing the typical, and tries to find general rules for how things happen. This is in contrast with history, which tries to analyse causally and account for individual actions, structures and personalities of cultural significance. The material, in the form of representative cases, for sociological conceptualisation is to a substantial extent, if not exclusively, borrowed from the realities of action that are relevant from the point of view of history too. Furthermore sociology forms its concepts and attempts

seems unlikely. The answer depends on reconstructions of the genesis of the book,[19] which was compiled after his death in its final form thanks to his wife Marianne Weber.[20] The editors of the modern critical edition of Weber's works deny the unity of *Wirtschaft und Gesellschaft* and have broken it up into sub-volumes (not all of which have appeared).[21] Their judgement has not gone unchallenged,[22] and even if it they were right, one could still regard the final product as a sort of collaboration between Weber and his remarkable wife, who understood his key ideas with great penetration, as well as anyone before or since,[23] and (I would argue) much better than the senior editor of the critical edition, who was led astray by his assumption that one could read Weber's political views into his later writings.[24] So let us regard the final version as a unity, whether the author was Max Weber or Max with Marianne.

It does indeed begin with very abstract ideal-types. Then the rest of Part I works through Economic Life, Authority and Power (= *Herrschaft*) and 'Status Groups and Classes'. Already the degree of specificity is greater. In Part II, however, the concreteness and specificity is so great that, whether or not we call it Sociology (and there is no reason why we should not) it is History too: just as much as (say) John Roberts's *History of the World* is history, though with a quite different structure, narrative where Weber's is analytical. The structure of this second part is not too different from that of Part I. The principal analytical categories[25] start once again with the Economy, Communities and Organisations in relation to the Economy, Ethnicity and Nationalism, Religious Communities, Law, Political Communities and Power in its various forms, and the City. The section on the City is typical of the general approach he surveys the world history of towns, and then points out what was distinctive about the history of the Western city: its relative cohesiveness. (So here his original preoccupation with the distinctiveness of the West admittedly still comes through very clearly.) Or again, to take an example

to establish its rules above all also in the light of the question of whether doing so can assist with the task of accounting in terms of historical causation for culturally significant phenomena' (*Wirtschaft und Gesellschaft*, vol. 1, p. 9, passage beginning 'Die Soziologie bildet' and ending 'einen Dienst leisten kann'.
[19] Cf. Whimster, *Understanding Max Weber*, 137–47, 247–8.   [20] *Ibid.*, 140.   [21] *Ibid.*
[22] *Ibid.*, on the criticism of the *Gesamtaufgabe* plan by Hiroshi Orihara.
[23] I regard the analyses of his thought in her biography of him (in other respects rather stilted) as outstandingly perceptive, and perhaps unsurpassed as a short summary: see Marianne Weber, *Max Weber: Ein Lebensbild* (Tübingen, 1984), ch. 10, 'Die neue Phase der Produktion', and ch. 20, 'Der Lehrer und Denker', 689–94.
[24] See Mommsen, *Max Weber and German Politics*.
[25] My comments can be checked against the 'Inhaltsübersicht' at the start of *Wirtschaft und Gesellschaft*, though I do not follow the chapter headings slavishly.

from below the chapter level: in some remarkable pages on sacred law[26] he works through Hindu law, Islamic law, Sunni and Shi-ite law, Jewish law, and Christian canon law, bringing out common and individuating features. This is Weberian comparative history, and also his sociology, at its virtuoso best.[27] The underlying question seems to be: how unique is x or y (say Hindu law or canon law) in world history? The answer is equally interesting whether or not it brings out a general pattern or a historical specificity. The very grouping of certain systems under the category of sacred law implies a common pattern, ultimately deriving from the divine underpinnings deposited in sacred texts of all the laws he collects in this section (except for Chinese classical law, to which he gives only a few lines at that point). On the other hand, he brings out the legal formality of Catholic canon law as a feature marking it off from the other systems discussed in the section.

Limitations and remit of the present work

Weber's (or the Webers') sociological comparative history is a massive *Summa*. The present work imitates the method but not the genre. It is only an essay and it concentrates on just one set of Weberian questions, though they are central in his thought. It takes as its starting point his brief, crucial and rather neglected comments on the interdependence or symbiosis (my word) of values and instrumental rationality,[28] then extends this approach to the relation of both to formal and substantive rationality, and to the mutual relation between these last two ideal-types of rationality. Thus four key concepts will dominate the book: instrumental, value, formal and substantive rationality. They do not exhaust the conceptual field of rationality but this study aims to open the subject out – empirically for social scientists, conceptually for historians – and not to wrap it up.

Each of the four ideal-types has a distinct analytical role. As will be argued below, conceptual confusion must arise from any equation of substantive rationality with values, or of formal and instrumental rationality. To anticipate, without escaping the risk of over-compression: a recurrent pattern is for value rationality to shape instrumental technique,

[26] *Wirtschaft und Gesellschaft*, 472–82.
[27] Not a universal consensus, as I know from combative discussion in the Bloomsbury Sacred Law Group that I run with colleagues from University College London, School of Oriental and African Studies, Birkbeck College and Queen Mary, University of London. This is a good place to thank Werner Menski, Sami Subaida, Yossi Rapaport, Ido Shahar, Lynn Welchman, Caroline Humfress and Andrew Lewis.
[28] *Wirtschaft und Gesellschaft*, 13: discussed in detail below.

which in turn, among other things, reinforces the values through rituals, mental imagery, mass meetings, processions, education, etc. Formal and substantive rationalities are also in a symbiotic relationship, the nature of which tends to be shaped by instrumental calculation within value parameters.

These ideal-types are used to generate questions for comparative history. The patterns that emerge are for the most part quite general features in the history of civilisations, but Weber's comments on the distinctiveness of canon law are reinforced by new data of which he could not have been aware, from the post-Tridentine 'Congregation of the Council'. This data responds particularly well to the questions about formal and substantive rationality, especially if we streamline his own very complex formulation of them.

Weber undoubtedly wanted later scholars to modify and develop his ideal-types and to use them on fresh material, rather than treating his writings like sacred texts. Similarly, as a thinker with the power to synthesise the apparently contrasting tendencies of his predecessors – the hermeneutics of Dilthey, classical economics, Marxist class analysis – he would have been interested to see how such apparently polar opposites as Rational Choice Theory and 'everything is culture and nothing is nature' anthropology can after all be reconciled with relative comfort within his framework.

As a Weberian study rather than a study of Weber, and an essay rather than a comprehensive survey, this book disclaims any attempt at a rounded presentation of his thought,[29] or its relation to his own psychology[30] or personal political,[31] or religious[32] convictions, or of his academic sociological treatment of religion,[33] even though religious rationalities are a particular focus of the present study.[34] It does not try to

[29] For good recent books see Ringer, *Max Weber* and Whimster, *Understanding Max Weber*.
[30] Radkau, *Max Weber*.   [31] Mommsen, *Max Weber*.
[32] Cf. Carroll, *Protestant Modernity*, 259, who claims that 'the architecture of Weber's theory of action has been shown [by Carroll himself] to be Protestant'. Weber drew ideas from all sorts of writers, and in German universities *c.* 1900 a high proportion of scholars were Protestants, but the level of value neutrality achieved in (above all) *Wirtschaft und Gesellschaft* strikes me as so high that I find Carroll's conclusion quite unconvincing, though his book is lively and stimulating.
[33] Recent works covering some of the ground that I pass by are Sharot, *A Comparative Sociology of World Religions* (very Weberian); Kippenberg and Riesebrodt (eds.), *Max Webers 'Religionssystematik'* (important collection of essays).
[34] Note, however, that religious rationalities are not segregated here from other kinds of firmly held world-view, and a subsidiary aim of the book is to bring out some common characteristics of the ways of thinking in world religions, non-literate world-views, and secular ideologies.

enter the 'Protestantism and Capitalism' debate.[35] On the rationalisation of the West as a developmental schema[36] it has little to say (except it shows how useful his concepts of rationality can be away from debates about the nature of 'modernity'[37]).

Theory wars

The book makes no attempt, furthermore, to enter into the 'theory wars' between Weberian and other kinds of social theorist. It can be surprisingly difficult to attain a state of mutual comprehension, let alone consensus, between theoretical approaches with different 'forms of reasoning'.[38] This may be because each tends to try first to fit the others into the framework of its own conceptual scheme – as if someone approached the oeuvre of Aristotle by asking not 'what did he mean?' but 'how can Aristotle's ideas be fitted within a Wittgensteinian framework'? – a worthwhile question, no doubt, but far harder to answer than the (hard enough) straightforward one.[39] In particular, a Durkheimian framework seems to complicate the task of understanding Weber.[40] As with 'waves' and 'particles' as alternative ways of thinking about physics, it may be that two different frameworks are ultimately complementary but hard to synthesise or even think about usefully at the same time. In principle, though, the Weberian line adopted here should be compatible with Durkheimian Functionalism[41] or with cultural evolutionary models.[42]

---

[35] For recent studies with further references to earlier work see Barbalet, *Weber, Passion and Profits*; Swatos and Kaelber, *The Protestant Ethic Turns 100*; and *The Protestant Ethic Debate*, ed. Chalcraft and Harrington.

[36] Schluchter, *The Rise of Western Rationalism*.   [37] See below pp. 19–21, and *passim*.

[38] Cf. a recent comment by a leading sociologist of religion: 'The meaning that social scientists and social theorists attribute to secularisation, for example, varies with their assumptions about whether it [i.e. religion] is a constitutive feature of social life, a contingent product of certain forms of social life, an anthropological constant or a psychological property. A characteristic logic or form of reasoning runs through each position making them virtually indifferent to arguments rooted in different positions.' (Beckford, *Social Theory and Religion*, 194.)

[39] A paradoxical result is that I have always found it easy to explain Weber's ideas about rationality to undergraduate and masters students, but not to other colleagues who are either suspicious of theory as such or so committed to a different one that the latter provides the categories for understanding Weber.

[40] See notably the Durkheim expert Steven Lukes's comment that 'The use of the word "rational" and its cognates has caused untold confusion and obscurity, especially in the writings of sociological theorists'; he adds that 'I think Max Weber is largely responsible for this. His uses of these terms is irredeemably opaque and shifting' (Lukes, 'Some Problems about Rationality', 207). It is remarkable how little (if anything?) Durkheim and Weber said about each other in print. The likely explanation is that neither could dismiss the other, nor yet see how the other's ideas could be integrated with his own.

[41] Thus see below, Chapter 2, p. 91; cf. 94–5.

[42] For one of the most important syntheses in this kind of framework see Runciman, *A Treatise on Social Theory*.

While these different frameworks are not easy to synthesise, they are not mutually exclusive either. Ideally, sophisticated and confident readers with a different theoretical approach should try to suspend awareness of their own conceptual schemes for a while, to see if the Weberian concepts continue to stimulate empirical understanding.

Historians, sociologists and philosophers

Similarly, the sophisticated empiricist, sceptical of all social theories, should suspend disbelief in Weberian concepts long enough to see if they can serve an empirical purpose. A study of this kind is a particularly hard sell to historians in a certain Anglo-American tradition. Many are theory-friendly, but even they like it to be kept in its place: in *bantustan* sections of the introduction, and in the servants' quarters of discreet footnotes to authoritative anthropologists, sociologists or literary theorists. The free intermingling of theoretical argument with empirical data throughout the public spaces of a history book definitely transgresses some invisible genre rules. But the friends of social theory are probably outnumbered in history departments by colleagues who regard it with scepticism. They anticipate an attempt to prove that 'we can never really know the past', and they feel uncomfortable with too much abstract logical reasoning. Students in history departments might also be excused for sharing the attitudes of many of their teachers. In the United Kingdom at least the curriculum often includes some 'theory' in the form of quick shots of anthropology (Geertz perhaps), sociology (Weber and Marx), some gender studies, and some discussion of – 'can we really know the past?' Incongruously, the 'Annales School' seems to qualify as 'theory'. What may strike undergraduates is how well they can do in their other papers without remembering much of what they studied in the 'theory' or general part of the course.

What should one say in answer to such sometimes quite aggressively formulated objections? First, that they are quite right – in the sense that excellent history is done at all levels without thinking about theory at all. Historical work of the highest distinction can be and often is innocent of any interest in sociology or anthropology (let alone in 'deconstruction' or postmodernism, with which the present study is not concerned at all). The kind of comparative sociological history practised in the present volume has no ambitions to convert the whole discipline to its ways. History does not *need* Weberian sociological theory.

What Weberian theory can offer is an extra dimension. No one is obliged to go into it, if they are not so inclined or if their minds do not work that way (just as cultural historians are not obliged to try to learn the mathematics required to understand some articles in the

Journal of Economic History). Few may feel the urge to produce this kind of history, but more should want to consume it. Certainly it seems bigoted to deny it a place alongside other ways of doing history, and narrowminded to translate personal taste into a denial that this other dimension exists.

So what is this extra dimension? It is an awareness of the more general social forms – not laws, at least as normally understood – embodied in the sections of the past on which historians usually concentrate. Thus, for example, it is a mind-enlarging experience to realise that the thought-forms of an Enlightenment philosopher have non-trivial and non-obvious structural features in common with those of an illiterate African tribe in the early twentieth century. It is instructive to consider within a common frame the strikingly similar opinion-forming technologies (using the word in both a semi-metaphorical and the literal sense) used by Christian evangelists, Buddhist monks, nineteenth-century German workers' movements and anticlerical politicians in the third French Republic, though this is not essential for understanding any of them individually. One can understand each of these separately but one understands them still better together.

Again, the interplay of discretion and legal formality is an important theme in the history of English law but in other legal systems also. It broadens a historian's mind to reflect on the oscillation between these two kinds of legal thinking in other times and places. Such reflection may also lead on to a heightened awareness of the specificity of this or that system – such as the one operated by the Congregation of the Council within the Catholic Church from the sixteenth to the twentieth century. Historians may acquire a sharper-edged conception of the individuality of a particular legal or administrative structure if they can analyse it as a unique arrangement of some building-blocks which can be found in many societies.

Comparison between very different societies cannot rely on 'the language of the time', for the simple reason that the words are in different languages. To find what corresponds to what in the thought forms of different cultures requires research concepts that mediate between the different cultures. Much of 'theory' is nothing more than the development of such concepts, which need to be as jargon-free as possible. Thus, for instance, the concepts of formal and substantive legal rationality enable comparisons to be drawn between legal attitudes in English common law (in its various stages), the Congregation of the Council, and classical China. Readers of Chapters 5 and 6 must judge whether such comparisons are feasible, but it would take a narrow-minded person to think them uninteresting even if feasible.

Awareness of general forms need not diminish sensitivity to the time-bound and contingent character of historical causation, or rather, it can draw attention to it by incorporating it. Take the following schema or ideal-type: if a system of convictions comes under attack at the same time, but independently, or is reinforced at the same time, but independently, from two directions, which may well be simply a matter of chance: then two plus two will make more than four and it will be immeasurably weakened or strengthened as the case may be. It will be argued that the essentially independent lines of objection to traditional biblical Christianity deriving from German Biblical Criticism and Darwinism were a disproportionately formidable combination.[43] This is a structurally almost identical photo-negative of the coincidence in the thirteenth century of a sophisticated theoretical rationale of miracles (developed by Thomas Aquinas) with the rigorous historical testing of them in canonisation processes from the same century: a combination which made belief in them the most reasonable thing in the late medieval world.[44]

If empirical historians are to take this extra dimension seriously, it is not a bad idea for their guide to be another historian. The comparative method used here has been worked out from within their own discipline. Historians are more at home with data from earlier periods than the majority of sociologists, and are more willing to work in archives. Then again, they are more used to studying large-scale societies and developments over long stretches of time than the majority of anthropologists. Some language is borrowed from other disciplines in the pages that follow, but the dialect and accent are those of a historian.

This could have its advantages also for readers who would identify themselves as social scientists. The examples used to bring out the theoretical argumentation may have an interesting unfamiliarity. The sad case from the Congregation of the Council discussed in the final chapter and the Appendix is not the kind of thing that would normally cross a sociologist's path, unless he or she were also a historian writing in similar genre to this one. Sociologists will also want to engage with a reading and application of Weber in which the problem of 'Modernity' is put on a back burner.

A couple of the arguments of the book violate the territorial waters of philosophers. In trying to explain why systems of conviction can repel attack so easily, the *structure* of Hume's argument about miracles is generalised to account sociologically for all world-views that (like Hume's) disarm refutation to the satisfaction of anyone within the system. Hume's ideas were fertile enough to generate arguments leading in directions he

[43] See below, Chapter 3, p. 103.
[44] See d'Avray, *Medieval Religious Rationalities*, index, *s.v.* 'miracles'.

might not have expected. Similarly, the chapters on formal and substantive rationality have some relevance to philosophy of law. Before any such distinctions can be drawn, however, a core definition of rationality is required.

The concept of rationality

The real starting point has to be a clarification of the core meaning of 'rationality' as used in this study: as an ideal-type, it should be reiterated, for, like the subcategories of rationality which will be discussed and applied in due course, the definition has to justify itself by its capacity to sharpen the edge of empirical research. The word is current in many different disciplines, notably anthropology, sociology, political science, economics and game theory, as well as history and Anglo-American analytical philosophy.[45]

On the whole, *grosso modo*, the same nexus of problems can be discerned behind all these outpourings into print. A lexicographical analysis, however, would only enhance the confusion. We need to shape the concept into a form that enables analysis rather than obfuscating it. One may start with that of the philosopher John Rawls, who describes his definition as the 'standard one familiar in social theory' (apart from his special assumption that a rational individual does not suffer from envy):

A rational person is thought to have a coherent set of preferences between the options open to him. He ranks these options according to how well they further his purposes; he follows the plan which will satisfy more of his desires rather than less, and which has the greater chance of being successfully executed.[46]

This definition sums up one of the largest academic traditions of writing about rationality discussed in this book: Rational Choice Theory, which is particularly strong in economics, game theory, political science and sociology. The definition covers a good deal of the thinking that will be

---

[45] For a convenient introduction to a range of philosophers' views on rationality, see Mele and Rawling, *The Oxford Handbook of Rationality*. Cf. also A. Millar, *Understanding People* and the studies it discusses. Despite the territorial violations just mentioned, philosophers' theories are used only unsystematically in the present study. Thus Robert Nozick has tried to 'link theories of rational choice more closely to anthropology's concerns' (Nozick, *The Nature of Rationality*, 32), which I also try to do, but in quite different though possibly compatible ways. My own approach is much closer to Hollis, *The Philosophy of Social Science*. Hollis's preface acknowledges the influence of Quentin Skinner. Many of my own lines of thinking could probably be traced back to a lecture course by Skinner on 'The Explanation of Action in the Social Sciences' (title from memory) that I followed as an undergraduate. Some of its themes are brought together in his 'Interpretation, Rationality and Truth'.

[46] Rawls, *A Theory of Justice*, 124.

called instrumental rationality in this book. It presupposes that rationality is essentially one and the same for all people. Thus the definition is in tension with the position of another philosopher influential in discussions of rationality, Peter Winch:

we start from the position that standards of rationality in different societies do not always coincide; from the possibility, therefore, that the standards of rationality current in S [i.e. some society other than ours] are different from our own.[47]

Winch is closer to anthropologists. Their discipline's interest in Rational Choice Theory is on the whole lukewarm. Winch's idea of rationality has much in common with the kind of thinking that will be called conviction rationality in this book – a concept which is a developed version of Weber's value rationality.

Can one usefully draw these different concepts of rationality into a common framework? If not, the chapters on instrumental and on value rationality in this book might arguably not belong between the same two covers. I would suggest that the concepts of rationality used by Rawls and Winch are not simply equivocal. They can even be understood as species of the same genus.

For one thing, they share an idea of rationality as logical consistency. Here another philosopher influenced by the Anglo-American analytical tradition is worth quoting, Charles Taylor:

What do we mean by rationality? We often tend to reach for a characterisation in formal terms. Rationality can be seen as logical consistency, for instance. We can call someone irrational who affirms both p and not-p. By extension, someone who acts flagrantly in violation of his own interests, or of his own avowed objectives, can be considered irrational.[48]

Taylor further explains this definition as assuming that a person 'has to know, in some sense, that he is frustrating his own goals, before we are ready to call him irrational' – he must have at least 'unconscious knowledge':

Thus logical inconsistency may seem the core of our concept of irrationality, because we think of the person who acts irrationally as having the wherewithal to formulate the maxims of his action and objectives which are in contradiction with each other.[49]

That is not the end of the story so far as Taylor is concerned. He goes on to argue for a richer conception of rationality, one which 'involves more than avoiding inconsistency', which allows for comparative evaluations

[47] Winch, 'Understanding a Primitive Society', 97.
[48] Taylor, 'Rationality', 87.   [49] Ibid.

of particular components of different cultures, though perhaps not for comparisons between the overall worth or success of the two cultures.[50] Still, he does not reject the consistency criterion of rationality. His minimalist definition is useful as a bridge between the idea of rationality as a ranking of preferences (with account taken of probabilities) and the idea of it as an internally coherent cultural system.

For a final element of a pared-down concept of rationality, that nevertheless ties the positions represented by Rawls and Winch together, one may turn to Kant, whose concept of rationality is useful whether or not one subscribes to the rest of his system: 'Everything in Nature operates according to laws. Only a rational being has the capacity to act *in accordance with the mental idea of the laws*, that is, in accordance with principles.'[51] Insofar as action or belief factors in general principles (not necessarily self-consciously or reflexively), I will call it rational. The ability to reason with the help of general principles may be a decisive difference between humans and animals.[52] These general principles need not be abstruse. They could include such generalities as 'A bird in the hand is worth two in the bush', 'Better to be a big fish in a small pond than the other way around', or 'Never give a sucker an even break' (on the instrumentally rational side of the line); or, in the realm of value rationality, 'Men and women should be treated equally', 'No one should be convicted unheard', 'No man is an island'.

Thus rationality will be defined here as 'thinking which involves some general principles and strives for internal consistency'. One further criterion of rationality is worth noting, because it is helpful in constructing a definition of 'irrationality'. John Elster has put his finger on it:

we should evaluate the broad rationality of beliefs and desires by looking at the way in which they are shaped. A belief may be consistent and even true, a desire consistent and even conformable to morals – and yet we may hesitate to call them rational if they have been shaped by irrelevant causal factors, by a blind psychic causality operating 'behind the back' of the person.[53]

---

[50] *Ibid.*, 105, and *passim*.
[51] 'Ein jedes Ding der Natur wirkt nach Gesetzen. Nur ein vernünftiges Wesen hat das Vermögen, *nach der Vorstellung* der Gesetze, d. i. nach Prinzipien, zu handeln' (Kant, *Grundlegung zur Metaphysik der Sitten*, 56).
[52] Animals, computers, and even keys can in some sense abstract, in the sense of detecting general structures: my key can detect the same structure in the lock of my door and that of the departmental office. Perhaps the distinctiveness of human reasoning could be expressed thus: we share conscious (maybe not self-conscious) awareness with animals; we share a practical ability to detect general structures even with keys; however, we do not share with other species self-conscious awareness of generalities and our power to abstract them. For an acute analysis of the role of generalities in instrumental rationality, from a different perspective, see Papineau, 'The Evolution of Means–Ends Reasoning'.
[53] Elster, *Sour Grapes*, 15–16.

Elster is quite close here to the philosopher Donald Davidson's analysis (not surprisingly, since they both took part in a 'Working Group on Rationality' at the Maison des Sciences de l'Homme in Paris[54]):

> In standard reason explanations...not only do the propositional contents of the various beliefs and desires bear appropriate logical relations to one another and to the contents of the belief, attitude, or intention they help explain; the actual states of belief and desire cause the explained state or event. In the case of irrationality, the causal relation remains, while the logical relation is missing or distorted...there is a mental cause that is not a reason for what it causes. So in wishful thinking, a desire causes a belief. But the judgement that a state of affairs is, or would be desirable, is not a reason to believe that it exists.[55]

With instrumental calculation, matching means to ends and so forth, there is often a discernible chain of reasoning which provides a prima facie explanation of the action in question. With conviction rationality on the other hand we may well want to know how a person or group came to hold their convictions. A paranoiac's world-view is consistent – the world is divided between open enemies and people who pretend to be friends – but probably has a psychological cause of which they are unaware. Perhaps a collective group can also become paranoiac or hold other internally consistent but fundamentally irrational world-views. Consequently, it is important to understand the dynamics and trace the formation of convictions – a task attempted in Chapter 3.

Irrationality

This study must skirt around the vast and admittedly crucial topic of irrationality. This too is a heterogeneous field. There is 'akrasia' – the problem of weakness of will[56] – surely a powerful force in most people's individual experience and therefore in history. Then there is the analysis of predictable and recurrent types of human mistake[57] – also sometimes treated under the heading of 'Bounded Rationality'.[58] Then again, experience would seem to show that rationality can be at the mercy of other forces – motivations of which the agent is not properly aware. There may be arguments in favour of a belief, but stronger and accessible arguments against it; actions may have reasons, but there may be better reasons for

---

[54] *Ibid.*, p. viii.   [55] Davidson, 'Paradoxes of Irrationality', 179.
[56] Cf. e.g. Stroud and Tappolet (eds.), *Weakness of Will*, or the fascinating G. Ainslie, *Breakdown of Will*.
[57] For a popular presentation, see Ariely, *Predictably Irrational*.
[58] See pp. 31–2. 'Bounded rationality' can also be understood to mean reasoning which aims not at an ideal solution but at one that is good enough for practical purposes.

alternative actions.[59] So the beliefs or actions may have to be explained by other causes: chemical imbalances, neuroses, manipulated preferences, and self-deception out of wishful thinking being among the important variants.

To explain how this can come about, Donald Davidson suggests that there are so to speak 'overlapping territories' or 'semi-autonomous departments' in the mind: thus it can happen that one of these two departments 'finds a certain course of action to be, all things considered, best', while the other department proposes a different course of action, which is actually taken.[60] He postulates a '"principle of continence" which says one should prefer (act on) the judgement based on all the considerations deemed relevant'.[61] This may be overridden by one of the mind's 'semi-autonomous departments'. This approach could take in not only actions but ideas: they are rational if a judgement based on all considerations deemed relevant leads one to adopt them, irrational if such a judgement is pre-empted by the wish to believe something else.

When people give themselves reasons which are different from the real causes of their ideas or actions (without understanding what they are about) we may speak of irrationality or at least diminished rationality. All beliefs and actions should be rationally explicable, but not all should be explained by rational motivation. Thus (to imagine an example) an attack in a pub may be better explained by inebriation rather than by the imagined insulting look which was the pretext for it in the mind of the aggressor. We can rationally account for his bellicose attitude in terms of his alcohol-fuelled and irrational impulses. Or (to take a real historical phenomenon) the belief that Jews habitually killed children ritually was irrational at least in its roots because there was insufficient warrant for the story when it started, and because its survival can be easily explained by the wish to find someone to blame when a child was murdered. Thus the blood libel is irrational and at the same time rationally explicable, psychologically and sociologically.

The concentration in this book on rationality rather than irrationality should not be mistaken for an assumption that the former predominates in history; on the contrary, irrationality or diminished rationality in one form or another is everywhere. The study of rationalities does at least pave the way for understanding irrationality. It is a good principle to attempt first to explain thoughts and actions as rational. Only if that cannot be done should one go on to seek an explanation – a rational explanation, as all explanations by definition are – in terms of non-rational causes. In

---

[59] Davidson, 'Paradoxes of Irrationality', 176.   [60] *Ibid.*, 181, and n. 6.
[61] Davidson, 'Incoherence and Irrationality', 194.

short, however much history may be a playground of irrational forces, the best practical methodology for explaining it is to start by analysing rationality. In order to do so, analytical categories about how people reason need to be defined as clearly and precisely as possible.

Weber and 'Modernity'

Although the book is an application of Weber's ideas and methods rather than an interpretation of his writings, a difference in emphasis at least from various modern readings of his sociology needs to be noted.[62] There is a tendency to suggest that instrumental and 'formal' rationality (of which more in Chapter 5) are especially associated with modernity. Thus Wolfgang Mommsen speaks of Weber 'extrapolating trends which point to the eventual emergence of social structures which are dominated by purely instrumentally-orientated forms of social conduct and formally-legal bureaucratic rule'.[63] Rogers Brubaker seems to associate the 'modern Western social order' with formal rationality and instrumental rationality,[64] whereas it will be argued here that these are not a special property of modern times. Under the heading of 'Modernity and Rationality', Anthony Kronman writes that 'Legal-rational bureaucracies . . . administer laws which are acknowledged to be the deliberate creations of human beings; indeed it is the artificiality of these laws – the fact that they have been intentionally posited or promulgated – which establishes their validity',[65] while it will be argued here that there is nothing specifically modern about this state of affairs. Cary Boucock's reading of Weber is also focused on 'modernity':

[62] Since my readings of Weber often differ from views which have become quite embedded in modern thinking about him, I often justify my interpretation of passages from his writings by quoting from him quite fully. It is normal for great thinkers to be read in different ways. As just one example of the continued vitality of Weber's influence see the various contributions to the recent 'Lire Max Weber' issue of the *Revue française de sociologie*, 46/4 (2005) (this includes both studies, texts and reviews of recent books about Weber).

[63] Mommsen, *The Age of Bureaucracy*, 21, argues that Weber 'was not satisfied' with doing this, but takes it as established that he did do it.

[64] Brubaker, *The Limits of Rationality*, 30: 'Certain thematic strands run throughout Weber's discussions of the rationality of the modern social order . . . One such theme, is that the rationality of modern capitalism, law, bureaucracy and vocational asceticism is purely formal, and that this very rationality may be judged highly *irrational* from a substantive or evaluative point of view' (p. 30); again, discussing intellectualisation as one of the 'thematic strands . . . of the rationality of the modern social order' (*ibid.*) in his reading of Weber, Brubaker discusses 'the increasing tendency for individuals to act on the basis of conscious reflection about the probable consequences of their action – a mode of orientation that Weber calls *zweckrational* (means–ends rational or instrumentally rational)' (*ibid.*, 31–2) – which he associates with self-interest, quoting Weber out of context, as it seems to me. Cf. also Brubaker, *The Limits*, 18.

[65] Kronman, *Max Weber*, 167.

Weber uses the concept of formal legal rationality as a tool to explicate the ideal-typical character of modern power and authority... [he] identifies fundamental difficulties with the rationalism of modern social arrangements. As a result, his ultimate judgment of the ethical significance of formal legal rationality for modern individual autonomy is riven with ambivalence.[66]

Boucock advocates 'linking the significance of Weber's concept of formal legal rationality to his account of the origins and developmental tendencies of modern society',[67] and proposes that 'what is specific and peculiar to the rationalism of modern law is the formalism of its relations and functioning' (as well as the 'positive quality of its norms').[68] Stephan Breuer plays down the extent of formal rationalisation before the French Revolution.[69] The medieval historian Gerd Althoff attributes to Weber a sharp distinction between traditional action and the instrumentally rational action associated with modernity.[70] He argues against the distinction but may be mistaken in attributing it to Weber. The foregoing citations out of context are vulnerable to the same kind of charge, in that they leave out the subtleties in the arguments of these commentators on Weber. They do, however, bring out an emphasis on 'modernity' as the crucial problem which Weber's concepts of rationality were designed to elucidate. Even if that problem was Weber's starting point and ostensible goal, the balance of his actual coverage of history by no means privileges 'modernity' and his conceptual framework is generally applicable and not in the last analysis 'developmental': that is, it need not go with the idea that human society develops in a sequence of stages.

Weber was certainly interested – passionately – in the modern West. At times he writes as if he thinks that the modern West has taken rationalisation further than any other civilisation (not that he necessarily means this as a compliment to the West).[71] This may indeed have been the starting point of his investigations of universal history. These led him, however, into the broadest possible view of cultures other than the West and to an appreciation of the variety of different rationalities. He indicates that there are many different kinds of rationalisation,[72] and the implication would seem to be that they are incommensurable. It impoverishes his contribution to reduce it to some sort of developmental schema leading

---

[66] Boucock, *In the Grip of Freedom*, 65.   [67] *Ibid.*, 6.   [68] *Ibid.*, 183.

[69] Breuer, *Bürokratie und Charisma*, 51–6.

[70] 'these Weberian distinctions between traditional action and, on the other side, instrumentally rational = modern action' ('diese Weberschen Unterscheidungen von traditionalem und auf der anderen Seite zweckrationalem = modernem Handeln'); Althoff, 'Zur Bedeutung', 371.

[71] This reading of Weber, which certainly catches validly one of his intellectual 'moods', is widespread among modern interpreters. See for instance Brubaker, *Limits*, 1.

[72] As Brubaker indeed recognised, *ibid.*, 8, though he does not pursue the line of thought.

up to 'Modernity', even when when we duly note his negative feelings about his own time, in which concern for external goods, for the early Protestant a thin cloak that could easily be cast aside, had become a casing as hard as steel, or 'iron cage', as it is often translated.[73] Scholars preoccupied with 'Modernity' are not necessarily mistaken about Weber but they tend to marginalise much of the most interesting matter which is to be found in two of his most important works (the opus magnum on 'Economy and Society' and his book-length essay on Hinduism and Buddhism[74]), and to underplay his key insight that there are many different kinds of 'Rationalisation'.[75]

Instrumental and value rationality: their symbiosis

A version of Weber's distinction between value and instrumental rationality, *Wertrationalität* and *Zweckrationalität*,[76] is central. For reasons to be explained below, however, I will treat 'values' as a subset of convictions. This modification is in tune with those analytical philosophers who question a sharp distinction between fact and value.[77] They argue that

---

[73] Weber, 'Die protestantische Ethik', 203: the German is 'stahlhartes Gehäuse'.

[74] *Gesammelte Aufsätze zur Religionssoziologie*, vol. 2: *Die Wirtschaftsethik der Weltreligionen*, 2: *Hinduismus und Buddhismus*.

[75] Not all modern commentators fail to see this: Tambiah, *Magic, Science and the Scope of Rationality*, 153, well understands Weber's idea that the great religions 'were historically subject in their own distinctive ways to a progressive systematisation and rationalisation by their religious specialists and reflexive elites, in regard to dogma, doctrine and practice'. But I do not recognise the Weber of *Wirtschaft und Gesellschaft* or of the *Religionssoziologie* essays in the representation of his sociology by Boudon, 'A propos du relativisme des valeurs', esp. 884–95, as one of 'progrès moral' (p. 893): towards the ideas that all individuals should be treated as citizens, that slavery is unacceptable, of the separation of powers, and of democratic institutions – ideas coated by Boudon with very un-Weberian positive value judgements; note, however, important qualifications on pp. 892–3. Boudon also has a good formula with his line that '"Rationalité instrumentale" et "rationalité axiologique" doivent être distinguées, mais ces deux formes de la rationalité sont organiquement liées' (*ibid.*, 888), though he might not approve of the way I understand and apply rather similar formulae.

[76] Weber, *Wirtschaft*, 12–13.

[77] On the history of the concept of 'Value' see e.g. Satris, 'The Theory of Value' (for a different perspective see Joas, *The Genesis of Values* – remarkably little overlap). On fact and value see notably Williams, *Morality*; Davidson, 'The Objectivity of Values', 49: 'we should expect people who are enlightened *and fully understand one another* to agree on their basic values. An appreciation of what makes for such convergence or agreement also shows that value judgements are true or false in much the way our factual judgments are'; it should be added that Davidson is very optimistic about the possibility of consensus, and also that the argument about 'fact and value' continues: see e.g. Smart, 'Ruth Anna Putnam'. Whatever the views of philosophers on 'facts' and 'values', I will argue that convictions about 'facts' and convictions about 'values' can produce effects which are sociologically indistinguishable. See now the issue of *Revue française de sociologie*, 47/4 (2006) devoted to the sociology of values (with special

the difference between 'is' propositions and 'ought' statements is not so fundamental as many philosophers since Hume have thought. This seems right: an 'is' conviction such as that 'all humans are equal' is similar phenomenologically – that is, when observed and described without presuppositions – to an 'ought' conviction such as that 'it is wrong to lie'.

The most useful litmus test for distinguishing the two rationalities is to ask whether there was more than one acceptable option allowed by the convictions of the people concerned. When people think torture is never an acceptable option, we are dealing with a value or conviction. If they think it permissible if the stakes are high enough, then the decision is instrumental. One man's value rational imperative is another man's instrumental calculation, even if it is made within a strong framework of values. But whenever the value system does not dictate a belief or pre-empt choice, instrumental calculation can come into play.

The belief that the pursuit of perfection involves certain absolute requirements can also be classed with values and convictions even where not everybody is expected to pursue perfection. The value is: if perfection, then this and only this way. For instance, there was a strong strand in early Buddhism in which the monastic order as a package had an absolute value as the exclusive path to salvation.[78] For those who thought that way, the choice to become a monk was value rational, granted a determination to pursue perfection in the first place. There was also a strong contrary tendency to regard the path of salvation as open to the laity.[79] (These two tendencies both go back very early and there seems no way to tell whether one was a reaction to the other or whether they were more or less contemporary.[80]) For this second category the choice to become a monk fell within the realm of instrumental rationality.

The monastic life once chosen, there would still be ample room for instrumental decision-making – so far as the mainstream of the Buddhist

reference to Europe). One idea of values discussed there is that they are 'l'expression des orientations profondes et des croyances collectives d'une société' (Galland and Lemel, 'Présentation', ibid., 683) – which would presumably include 'croyances' about facts as well as values; it is a helpful definition except for the implicit exclusion of individual 'croyances'.

[78] Gombrich, *Theravada Buddhism*, 73; a careful recent study speaks of the 'Claim of the order to exclusivity with regard to the way of salvation' ('Anspruch des Ordens auf Exklusivität im Hinblick auf den Erlösungsweg') (Freiberger, *Der Orden in der Lehre*, 239).

[79] 'On the other hand, in a series of passages the possibility is explicitly presented of the lay followers having their own "spiritual" evolution capable of leading them to salvation. The common notion that these cases are to be regarded as exceptions cannot be endorsed in view of the large number of passages and of the formulation of their contents' (passage beginning 'Zum anderen wird an einer Reihe von Stellen' and ending 'nicht bestätigt werden') (ibid., 239).

[80] *Ibid.*, 240–3.

monastic tradition was concerned. According to Richard Gombrich 'the first schism, albeit a temporary one, is said to have occurred when a wicked monk proposed to the Buddha that five practices be made compulsory: subsisting on alms; vegetarianism; wearing only rags; living only in the jungle; living only at the foot of a tree'.[81] The Buddha refused. Presumably the schismatic monk saw these rules as absolute values for the perfect life of renunciation. If the schismatic monk had not existed – and indeed we cannot be certain he did[82] – perhaps Buddhism would have had to invent him to make the point that the austerities of the monastic life are a means to an end. The tradition of Buddhist monasticism that triumphed did not identify observance of monastic discipline with virtue *tout court*: 'the Buddha is constantly reminding his hearers that it is the spirit that counts',[83] intention being the key to morality,[84] and the rules went with explanations that relativised them.[85] One could add that decisions about when to suspend slavish observance of the rules would thus be an instrumental calculation, just as the rules themselves were, in a sense, instrumental devices to promote the core values of Buddhism.

This case illustrates the kind of distinction being drawn here between instrumental and value-instrumental rationality. It is not between one kind of proposition and another (say between 'ought' and 'is' propositions). It is a line between beliefs or conduct about which there is only one choice, and beliefs or conduct where several legitimate options are open in principle, so that calculations of consequences can be made without the constraint of fixed conviction. When monastic rule is not an iron ethical law, it is likely to be an ascetic instrumental technique in the service of religious values.[86] When exceptions are made from the rule,

---

[81] Gombrich, *Theravada Buddhism*, 94. Cf. Silber, *Virtuosity, Charisma, and Social Order*, 110: 'Not only did the Buddha oppose systematic mortification, but connotations of schism and heresy were soon attached to the idea of greater ascetic rigor in the canonical precedent of Devadatta, who threatened to split the Sangha by advocating that additional ascetic practices (*duthunga*) [*sic* for *dhutanga*] and more reclusive living be made obligatory – which the Buddha refused to do. *Duthunga* practices thus ever remained optional . . . Moreover, the stringency of *duthunga* practices was qualified by degrees of rigor (traditionally three), and by the fact that they were practiced only one or a few at a time.' Or again Bailey and Mabbett, *The Sociology of Early Buddhism*, 163: 'Despite the Buddha's rejection of severe austerities, in places he is represented as accepting some of the *dhutangas* if they are practised without selfish intent . . . In one place the Buddha is said to have adopted a pragmatic attitude to the practice of austerities – it all depended whether profitable states arose in the practitioner. Modern scholars are divided on the importance of these practices to the Buddha. In fact, what probably counted was motivation.' All this puts early Buddhist asceticism firmly in the sphere of ends–means calculation.
[82] Or that he held the views attributed to him, as Prof. Gombrich pointed out (personal communication).
[83] Gombrich, *Theravada Buddhism*, 88.   [84] *Ibid.* 67.
[85] Harvey, *An Introduction to Buddhism*, 224.
[86] See d'Avray, *Medieval Religious Rationalities*, ch. 4(b).

these too can be instrumental calculations in the service of the same set of values. Call the rule 'formal rationality' and the exception 'substantive rationality', and it becomes clear that this second set of concepts cannot be folded into the first pair (instrumental and value rationality) without obscuring the interplay between four distinctive but closely connected ways of thinking – around which, as already noted, most of this study revolves.

Concepts and explanations

As well as producing an unmuddled terminology, such analysis of concepts can lead on to explanations: once different kinds of thinking have been distinguished, typical causal relations between them become comprehensible. The reproduction of convictions from one generation to the next can be explained in part by the instrumental technique employed. Different systems of convictions and values generate forms of reasoning so different from those of the modern West that their instrumental character cannot easily be recognised without clear-cut concepts as tools of analysis. Values colour instrumental reasoning, and through it the relation between formal and substantive rationality. Clear concepts are needed to bring out these flows of causal influences.

The ideal-type of 'conviction rationality' developed later in this study[87] makes it easier to understand why certain positions (varying from Azande belief in magic to Hume's rejection of evidence for miracles) can be entirely immune to empirical evidence without being irrational. Similarly the remarkable parallels between different religions at the level of devotional and ritual practices become easier to understand once one recognises the hidden universal character of instrumental rationality. Again, when actions are partly irrational one has not understood their real cause if one takes the agent's explanation at face value: consequently, clear notions of what rationality is, and an ability to distinguish coherently between irrationality and a world-view that we personally find alien, are desirable for the sake of causal analysis as well as to avoid the muddy waters of conceptual confusion.

Explanations in terms of rationality are explanations in terms of motives: so they are causal even though they are also and in the first instance explanations in terms of meaning. The latter sort tend to be known in the social sciences under the grander titles of 'hermeneutic'[88]

---

[87] See below, p. 92.
[88] Cf. for instance Giddens, *New Rules of Sociological Method*, 65, 86.

or *Verstehen*[89] explanations. The pedigree of this approach goes back to Dilthey, whom Weber used and made useful for social science.[90] The 'causal' approach in its extreme form – not Weber's – can be described as a case of 'physics envy'. It takes the natural sciences (as understood by non-practitioners) to be the model of proper explanation. Though Weber started the hermeneutic tradition in sociology he believed it to be compatible with a soft form of causal explanation and did not like the 'us and them' attitude to natural scientists. He noted that people are most predictable when they are most rational and free (by contrast, say, with people in the grip of overpowering emotion).[91]

A generation ago, in the third quarter of the twentieth century, this reconciliation of causal and *Verstehen*-type explanations could seem primitive. A sympathetic account by W. G. Runciman of his thought on method speaks of an 'immediate philosophical difficulty which Weber never clearly resolves': Weber 'is presumably committed to the view that motives are causes', but 'he never says so in so many words'.[92]

He doesn't explicitly advance the view of the traditional English empiricists that motives are identifiable mental events which consistently precede, and must therefore be held to be the causes of, identifiable items of behaviour – 'ghostly thrusts', as they were effectively caricatured by Ryle. But nor does he advance the opposite view that the connection between motives and actions is merely a logical one which therefore cannot (or so it is sometimes argued) be a relation of cause and effect at all. The likely answer is that he never considered the question

---

[89] For an overview see Martin, *Verstehen*.

[90] For key footnotes showing Weber's use and transformation of Dilthey's concept of *Verstehen* or *Deutung*, see Weber's 'Roscher und Knies und die logischen Probleme oder historischen Nationalökonomie. II Knies und das Irrationalitätsproblem', in his *Gesammelte Aufsätze zur Wissenschaftslehre*, 42–145 at 91 n. 2, and 93 at n. 4.

[91] 'The more "freely" the 'decision' of the person acting is made, that is, the more it is made on the basis of the person's "own personal" calculations, unclouded by "external" compulsion or irresistible "affectual impulses", the more fully motivation – other things being equal – can be fitted into the categories of "End" and "Means"; the more completely and successfully, then, can the rational anaysis of it and, where applicable, the classification of it within a schema of rational action be carried out; and, in consequence, the greater is the role played – on the one hand with respect to the person acting, and on the other hand with respect to the researcher conducting the analysis – by a social science that invokes general laws; and the greater the extent to which the behaviour of the person acting is 'determined' so far as the choice of means is concerned.' (Passage beginning 'Je "freier"' and ending 'in bezug auf die "Mittel".') *Ibid.*, 132. The passage which then follows completes this distinctively Weberian argument by relating this instrumentally rational action to the agents 'letzten "Werten" und Lebens-"Bedeutungen"' – all of which should become clearer in the course of the present book. As argued above, it seems to me that 'Lebens-"Bedeutungen" cannot be confined under the rubric of 'ought' propositions: so I do not think Weber's 'ends–means' language in the passage translated should be pressed too far (but if he did mean that literally, my schema reshapes his somewhat).

[92] Runciman, *A Critique of Max Weber's Philosophy*, 25.

in this way: after all, he could hardly have been expected to foresee the spate of discussion which it was to arouse among English-speaking philosophers of the 1950s and 1960s.[93]

Runciman spoke too soon. Even around the time this passage was written, one of the greatest of English-speaking philosophers was putting in place a synthesis with a strong affinity to Weber's. Donald Davidson argued powerfully that explanations in terms of reasons can be causal.[94] While staying well away from 'physics envy', Davidson admitted the possibility of soft and loose laws,[95] and here he does not seem very far from Weber, many of whose 'ideal-types' are in effect soft and loose generalisations about rational motivations. I am not sure that anyone has noticed the strong affinity between their conceptions of Rationality, but it should enhance our confidence in Weber's instinctual philosophical sophistication.

Since motivations are causes, different kinds of motivation imply different explanations. Like wires in a complicated machine the different sorts of motivation are tangled up together and one needs to identify which is which to understand how the machine works. The distinctions between different kinds of rational (and irrational) motivations developed in this book are analyses of different kinds of causes.

Modern research on rationality tends towards one or other of two poles; assuming either that there is one kind of rationality, or that there are many different sorts (none demonstrably superior to the rest). As will be clear by now, the position adopted here is Weber's view that one can indeed have it both ways. Nevertheless a great deal has been written on either side of the divide since he wrote, and needs to be surveyed at least cursorily before moving beyond the summary of theories to an independent formulation of a broadly Weberian approach and its application to concrete problems.

Chapter structure

Chapter 1 concentrates on theoretical writings since Weber: first on Rational Choice Theory and other approaches which take a universal rationality for granted, then on ideas about the specificity of rationalities. It ends by suggesting how both lines of thought can be fitted within Weber's framework. On the one hand, Rational Choice Theory is about

[93] *Ibid.*, 25–6.
[94] Davidson, 'Problems in the Explanation of Action', 109. Cf. Davidson's summaries in his *Essays on Actions and Events*, xvi–xix.
[95] *Ibid.*, 112, 114–15.

what he calls instrumental rationality; on the other, 'culture all the way down' social anthropology, which emphasises the irreducible plurality of rationalities and calls into question the assumption that they are all based on a common 'human nature', is about what he calls value rationality. The important thing is to study them together, for in history they constantly interact.

Chapter 2 clarifies the notion of conviction rationality – Weber's 'value rationality' adjusted to include some 'is' as well as 'ought' beliefs. It is the rationality of world-views: 'liberty, equality and fraternity'; 'my country right or wrong'; 'God is God and Muhammad is his prophet'; 'Dharma, Karma and Samsara'; etc. The various elements of such systems support each other logically, enhancing the prior probability of the rest being true. Coherence is crucial to their rationality. From within, the probability of an objection to any one element of the system being right is low, however speciously plausible the objection, because the rest of the system creates a strong antecedent probability that the element under attack must be right. Immune systems capable of seeing off empirical evidence can be sophisticated and not necessarily illogical: Hume's essay on miracles is a case in point. Furthermore, conviction rationalities tend to be toughened by strong mental images, derived from experience, rituals, and other methods of turning abstract into concrete thought.

Chapter 3 asks how far conviction rationalities can change, and how they reproduce themselves. It will be argued, for instance, that changes in values and convictions are often only apparent; that when they do happen, often experiences (individual or collective) are the explanation; that crises can be generated by the internal development of a value system as well as by a threat 'from outside'; and that there is an 'events history' of value change, in which contingencies of timing, and coincidence of unrelated threats to a world-view, can be decisive.

Chapter 4 analyses the interdependence of instrumental and conviction rationality. The relationship between them seems to be symbiotic. On the one hand, the advances, retreats, and reproduction over time of systems of values and convictions are often explicable in terms of instrumental rationalisation: mass communication, education, rituals, etc. have much to do with a system's thriving or withering in the face of a competing system. On the other hand, different systems of value generate instrumental rationalities which share some common features – understanding of cause and effect and of basic logic – but which are shaped and coloured by the values and convictions of which they are an extension. The chapter concentrates on Buddhist monasticism and revivalist preaching. There is an instrumental rationality of asceticism just as there is of bureaucracy or factory capitalism. Weber well understood the instrumental rationality of religion, and the reader is pointed to some seminal passages in his oeuvre.

Chapter 5 pursues a similar line of argument in relation to formal legal rationality: often associated with modernity, it can equally well be an instrument serving religious ends. Legal formality is understood as the abstraction of legal rules and principles from all other considerations, whether ethical, political or indeed utilitarian (so: not just from 'values'). Formal legal rationality has been closely identified with secular modernity.

To correct this assumption I discuss the formal rationality of the 'Congregation of the Council', an institution created in the sixteenth century to implement the Council of Trent's decisions, and which then went on working for almost three centuries. A snapshot of a mid-nineteenth-century phase of this interesting institution is provided.

Chapter 6 turns to the relation between formal and substantive legal rationality: between sticking to the rules firmly to provide certainty or predictability and consistency, and overriding them when they seem to defeat their own objects. I argue that the border between formal and substantive legal rationality is policed by instrumental judgements, which are guided in turn by values. So this is a good example of the symbiosis of different sorts of rationality. The principal case study is once again the Congregation of the Council. This chapter includes some fresh research in the Congregation's archive, now part of the Vatican archives.

1   Universal and specific rationalities: theories

Rationality as universal: Rational Choice Theory

At one end of the spectrum of ideas about rationality is the view that rationality is one, not multiple: that all societies have essentially the same rationality so that human action generally can be analysed in terms of universal modes of reasoning.[1] 'One rationality' scholarship takes many forms but one of the most influential is Rational Choice Theory (RCT), which tries to build all thinking on (a) preferences and (b) estimates of the probability of obtaining this or that. It has been fruitfully combined with institutional analysis.[2] RCT is hugely influential in such subjects as political science, sociology, and law, and has even been known to penetrate into literary criticism. The austere economists' version avoids many of the claims of the political scientists and sociologists who use RCT.[3] Rational Choice Theory proves its worth most clearly by showing (for instance) how a series of rational individual decisions can together amount to a collectively irrational process, such as economic booms and crashes. On the other hand, the concept of 'preferences' is overworked in some forms of RCT, being forced to stand for convictions and values as well as for preferences in the more normal sense.[4] It will be argued

---

[1] This section is heavily indebted, conceptually and bibliographically, to the help of my colleague Ken Binmore; my thanks also to Steffen Huck.

[2] Cf. the review article by Ostrom, 'Rational Choice Theory'. The institutional analysis approach seems not to focus particularly on 'world-view' convictions.

[3] For a presentation of the economists' version by a leading exponent I have relied especially on K. Binmore, *Rational Decisions*. As representatives of sociology and political science RCT I have used especially Coleman, *Foundations of Social Theory*, and Shepsle and Bonchek, *Analyzing Politics*.

[4] For example: 'moral and cultural judgments affect choices by influencing the personal and social capital included in a single extended utility function. Second-order meta-preference rankings may help to articulate the moral judgments that underlie behaviour . . . However, I do not believe that higher-order rankings are either necessary or useful in understanding behaviour since ethics and culture affect behaviour in the same general way as do other determinants of utility and preferences.' Becker, *Accounting for Tastes*, 17–18.

below that preferences do differ from convictions: for one thing the latter involve general principles that can lead to unexpected and up to that point undesired applications.

Anyone who does a title or keyword search in the catalogue of a great library or database of academic journal articles is likely to be astonished at the number of entries containing the phrase 'rational choice'. The literature is too voluminous to be surveyed here or mastered by anyone for whom the discipline is not a central intellectual vocation (perhaps not even in that case). The approach is represented by innumerable practitioners. It has also attracted some harsh criticism.[5] Scholars outside the disciplines that have fallen under the spell of RCT are inclined to view it as a waste of time. It cannot be dismissed too summarily, however, as it is probably by far the largest bibliographical block among recent works on rationality. The sheer scale of the enterprise earns it an extended hearing.

Rational Choice Theory seems to have come out of game theory[6] and neoclassical, free-market, economics – though its implications are potentially subversive of faith in the 'invisible hand' that turns self-interest into common good. It takes an approach which has long been applied to the market and political economy and applies it to any sphere of life: marriage and divorce, average family size, crime, ideas, etc. It is striking how often James Coleman, one of the leading Rational Choice theorists in the field of sociology, draws on the policies of economic corporations for analogies to explain individual behaviour.[7]

'The theory of rational action of [*sic* for 'or'?] purposive action is a theory of instrumental rationality, *given* a set of goals or ends or utilities.'[8] So runs this sociologist's definition of his discipline. What does this really mean? As noted above, one could define RCT as the attempt to explain human behaviour by two variables: first, preferences, and second, estimates of the probability of a given action realising a given preference. Such estimates are called 'beliefs' in the rational choice world. A textbook of Rational Choice Theory deriving from a course in the Harvard core curriculum defines a belief as 'a probability statement relating the effectiveness of a specific action (or instrument) for various outcomes'.[9]

[5] Cf. Green and Shapiro, 'Pathologies Revisited', rebutting responses to their attack on Rational Choice Theory in their *Pathologies of Rational Choice Theory*; Bruce, *Choice and Religion*.
[6] According to my RCT mentor Ken Binmore, the archetypal reference is Luce and Raiffa, *Games and Decisions* (1957).
[7] Coleman, *Foundations of Social Theory, passim.*
[8] *Ibid.*, 516. For an interesting and constructive critique of Coleman's framework see Favereau, 'The Missing Piece'.
[9] Shepsle and Bonchek, *Analyzing Politics*, 32.

This is a potential source of (purely verbal) confusion since in other realms of discourse (anthropology, for instance) 'beliefs' would more naturally be taken to mean religious convictions[10] or world-view-type convictions.

Rational Choice Theory makes some basic assumptions: that the desirability of available outcomes can be ranked; that they are weighed against one another before one acts; that the likelihood of achieving what one desires is factored into the choice; that each choice shoulders aside discarded choices; and that what appear to be changes in goals can be explained in other ways, so that, to take a rather obvious example, a switch from whisky to beer might be explained by higher tax, not change of taste.

Bounded rational choice

The variant of Rational Choice Theory known as 'bounded rational choice' does not (as its name might suggest) build value systems into the theory as constraints on rational choice. Bounded rational choice seems to have grown out of the notion of *satisficing*: enough is as good as a feast, so individuals will be satisfied with less than the ideal rational solution in some circumstances – say if that solution is troublesome to discover.[11] Thus, for instance, a Bounded Rationality theorist has pointed out that people are likely to make some sacrifice of full rationality when choosing from a large catalogue: they tend to pick something near the beginning. The formulation of this point can, incidentally, serve as an illustration of the discourse of RCT:

If the alternatives are a, b, and c, the preference ranking is $b>a>c$, and the ordering O is alphabetical, then the alternative a will be chosen from among $\{a, b, c\}$ and b from among $\{a, b\}$, a choice conflicting with the consistency condition.[12]

Bounded Rational Choice Theory includes all sorts of decision-making under less than perfect conditions. On the one hand, it identifies the varieties of rule of thumb or practical logic that operate in real-world

[10] e.g. Kirsch, 'Restaging the Will to Believe'.
[11] As the following succinct characterisation suggests: 'It has been a long time since Herbert Simon pioneered the investigation of economic theories of bounded rationality by introducing the notion of *satisficing*, but advances in this area remain notoriously elusive . . . In satisficing models, the players don't optimize down to the last penny. Rather than spending time and energy looking for something better, they declare themselves satisfied when they come across a strategy that is only approximately optimal' (Binmore, *Playing for Real*, 164). The subdiscipline has not developed entirely as Simon wished. He thought it should be based on the systematic collection of experimental data.
[12] Rubinstein, *Modeling Bounded Rationality*, 15.

decision-making: the previous example, saving time when choosing from an inconveniently large catalogue, being a case in point. On the other hand, it can identify characteristic fallacies in the real world of decisions – such as the inconsistencies deriving from the way in which a problem is framed.[13] Here is an example:

Subjects were told that an outbreak of a disease will cause six hundred people to die in the United States. Two mutually exclusive programs, yielding the following results, were considered:
A. two hundred people will be saved.
B. With a probability of 1/3, six hundred people will be saved; with a probability of 2/3, none will be saved.
Another group of subjects were asked to choose between two programs, yielding the results:
C. four hundred people will die.
D. With a probability of 1/3 no one will die; with a probability of 2/3 all six hundred will die.

Although 72 percent of the subjects chose A from $\{A, B\}$, 78 percent chose D from $\{C, D\}$. This occurred in spite of the fact that any reasonable man would say that A and C are identical and B and D are identical! One explanation for this phenomenon is that the description of the choice between A and B in terms of gains prompted risk aversion, whereas the description in terms of losses prompted risk loving.[14]

As one would expect with such an active field, Bounded Rational Choice theorists do not all speak with one voice. In particular, there is a division between Herbert Simon's view that theory should be based on 'careful observation and experimentation',[15] and a more theoretical approach in the genre of mathematical economic theory.[16]

---

[13] Not everyone is happy with including such fallacies under the rubric of bounded rationality, or more generally with the range of ways in which the phrase is used: see e.g. Gigerenzer and Selten, 'Rethinking Rationality', 4: 'bounded rationality has become a fashionable label for almost every model of human behaviour . . . Bounded rationality is neither optimisation nor irrationality. Nevertheless, a class of models known as *optimisation under constraints* is referred to in the literature as "bounded rationality", and a class of empirical demonstrations of so-called errors and fallacies in judgment and decision making has also been labeled "bounded rationality". The fact that these two classes of models have little if anything in common reveals the distortion the concept of bounded rationality has suffered.'
[14] Rubinstein, *Modeling*, 17; here rational choice deals with matters elsewhere discussed under the rubric of irrationality: for a popular introduction see Ariely, *Predictably Irrational*.
[15] Letter from Simon, quoted in Rubinstein, *Modeling*, 188.
[16] Rubinstein dealing with Simon's criticism: 'Thus, the satisficing procedure of Simon is an interesting concept, not because it was empirically shown to be popular but because it sounds like a reasonable ingredient of our decision making. This by itself justifies those beautiful studies that draw analytical connections between, for instance, the satisficing criterion and optimisation when taking search costs into account.' *Ibid.*, 193.

'Social Analysis 46'

The civilised divergence between pure and applied Rational Choice theorists in Economics is relatively minor compared with the contrast between the cultures of the Rational Choice communities in economics and in political science. To give a flavour of the political science version of Rational Choice Theory in an elementary but ably presented form it is worth looking more closely at the textbook which has been used in the Harvard core curriculum – 'Social Analysis 46' – mentioned in connection with that discourse-specific definition of belief. This lucid survey by Shepsle and Bonchek is refreshingly sensible. For instance, although the authors assert that 'Rational individuals choose from the top of a set clearly ordered according to preference',[17] they are aware that the conditions required for rational choice calculations do not always obtain. Comparability between the options is necessary, but there are 'situations in which comparison doesn't make sense to the chooser' (p. 28). RCT also requires 'transitivity': if I like watching TV more than novel-reading and novel-reading more than going to the gym, I should like TV more than going to the gym. They are aware that transitivity should not be just assumed, giving the example of an imaginary voter in the American Election of 1992 who preferred Clinton to Bush (Senior) and Bush to Perot, but Perot to Clinton, and explaining that she may have had domestic issues and the economy in mind when she compared Clinton to Bush, and foreign policy in mind when she compared Bush to the inexperienced Perot; but character may have seemed decisive to her when she compared Clinton and Perot (p. 27 n. 7). Thus they show awareness of the limitations of Rational Choice Theory.

Another of the merits of the book is that it explains the quasi-mathematical notation that fills books and articles from the rational choice stable. (Historians out of sympathy with the rational choice approach may not mind this barbed-wire fence of notation because it is calculated to keep nearly all of their undergraduate students well away from that sector.) It turns out that:

- '$x \, P_i \, y$' means that Mr i prefers x to y;
- '$x \, I_i \, y$' means that Mr i is indifferent between x and y (p. 25);
- '$x \, R_i \, y$' means that Mr i either strictly prefers x to y or is indifferent between them (p. 25 n. 3);
- '$u(x)$' means that the utility you attach to an outcome is the number which you substitute for the algebraic x to indicate its value over against those of other possible outcomes (p. 33);

---

[17] Shepsle and Bonchek, *Analyzing Politics*, 31. Further references are given in the text.

- That 'action A led to a fifty-fifty chance of x or z' can be expressed as $Pr_A(x) = \frac{1}{2}$, $Pr_A(y) = 0$, and $Pr_A(z) = \frac{1}{2}$ (p. 34).

By supplying numbers for the x that stands for the ranking order and for the x that stands for the probability of an outcome it is in principle possible to quantify the desirability of different courses of action.

While it is hard to imagine historians supplying numbers to get quantitative outcomes in this way while keeping a straight face, there is an insight here: the considerations that influenced rational people in the past in choosing this or that course of action were a combination of how much they wanted it and how likely they thought they were to achieve it. Thus one might be desperate to free oneself from a manorial lord but judge that there was no hope of a successful resistance. Or one might feel that the rebellion had a good chance of success but that the new status it could bring about might not be all that much better than the old. Every combination in between is thinkable. Once reduced to ordinary prose, of course, rational choice analysis can look rather obvious.

Some of the results are not at all obvious, however, when they turn to the analysis of voting patterns. They repeatedly show that apparently democratic voting systems in which individuals act rationally enough can produce strange and paradoxical outcomes at odds with the representative ideal. 'Arrow's Theorem' shows that when there are more than two voters and more than two possible outcomes there 'exists no mechanism for translating the preferences of rational individuals into a coherent group preference' and at the same time satisfying a handful of conditions (which he specifies but which need not concern us) that seem reasonable in themselves.[18]

Again, they point out that to succeed in a democratic process it may be necessary to vote against one's convictions, say by supporting an amendment to a bill which is calculated to get the whole bill defeated.[19] They introduce the student to 'Heresthetic', the redefinition of the field of political conflict.[20] As an example they cite the theory that slavery was made an election issue in the USA by opponents of a coalition which was 'united principally by the issue of agrarian expansionism':

[18] e.g. that each member of the group 'may adopt any strong or weak complete and transitive preference ordering' of the alternatives and that if 'every member . . . prefers j to k (or is indifferent between them), then the group preference' must reflect the same ranking (*ibid.*, 65). Ken Binmore comments that 'the assumptions of Arrow's theorem do not allow the strength of the players' preferences to be compared. So any compromises made by bargaining *are* excluded' (pers. comm.).

[19] *Ibid.*, 153–4. They cite the Gibbard–Satterthwaite Theorem, the climax of which is that 'every nondictatorial social choice procedure . . . is manipulable for some distribution of preferences': i.e. no method of group choice is immune from manipulation (p. 153).

[20] *Ibid.*, 160–4.

Slavery worked as a strategic manoeuvre because it divided the members of an existing winning coalition, some of whom tolerated slavery and some of whom opposed it. Once the northern elements of the...coalition came to fear that support of slavery on which their southern coalition partners depended would be their own personal undoing, the coalition could no longer hold.[21]

The use of this volume as a textbook to be studied by all Harvard undergraduates is an interesting index of the extent of Rational Choice Theory's intellectual empire. It is an empire with many different sorts of provinces, some of which can look eccentric from outside. A case in point is the attempt to account for religious fervour in rational choice terms.

Rational choice and religion

A Theory of Religion by R. Stark and W. S. Bainbridge builds up a system through a series of propositions like the following:

Schisms in groups will most likely take the form of secessions which appear to preserve the investments of the individuals seceding.

Schisms in groups will most likely take the form of secessions which appear not to require great new investments on the part of the individuals seceding.[22]

Or:

The period of initial organisational formation is a time of high exchange of positive affect in a new sect or cult.

Def. 98 'Affect' is the intense expression of evaluations (p. 264).

They think they can prove that 'secularisation is a self-limiting process' (p. 311), for 'the ultimate source of religion is the fact that humans greatly desire rewards which are not to be found in this material world of scarcity, frustration and death' (p. 312). It is likely to prosper where there is 'a free market of faiths, as found in the United States and other non-repressive industrial nations. Those citizens who wish high-tension [they borrow a definition of 'tension' as 'strong, unmet desires' (p. 204)] sectarian religion can easily find it, while those who wish only a vague generalised sense of hope and fellowship, as offered by low-tension denominations, have several to choose from' (p. 312). What Stark and Bainbridge's quasi-Euclidean system fails to explain is the difference between the USA,

---

[21] *Ibid.*, 163.

[22] Stark and Bainbridge, *A Theory of Religion*, 131. Here and below the passages in italics are quotations with the numbering omitted. Further references are given in the text.

where religious groups prosper, and Western Europe, where they seem to be on the defensive. Furthermore, the blanket elimination, in 'Rational Choice Theory of Religion', of genuine altruism from the understanding of religion has drawn forceful criticism.[23]

Behind the scientific language there seems to be an ideological agenda driving the rational choice analysis of religion by Stark and Bainbridge. It does not have to be so. Rational Choice Theory could be stated in value-neutral terms so far as religion is concerned. A Rational Choice theorist could simply treat the religious convictions of the people studied as a given, without endorsing or undermining them. In the same way, Rational Choice Theory should in principle be able to embrace a wide spectrum of political standpoints.

Rational choice and politics

Rational Choice Theory has tended to flourish in intellectual climates also friendly to free-market economics. They do share some key assumptions: that individual choices are crucial in society; that they result from ranking outcomes and estimating the chances of obtaining them. Still there is no necessary connection between the two intellectual currents, and no intrinsic reason why RCT should be a 'right wing' discipline. A kind of RCT has been developed by the important Marxist philosopher G. A. Cohen.[24] The political scientist Keith Dowding argues on rational choice grounds against the [British] Conservative Party's elevation of 'choice' as something desirable in itself:

Where we are not sure about the value of the alternatives to us then we may not want a choice . . . whatever the merits of Conservative policies, claims to have 'increased choice' need careful examination. Increased choice, as opposed to better products or efficient markets, is not necessarily something to be valued at all . . . Rather, what we value is getting what we want . . . The value of choice in the market is merely instrumental in that it enables preferences to be revealed or discovered. Unless one revels in making choices and prefers weighing up alternatives to actually having them, 'increasing choice' itself is valueless.[25]

---

[23] Notably Jerolmack and Porpora, 'Religion, Rationality and Experience'. I owe this reference to Daniel Monsell.

[24] Cohen, *Karl Marx's Theory of History*, 152, 155. For a respectful critique of Cohen and an attack on rational choice Marxism generally see Callinicos, *Making History*. With both Callinicos and Cohen the cross between Marxist convictions and Oxford philosophy produces insights that non-Marxists cannot afford to ignore.

[25] Dowding, 'Choice', 314.

Rational choice and a fallacy of laissez-faire theory

Far from giving free-market economics unqualified support, Rational Choice Theory helps explain how the Invisible Hand can drop the ball, as for instance in the case of a stock market crash. Sometimes stock markets appear to be in the grip of an irrational panic, so that shares go into a tailspin even when they and the economy are fundamentally strong. The natural explanation seems to be an irrational collective panic, but Rational Choice Theory shows how a crash that looks like the product of hysteria can result from a series of individually rational decisions by stockbrokers. It makes it clear how individual rational choices can produce a collectively irrational outcome. There is a rumour in the market which suggests shares may go down. Mr X the stockbroker knows that the best thing for everyone would be for *everyone* to hold on to their shares for the time being. Let us even suppose that he knows that the rumour is based on mistaken information and that the shares are genuinely sound. What he does not know is whether the other stockbrokers will buy or sell. If he waits and they sell, share prices will plummet. When he finally sells, they will be worthless. 'Better safe than sorry' he may reason. He sells immediately. But everyone else reasons quite logically in the same way. The stock market crashes and perfectly good stocks become worthless. No individual acted irrationally but the outcome is an economic collapse. It was not caused by panic but by individual rationality.[26]

This is not to say that the 'better safe than sorry' principle is rational in all cases. On the contrary, it may be temperamental timidity, or visceral instinct. The point is that the sequence of actions outlined above *could in principle* follow on from pure rational calculation; it is surely a common enough phenonenon in the real world too.

Individual rationality and collective irrationality

The theory that individual rationality can lead to collective irrationality can be demonstrated by two game theory examples. The first is the famous 'Prisoner's Dilemma', which is actually quite close to real life as well as to numerous police interrogations on television programmes. Let us say that two suspected hitmen are under interrogation because they almost certainly began an attempt to assassinate a politician. They have been caught in the grounds of his country residence carrying firearms,

---

[26] The economic crisis of 2008 has given extra relevance to this line of reasoning. Quite apart from irrational exuberance or its opposite, and apart from greed, etc., a partial explanation of the crash is that perfectly rational individual choices, left to themselves, do not add up to an optimum outcome.

for which they have a licence. They can be sentenced to a year for tres-
passing, but naturally the interrogators want more. There has been too
much publicity for them to get away with torture. Obviously the police
interrogate the suspects separately. They offer each suspect a mere five
years in a relatively comfortable prison if the suspect confesses and impli-
cates his partner. The interrogators warn each suspect that if they stay
silent and the other confesses, they will be executed or go to prison for
life. If they both stay silent, they both escape with one year – but the risks
of the other confessing are an incentive to confess first. If each prisoner
consults his own interest and assumes the other will do the same, then it
will be a race between them to confess first, once they have understood
the situation.

There are some important provisos if the scenario is to play out like
that. The prisoners must put their own interest first, their preferences
should not include proving their constancy whatever the cost, they must
not be so devoted to the cause as to sacrifice everything to it, they must not
be terrified of reprisals for betrayal, and so on.[27] The thought-experiment
works with professional hitmen not too afraid of their employers, not so
well for *mafiosi* or terrorists who see themselves as freedom fighters or
servants of a religious cause.

The game 'Shaft or Share' is a simpler form of the prisoner's dilemma
that any university teacher can play with students while funds last. The
teacher picks two students from a group. Each decides independently
whether to shaft or to share. If both share, they get 5 each. If both shaft,
they get 4 each. If one shafts and the other shares, the shafter gets 9 and
the sharer gets nothing. Note that the aggregate profit of the students is
smaller than if they had shared. Even aside from any question of doing
the right thing, individual self-interest generates less overall gain than
social solidarity or distribution by a fair-minded authority would have
done. This outcome does depend on the ratio of rewards offered for
shafting or sharing. It also depends on each player's estimate of what the
other is likely to do. If the monetary advantage of shafting is derisory
or if each player trusts the other the outcome will be different. The
point of the experiment is to show that there are some amounts and
some estimates of probability such that the individual rational choice
produces the collectively irrational result – one could call them 'inferior
state equilibria'. In my experience, it is common for both students to
shaft or for one student to shaft and the other to share, the former
making a nice profit. If the two students are from the same tutorial group,
however, one would not bet on their shafting. A sense of solidarity might

encourage them to share.[28] Students from different sections have never both chosen to share, in my experience.

The 'Shaft and Share' game is no more than a playful flirtation with empirical observation, but there is in fact a massive body of empirical research into prisoner's dilemma-type games.[29] One might have expected that players of reiterated prisoner's dilemma-type games would learn over time that it paid to cooperate. Apparently no such clear-cut result has emerged.[30]

These imaginary, playful and serious scientific experiments can all point to some useful general rules of thumb. If there is nothing but self-interest to hold a group together, the individual rational choices do not *necessarily* produce the outcome most advantageous for the group on the aggregate. If the parameters are not set right, the Invisible Hand may prove clumsy. To maximise collective satisfaction something more than individual calculations of interest may be required.

This has implications for political thought. The fact that it is in the aggregate interest to work together under a central authority may not be enough to make individuals do so. Each individual may reckon that if he cooperates and the others look out for themselves, he will be worse off than if he too had looked out for himself. He would be like the suspect who did not confess in the prisoner's dilemma, or the sharer who was shafted.

Something is needed on top of self-interest to make individuals cooperate *even if* they know that it is in the aggregate interest for everyone to do so. The something can be fear of punishment (by God, or the state, or the mafia) or ideology: belief in the legitimisation of authority by God, say, or by a social contract combined with belief in the special legitimacy of a numerical majority of individuals. In societies where most individuals share neither of these beliefs, central authority is likely to be in trouble unless it has an unmistakable monopoly of force or unless there is some other extra ingredient on top of individual rational choice.

Civil wars

These general considerations can perform a small service for historians by clarifying their minds about periods of civil war. On a crude but

[28] Richard Kieckhefer pointed out to me in this connection that 'the psychological factor of self-esteem governs much human behaviour. People will act out of evident self-disinterest because they feel better about themselves if they behave in ways that others will approve and admire.'

[29] 'The prisoner's dilemma has motivated literally hundreds of experiments'; Roth, 'Introduction to Experimental Economics', 26.

[30] *Ibid.*, 26–8.

not entirely inaccurate model of pre-industrial landed societies, powerful landowners might frequently have half a mind to acquire pieces of each other's landed property. In normal times anarchy was kept away by fear of a ruler, a king or emperor, and belief in his legitimacy. When there was no doubt about the identity of the legitimate ruler, and when he was a lot mightier than any other individual subject, then any individual landowner could make a fair bet that his rivals would play more or less within the law. That was in the aggregate interest anyway, but the belief in legitimacy and power were required *on top of* awareness of the aggregate interest in cooperating, *and not simply as an inference from that awareness.*[31] In cases of disputed succession, when there was more than one claimant to royal legitimacy and where the rival claimants had comparable military and economic resources, a classic prisoner's dilemma situation is created and each landowner has to look after his own interest. The extra ingredient of unrivalled royal legitimacy would not on its own make people cooperate, but if it is endowed with some material power and added to individual rational choice calculations the latter can operate in a climate of mutual trust and a free-for-all be avoided.[32] The critical point is that a general desire to avoid a free-for-all is not enough unless there is an atmosphere of mutual trust created by ideology, fear, or some other ingredient x.[33]

Weaknesses of Rational Choice Theory

Though Rational Choice Theory can clarify the mind about some problems, it has shortcomings as a general account of how society works. The theory seems uncomfortable with the explanation of irrational behaviour: the behaviour of crowds, waves of emotion, collective and individual self-deceptions and illusions. A rational choice approach can be adapted to account for some apparently self-destructive behaviour.[34] Still, it would probably be true to say that hard-core Rational Choice scholars tend to overestimate the extent to which rational calculation explains social

---

[31] Is it not a problem with Hobbes's political philosophy that he seems to assume that a social contract will simply arise from the awareness of all the individuals that without a state life will be nasty, etc.?

[32] Medieval peace movements were another way in which an atmosphere of trust might be created, for a time.

[33] There may be a certain tension (not necessarily irreconcilable) between the argument of this paragraph and the 'folk theorem' that indefinitely repeated interactions will lead to an equilibrium in the form of a self-sustaining social contract. That may be so in principle, but in history the game repeated is never the same, so something on top of reciprocal interest seems necessary for an equilibrium. On the 'folk theorem' see Binmore, *Natural Justice*, 10–11.

[34] See notably Ainslie, *Breakdown of Will*.

behaviour, and would do better to focus more of their interest precisely on areas where their favourite methodology falls short of adequate explanation.[35]

As noted above, Rational Choice Theory does not provide much help with the explanation of behaviour apparently motivated by altruism and/or ideology. The problem is not just to explain altruism, for which evolution might account, but to make sense of the variety and content of the ideological convictions that affect people's choices, overriding personal interest in different directions. This is not necessarily a criticism of the theory, if does not pretend to do more than it can.[36] It is a criticism insofar as there may be a tendency of some Rational Choice theorists, in an 'of that which one cannot speak, thereof one must stay silent' spirit, to regard convictions as beyond the realm of explanation.

'Rational choice explanations of group phenomena . . . tend to give short shrift to ideological explanations, principally because they beg the question of where a particular ideology originates' – so the Harvard textbook.[37] Its authors try to face this difficulty. They argue that some actions that don't seem to come under the rubric of instrumental rationality are satisfying in themselves. They call such actions 'experiential' behaviour.[38] This they describe as a 'consumption activity' as opposed to an 'investment activity', instrumental rationality being the latter. They admit that 'We still will not have answered the question of where such beliefs and values originate nor why they survive. But economists do not tell us where consumer tastes originate either, and yet make central use of those tastes in constructing their theory of price.'[39]

This is doubly unsatisfactory. For one thing, the formation of tastes is in principle susceptible to explanation of the kind that historians and social sciences offer. Perhaps a sharp, deep, and narrow economist might be forgiven for ignoring this, but social scientists with a broader remit

---

[35] J. Friedman therefore sensibly comments that 'Rational choice theorists should do more than tolerate alternative forms of explanation. Properly understood, their greatest contribution may be to demonstrate how *infrequently* political behaviour exemplifies instrumental rationality – let alone the instrumentally rational pursuit of self interest.' Friedman, 'Introduction: Economic Approaches to Politics', 21.

[36] As Ken Binmore wisely comments: 'rational decision theory is only a useful positive tool when the conditions are favourable. Economists sometimes manage to convince themselves that the theory always applies to everything, but such enthusiasm succeeds only in providing ammunition for skeptics looking for an excuse to junk the theory altogether' (Binmore, *Rational Decisions*, 24).

[37] Shepsle and Bonchek, *Analyzing Politics*, 247.

[38] *Ibid.*, 247–8.

[39] *Ibid.* They cite a paper which 'shows that ideology can be incorporated into a rational choice account of political behaviour' (p. 250): Knoke, 'Incentives in Collective Action Organisations', esp. p. 326.

should not just walk away from the problem. For another thing, it is arbitrary to assume that beliefs and values are formed in the same way as 'tastes'. If they are not, this difference in genesis could affect the way they are applied to concrete cases – on which more below.

There is not much difference apart from words between the Harvard textbook's account and the Rational Choice theorists who describe idealistic motivations as 'preferences'. As we have seen, there is nothing to stop the Rational Choice theorist from doing just that, but one then comes back to the problem of the genesis of the preference, and how to account for the differences between the altruistic preferences of different societies. In medieval Europe, especially from the eighth century on, the living were altruistic towards the dead on a massive scale. The altruism was probably mixed with other motives in most cases: one could gain status by commemorating the dead generously and presumably lose status by failing to do so. Still, rational choice does not explain why spending wealth on services for the dead was a source of status in the Middle Ages. In modern Western societies the principle of equality compels some status groups to surrender massive advantages over others. Are these just preferences, like the preference of one half of the USA for Minute Maid orange juice and the other for Tropicana? The historian should be uncomfortable about describing as mere preferences the deeply rooted convictions, entwined with world-views, that make societies (and individuals) so different from each other.

The influential rational choice sociologist James Coleman does try to answer this. He suggests that the self can expand to include others in some circumstances: when one is benefiting them, when they are successful (supporting a successful team), when one has undergone a common experience, when one is dependent on the other people in question.[40] There is some plausibility about these explanations of some unselfish behaviour, and they could be developed into an account of how individuals sacrifice themselves to particular ideological causes. However, the whole concept of an 'expansion of the self' might be taken as metaphorical language to gloss over a fundamental weakness in the whole assumption that self-interest is enough to explain social action.

There are cases that Rational Choice Theory cannot easily explain – only set to one side, by saying that the goals people set themselves are not the business of the theory. What of the suicide bomber? The theorist can counter that he is pursuing his interest in the next life. How then does he or she come to believe that indiscriminate killing will be of help in another life? We have looked at the rational choice account of

---

[40] Coleman, *Foundations of Social Theory*, 518–19.

religion by Stark and Bainbridge and found it deficient. Moreover, one could move on to the case of a captain who goes down with his ship out of a sense of duty, without thought of reward even in an afterlife, and when his contemporaries thought such heroics out of date. If this is a 'preference', it pushes the limits of the word. The Rational Choice theorist may counter that the word 'preference' means only 'what someone wants' and that the theory does not need to distinguish between different kinds of preferences to deliver its explanatory goods. In fact, however, it is possible to distinguish between the ways in which preferences and values work.

Preferences distinguishable from values

It is problematic to use the concept of 'preference' as a label for any kind of choice – at least unless ordinary preferences are distinguished from another kind which it is convenient to describe as 'values'.[41] The conceptual distinction needed has long been at hand in Kant's definition of a moral act. There are choices made just because one desires the outcome, on the one hand, and, on the other, choices made via reference to a general principle. Call the former preferences and the latter values. (In fact there is a lot more to a useful definition of values than 'general principles', as will be argued below, but such principles are at any rate a component of such a definition.) In some cases *the application of the general principle to unforeseen circumstances might lead to choices cutting right against the grain of preference.* The principle that one must keep one's word might lead a politician into a politically suicidal course of action for which he might not necessarily receive any credit from the people who mattered to him. This distinction between types of act, preferences and principled action ought to be quite banal but Rational Choice theorists in effect ignore it when they use 'preference' as a one-size-fits-all concept.

---

[41] Binmore, *Just Playing*, 357–73, draws a distinction between tastes and values that at first sight resembles mine between preferences and values, but the terminology is not in fact the same. 'Tastes' in Binmore's vocabulary are not the same as preferences, and they are essentially personal and private. By 'values', furthermore, he means the version of fairness which has enabled a given society to reach an equilibrium or social contract, as individuals empathise what might be necessary to get along with one another. I use 'values' in a different though also semi-technical sense (as the next chapter will make clearer): to mean convictions which are part of a world-view and reinforced by its other elements, which involve general principle and are also concrete, filled out by experience or simulacra of experience or strong mental images. In principle, a value system so defined could be invented by and confined to an individual – so, not public. Into Binmore's vocabulary one could translate this as a new meme which failed to catch on.

In any case it is useful to distinguish preferences and principles in the same way that it is useful to have separate terms for the army and the police in describing the forces entitled to use legal violence in modern states. One could choose to call both the army, or both the police, or both the armed forces, but that would be conceptually inept and make it harder to put one's finger on non-trivial differences.

There is a rule of thumb for distinguishing preferences from values: values involve a casuistry, in the sense of the application of general principles to concrete cases whose relation to the principle is not immediately self-evident. With a preference, one does not need to think about how to apply a general rule. If one likes spicy food, one can take a straight line from preference through recognition to choice. On the other hand, if you think it is wrong to work on the Sabbath, casuistry comes into deciding whether it is wrong to turn on the oven, to turn on the TV, or to take a taxi to the synagogue. If you believe intoxicating liquor is wrong, does that apply to low-alcohol beer? Could a patient undergoing amputation without anaesthetic drink to deaden the pain? Is morphine an intoxicant or a painkiller? If all people are equal, is it wrong to know the age of an applicant? Such decision-making is a long way from the pursuit of preferences.

Another way of stating the same point is that evaluation carries with it the possibility of making a mistake in the application of values. One can't be mistaken about preferences in the same sense. One can be mistaken about the consequences of a preference – say, believing that wine at midday doesn't affect one's concentration afterwards – but it's harder to be mistaken about enjoying the wine. One can perhaps be the subject of self-deception or wishful thinking. One might convince oneself one likes a form of art or music because one wants to belong to a group. This is not the same as making a mistake in applying a value to a particular case, where the mistake is a genuine error rather than a self-induced one. The relation between the idea of a value and the possibility of making a mistake has been well brought out by the analytical philosopher Donald Davidson,[42] and his insight draws a wedge between values and preferences.

Davidson is not alone in drawing this kind of distinction between preferences and values. A rather similar point has been made by Elizabeth

---

[42] 'predicates like "good", "right", "honourable", and "cruel" stand for concepts. For a creature to have a concept it is not sufficient that it react differentially to things that fall under the concept: it requires that the creature be able to classify things it *believes* fall under the concept while aware that it may be making a mistake. To apply a concept is to make a judgement, and judgements may be true or false according to the creature's own understanding of the concept. If I judge that some act is immoral, I assign it

Anderson.[43] Then, from within the camp of the economists themselves, there is the critique of Rational Choice Theory by Amartya Sen.[44] Sen points out that the very name 'Rational Choice Theory' assumes a lot, comparing it in that respect to the beer which calls itself 'Best Bitter' in England, and he refers to the theory by the acronym 'RCT' to defuse that rhetorical strategy[45] (he doesn't say if he calls 'Best Bitter' 'BB'). His position is very close to the one developed above (or vice versa):

> RCT has denied room for some important motivations and certain reasons for choice, including some concerns that Adam Smith had seen as parts of standard 'moral sentiments' and Immanuel Kant had included among the demands of rationality in social living (in the form of 'categorical imperatives') . . . RCT does not at all allow these values and motives to be invoked in that form in interpreting either rational or actual choice. Insofar as moral or socially principled behaviour is accommodated within RCT, this is done through the device of complex instrumental arguments that are combined with ultimately self-interested behaviour . . . This has given the explanatory role of RCT an almost forensic quality, focussing on the detection of hidden instrumentality, rather than any acknowledgement of direct ethics. Things, it is darkly hinted, are not what they seem (or at least seemed to simple-minded observers like Smith or Kant). (pp. 28–9)

For Sen, this neglects 'the discipline of self-assessment and reasoning' (p. 33). It is possible to 'examine one's values and objectives and choose in the light of those values and objectives . . . We can ask what we want to do and how, and in that context also examine what we should want and how' (p. 36). 'A person can indeed choose to be mean without being irrational, but rationality does not actually *require* such meanness. To assume some inevitability here would amount to denying a central

---

to a class whose membership is determined by whatever criteria I have, but it is my criteria that determine whether the act belongs in that class, not my assignment in any particular case. Evaluative concepts no doubt differ in many ways from other concepts, but if they are concepts at all, if they are eligible for employment in judgements and can form part of the content of meaningful sentences, then they must allow the distinction between what actually falls under the concept (as understood by its user) and what the user judges in particular cases to fall under the concept.' Davidson, 'The Objectivity of Values', 54–5.

[43] Distinguishing likings from rational evaluations, and factoring in the role of social norms in forming evaluative attitudes, she asks: 'Should Pete Rose be admired as a great baseball hero, even though he betrayed the game by betting on it? Here, demands for justification come to the fore, where people offer reasons for and against rival proposals.' Anderson, *Value in Ethics and Economics*, 93. She goes on to argue that one of the conditions for a claim arising from a process of justification to be objectively valid is 'the possibility of error or deficiency' (*ibid.*).

[44] Sen, *Rationality and Freedom*, 26–37. For discussion of Sen's ideas with a final comment by Sen himself see Peter and Schmid (eds.), *Rationality and Commitment*. Ken Binmore argues forcefully that the Rational Choice Theory attacked by Sen is a straw man rather than the orthodox version set out in his *Rational Decisions* (pers. comm.).

[45] Sen, *Rationality and Freedom*, 27. Further references are given in the text.

feature of the "self" – the capacity to reason and to undertake scrutiny. The reach of one's self is not limited to self-interest maximisation' (p. 37). What this amounts to is the assertion that a sane analysis of the self must include not only self-interest however broadly defined, but also the possibility of critically examining what one's interest ought to be.

Other theories of universal reason: Obeyesekere

What much of the foregoing boils down to is that Rational Choice Theory is not good at explaining values. In this it resembles modern academic economics, the discipline to which it probably owes most. Though an economics Nobel Laureate, Sen was cutting against the grain of his discipline. But even economists would do well to treat some of their 'laws' as local rules.[46] Still, the approach works better for buying and selling than for marriage and attitudes to life and death, for instance. Subtler arguments for universal rationality have come from the anthropologists' camp.

Interesting insights in a polemical cloud can be found in the high-profile debate about whether the Hawaiians thought Captain Cook was a god when he first arrived.[47] The contestants were Gananath Obeyesekere, who argued that the Hawaiians had too much common sense to think anything of the kind, and Marshall Sahlins, who had argued that in the circumstances of Cook's first arrival he exactly fitted a Lono-shaped space in the Hawaiian ritual cycle. The interesting issues in that debate got hidden behind the acrimony: each anthropologist accused the other of being culture-bound and wedded to a Western understanding of rationality. The real issue was about the universality of rationality, as was noted in the previous chapter. Sahlins's position seemed akin to that of Winch: each culture has its own rationality,[48] as each game has its own

---

[46] Cf. Davis, *Exchange*.

[47] Obeyesekere, *The Apotheosis of Captain Cook*; Sahlins, *How 'Natives' Think*. For a good overall sense of the debate see Borofsky, Kane, Obeyesekere and Sahlins, 'CA Forum on Theory in Anthropology'.

[48] An eloquent credo of Sahlins' is worth quoting: 'Something like cannibalism or the eucharist can ... become anthropologically intelligible even if it is not to everyone's taste. But then, cultural relativism has never meant for anthropology the vulgar moral relativity for which it is criticized by the defenders of Western-cum-universal virtues. It does not mean that any peoples' values are as good as any others', if not better. Relativism is the simple prescription that, in order to be intelligible, other peoples' practices and ideals must be placed in their own context, thus understood as positional values in a field of their own cultural relationships, rather than appropriated in the intellectual and moral judgments of our own categories. Relativism is the provisional suspension of one's own judgments in order to situate the practices at issue in the historical and cultural order that has made them possible. Then something like cannibalism achieves

rules and each language its own grammar. Obeyesekere's position was not as crude as one might think from reading Sahlins's account of it.[49]

Obeyesekere recognises the 'otherness' of the Hawaiian world-view, but believes it allowed space for reasoning that is recognisably the same as ours. Thus, for instance, Hawaiians could deduce that Captain Cook was not the god Lono even starting from the axioms of their own system of thought: Lono was supposed to arrive in a canoe rather than in such a massive vessel, etc.

The approach to universal and 'other cultures' proposed by Obeyesekere has much in its favour as a framework even if he is mistaken about the Hawaiian situation, Sahlins's special field. Values and beliefs may be specific to the culture, but the reasoning based on them is very similar to the way modern Westerners reason on the basis of their very different culture (or rather their cultures, since the modern West is a mass of competing value rationalities). Obeyesekere's polemical tone and perhaps his particular thesis about Hawaii should not divert attention from the underlying conceptual structure, which owes much to Weber and with which I would substantially concur.[50]

Habermas

Another version of the 'universal rationality' theorem comes from the influential German philosopher-sociologist Jürgen Habermas. To quote an astute and sympathetic critic:

Habermas claims . . . that 'Strict discourses' such as moral argumentation contain rules of inference that make it legitimate to assume that *'in principle* a rationally motivated agreement must always be reachable' . . . The idea is presumably that if all moral questions are resolvable, given world enough and time, then any given failure to reach consensus can be explained away in terms of the limitations imposed by the circumstances under which the discourse was held, for example, lack of time, lack of knowledge, irrationality of participants, and so on.[51]

This claim by Habermas has wishful thinking written all over it. Even long and patient debates, such as do occasionally occur between friends, tend to remain unresolved when ethical and other fundamentals are concerned. Intrinsic implausibility apart, there is a logical problem, pinpointed by Heath. Habermas distinguishes between proper moral

---

an anthropological status: it appears as humanly *logical* – if not universally likeable' (Sahlins, in Borofsky *et al.*, 'CA Forum', 274).

[49] Sahlins's rather intemperate reaction may perhaps be excused by the fact that his empirical knowledge of Hawaiian anthropological history had much deeper roots than Obeyesekere's. It must have been irritating to be criticised by a newcomer to the field.

[50] Obeyesekere, *Apotheosis*, 19–21.   [51] Heath, *Communicative Action*, 219–20.

arguments and 'ethical' differences about 'values', which he regards as norms internalised in the process of socialisation: they have become part of the personality but they are an obstacle to moral argumentation – not the real 'moral' thing, in his terminology – which distinguishes 'moral' and 'ethical' questions, linking the latter with collective identity.[52] Only real moral issues can be decided rationally. Only there is consensus achievable. Heath points out that this is a circular argument: 'Any dispute in which agreement cannot be achieved is *eo ipso* reclassified as ethical.'[53]

Donald Davidson

Several rather different cases for a universal rationality have been presented: the army of Rational Choice theorists, lapsing into mathematical notation given half a chance; the common-sense defence of universal common-sense reasoning by an anthropologist embroiled in controversy; and a dialogue *à la* Habermas between sociology and linguistic philosophy. The last of these has affinities with the ideas of Donald Davidson, a dominant figure in the analytical philosophy of the later twentieth century. He advocates a 'coherence theory of truth', in which the truth or falsehood is tested by compatibility with our holistic view of the world and of reasoning, outside of which no one can penetrate, but combines this perhaps potentially relativistic approach with a philosophy of rationality as common to all enlightened humans when it really counts.[54]

He takes on what looks to the historian or anthropologist like the hardest task: to show that even norms and values cannot be totally different from person to person and society to society. He argues for a core of common rationality: 'we should expect enlightened values – the reasons we would have for valuing and acting if we had all the (non-evaluative) facts straight – to converge; we should expect people who are enlightened *and fully understand one another* to agree on their basic values'.[55] This sounds like the familiar culture-bound assumption that everybody thinks in the same way, but Davidson's view is subtler and to be taken very seriously. The very possibility of communication presupposes a good deal of common rationality

'With respect to the simplest and plainest logical matters', he argues, 'a sharing of norms of rationality is an inescapable artefact of interpretation ... Having made a start by assuming consistency, finding it where

---

[52] *Ibid.*, 234, 236–7.   [53] *Ibid.*, 237.

[54] For a general analysis of this approach to truth and different philosophers' versions of it see Walker, *The Coherence Theory of Truth*.

[55] Davidson, 'The Objectivity of Values', 49. Further references are given in the text.

we can, we prepare the ground for making the fallings off from rationality in others intelligible. We expect failures in reasoning when memory plays an important role, when sentences become complex, when distractions and temptations are part of the picture' (p. 50). Differences in norms cannot all be explained away along those lines. Even when people really understand each other there can be differences, but only 'as long as the differences can be seen to be real because placed within a common framework. The common framework is the area of overlap, of norms one person correctly interprets another as sharing. Putting these considerations together, the principle that emerges is: the more basic a norm is to our making sense of an agent, the less content we can give to the idea that we disagree with respect to that norm' (p. 50).

This puts values on the same level roughly as factual description. In both cases differences are explicable. 'When we find a difference [in values] inexplicable, that is, not due to ignorance or confusion, the difference is not genuine; put from the point of view of an interpreter, finding a difference inexplicable is a sign of bad interpretation' (pp. 50–1). The essence of the argument is that unless we have a body of shared beliefs and values we cannot 'make sense of the idea of a common standard of right and wrong, true and false' (p. 51).

Davidson is not pretending that 'there is more agreement than meets the eye', let alone that 'what we agree on is therefore true' (p. 51). He is not saying 'that there can be no real differences in norms among those who understand each other. There can be, as long as the differences can be seen to be real because placed within a common framework.' However, 'the principle that emerges is: the more basic a norm is to our making sense of an agent, the less content we can give to the idea that we disagree with respect to that norm' (p. 50). We should thus concentrate on his claim that disagreement about a norm becomes difficult when it is required to make sense of someone else's thoughts and actions.

Perhaps one could respond as follows: common norms are basic to making sense, but not basic *tout court*. For some disagreements are surely about values basic to how people view the world and think they should act in it, and which nonetheless resist amicable resolution. Here are a few fundamental questions that have received fundamentally different answers over the course of History, and still do: (a) What is human person? Some say a body with a brain, some say an immaterial soul that survives the body's death. Some say that the soul existed before it entered the body, some say a person is a combination of body and immaterial soul. (b) Is there a God? Some say: 'obviously not'; others: 'more than one!'; yet others think God is the totality of things. People who do think there is a God disagree about whether this is an impersonal first cause or a God with an active interest in the human race's history. (c) What kind of 'marriage' should the State legitimise? Some say it should be between a man and a woman and for life, others that it can be dissolved. Others say that it can be between two people of the same sex if they love each other, others again that love can be left to after marriage and that the parents can arrange the whole thing for their children. A high proportion of the world's population see no reason why marriage should be between two people only.

These are big differences. I doubt if they are due to confusion and misunderstanding, despite the name-calling that sometimes goes on when people disagree. Yet these disagreements are barbed-wire fences between our different 'rationalities'. To explain them may require more than Davidson gives us. His philosophical point may be valid in its way, but it does not solve the problem that faces anthropologists, sociologists, and historians of explaining why different rationalities are so well defended against one another. What we seem to find in practice, especially but not only in other cultures and in other periods, is a plurality of rationalities.

Advocates of a plurality of rationalities

At this point we must turn to the other end of the spectrum of views about rationality, where there are many scholars, above all anthropologists, who stress the particularity of rationality: 'cannibalism for cannibals, liberalism for liberals'. Properly speaking they analyse rationalities in the plural, rather than universal rationality. Their views provide a corrective to the universalist theories described in this chapter.

Godelier

Belief in the universal 'economic Man', *Homo oeconomicus*, whose rational decision-making transcends societies, is the bête noire hunted by Maurice Godelier in his powerful study of rationality and economics.[56] He argues that

There is no rationality 'in itself', nor any absolute rationality. What is rational today may be irrational tomorrow, what is rational in one society may be irrational in another... In the end, the idea of rationality obliges us to analyse the basis of the structures of social life, their *raison d'être* and their evolution.[57]

---

[56] Godelier, *Rationality and Irrationality in Economics.*   [57] *Ibid.*, 317

More specifically:

> there is no economic rationality 'in itself', nor any definitive form of economic rationality, that economic rationality is only one aspect of a wider rationality, that of social life, that this aspect plays an ultimately determining role, and that it is always provisional and relative – what is rational today becoming irrational tomorrow.[58]

Apparent irrationality thus turns out to be a different rationality, to understand which we need an anthropological analysis of each culture's overall social rationality.[59] The rationality of the society's social hierarchy creates a specific kind of economic rationality quite different from that of 'economic man'.[60]

It can be noted in passing that Godelier's approach is similar to and compatible with, yet distinct from a central argument of the present book, viz. that value rationality shapes instrumental rationality. Godelier would accept that but he is primarily interested in a subset of instrumental action: economic rationality. He makes a convincing case for its dependence on the structures of the society around it: and these structures are not universal. At the risk of distorting Godelier's thought by translating it into Weber's concepts, his 'structure of social relations' would embody values but could not be simply identified with 'value rationality', for the values in social relations would be mixed in with instrumental rationality, though not of the kind that a classical economist would recognise. If this is 'relativism', it is the right kind. Because the present study does not

---

[58] *Ibid.*, 102.

[59] 'On the basis of this overall social rationality revealed by anthropological analysis, the economic mechanisms can be reinterpreted and better understood. A kind of economic behaviour that seems to us "irrational" is found to possess a rationality of its own, when set in its place in the overall functioning of society.' *Ibid.*, 316.

[60] 'The economic *optimum* is not the *maximum* possible use of the factors of production, but the use of these factors that is best adjusted to the functioning of society's structure. The time taken for – the pace of – the development of the productive forces thus varies from one type of society to another in consequence not only of its production-relations but of *all* its structures. The intentional rationality of the economic behaviour of a society's members is thus always governed by the fundamental, unintentional rationality of the hierarchical structure of social relations that characterises this society. There is therefore no such thing as economic rationality "in itself", not any "definitive form" or "model" of economic rationality.' *Ibid.*, 99. Cf. p. 45: 'we can see the rationality of the economic behaviour of individuals as one aspect of a wider, social rationality, based upon the internal relationship between economic and non-economic structures in different types of society. We can already perceive that there is no such thing as economic rationality *per se*, nor any "definitive" form of economic rationality . . . it is clear that one cannot start from individuals in order to explain the content and hierarchical order of their needs, their values and their purposes . . . *without a scientific knowledge of the internal relations* of social structures, the economist *cannot acquire more than a statistical knowledge of individual preferences*, which necessarily appear to him as matters of taste, in relation to which the question of rationality does not arise.'

plough precisely this Godelian furrow (and must now turn in a different direction), it is important to stress its conceptual fertility for historians, before leaving it to others to cultivate.

Peter Winch and the rationality debate

Godelier's work on rationality appeared in French in 1966[61] and in English six years later. At around this time debate among anglophone anthropologists and philosophers about rationality and relativism was coming to the boil, with key contributions being brought together in 1970 by the sociologist Bryan Wilson.[62] One of the central figures was Peter Winch.[63] On his view, Rationalities are like games which cannot be faulted for violating the rules of different games, or like languages each with their own grammar, whose rules cannot be used to criticise another language. Peter Winch developed a Wittgensteinian version of this line of thought: just as Wittgenstein used games as an analogy to explain language, Winch took 'language-games' as a model for the rationalities of societies.[64] Wittgenstein had tried to answer the question: what is language? His first answer was: language is like a picture. Later he came to think that there was no one element common to all linguistic practices.[65] Linguistic practices are like games. Just as there is no rule or set of rules common to all games, so too there are no rules common to all linguistic practices. Winch took the reasoning further. He regarded the rules of games and of linguistic practices as special cases of societies generally. There is no set of rules that can apply to all societies.

Winch was reacting against a different tradition in social science: the attempt to find general laws of society. Just as natural scientists discovered laws of nature, social scientists would discover laws of society. So it was thought and sometimes still is. There was disagreement, however, even about the general character of these laws. Some looked for evolutionary laws.[66] Others looked for functional laws, like those of physiology, so

---

[61] Godelier, *Rationalité et irrationalité en économie.*
[62] See Wilson (ed.), *Rationality*, and Hollis and Lukes, *Rationality and Relativism*; Hollis, *The Philosophy of Social Science*, 151–7. Historians were not much involved in the discussion, though note the very important contribution of Skinner, 'Interpretation, Rationality and Truth', 36–40: pages of clarity and common sense.
[63] Winch contributed chapters 1 and 5 to Wilson (ed.), *Rationality*.
[64] Winch, *The Idea of a Social Science*, and 'Understanding a Primitive Society'.
[65] He did think that there was a series of family resemblances linking linguistic practice, even if no one feature was common to all, but this aspect of his thought is less relevant here.
[66] A tradition still alive today, in the thought of the sociologist W. G. Runciman and in a whole school which tries to link together the study of society and the study of biology.

that a social institution would be explained by its function just as a bodily organ would be explained by its contribution to the working of the body.

For Winch, there are no general, natural science-type laws for society and history. To look for them is misguided, like looking for laws governing both rugby and solitaire. This applies to rationality too. Modern Western rationality is one set of rules. It cannot be set over another set, say the rationality of an African tribe. Our rationality cannot sit in judgement on their rationality any more than theirs can on ours – so thinks Winch.

The rationality of Azande poison oracles

Winch applies this framework to Azande poison oracles, as studied by E. E. Evans-Pritchard in a famous book of which more must be said in the next chapter. Without actually believing in oracles personally, Evans-Pritchard showed how sensible the practice of governing one's life by giving poison to chickens could look from inside the system. The Azande poison chickens are used to arrive at decisions. Death of the chicken gives one answer, survival another. Evans-Pritchard used the same system of decision-making during his fieldwork and maintained that it worked as well as Western ways of solving dilemmas. According to Evans-Pritchard (writing between the wars), 'No important venture is undertaken without authorisation of the poison oracle. In important collective undertakings, in all crises of life, in all serious legal disputes, in all matters strongly affecting individual welfare, in short, on all occasions regarded by Azande as dangerous or socially important, the activity is preceded by consultation of the poison oracle' (pp. 121–2).

Azande oracles are a key method of detecting witchcraft. 'All death to Azande is murder' (p. 125). If the killer is known he can be executed (pp. 25–6), but if he is not, he must be discovered with the help of magic and the poison oracle. Natural causes of death are recognised but deemed to be compatible with murder by witchcraft, which is described metaphorically as 'the second spear' (p. 25). So when a person dies the poison oracle is asked to choose two people: someone to observe certain taboos, notably sexual taboos, and send the magic on its way to punish the witch; and a magician to provide the magic to be used to this end (p. 223). After an appropriate period of time someone dies and the oracle is asked if that was the guilty person. If the answer is affirmative the poison oracle of the priest is consulted to endorse the answer or send the relatives back to wait for the death of the culprit (pp. 224–5).

See notably Runciman, *A Treatise on Social Theory*, vol. 2: *Substantive Social Theory*, or P. Boyer, 'Functional Origins of Religious Concepts'.

Evans-Pritchard asks us to take all this seriously:

> I hope that I have persuaded the reader of one thing, namely, the intellectual consistency of Zande notions. They only appear inconsistent when ranged like lifeless museum objects. When we see how an individual uses them we may say that they are mystical but we cannot say that his use of them is illogical or even that it is uncritical. I had no difficulty in using Zande notions as Azande themselves use them. Once the idiom is learned the rest is easy, for in Zandeland one mystical idea follows on another as reasonably as one common-sense idea follows on another in our own society. (p. 22)

To take the Azande system seriously is one thing; to say that it is really and truly no more nor less correct than 'Western' ways of thinking is another. Winch takes the further step. For him, Azande magical rites

> do, or may, express an attitude to contingencies; one, that is, which involves recognition that one's life is subject to contingencies, rather than an attempt to control these. To characterise this attitude more specifically one should note how Zande rites emphasise the importance of certain fundamental features of their life... We have a drama of resentments, evil-doing, revenge, expiation, in which there are ways of dealing (symbolically) with misfortunes and their disruptive effect on a man's relations with his fellows, with ways in which life can go on despite such disruptions.[67]

Empirically, this account of Azande magic's rationale may not stand up. One can object to Winch that he has to present the Azande system as expressive rather than (putatively) effective before he can say that it is no less right than the Western one. It is true that such an intellectual strategy can sometimes have much merit. A Martian anthropologist observing the Changing the Guard outside Buckingham Palace would be missing the point if he saw it as a defensive measure. Winch draws a comparison with Judaeo-Christian prayer. Central to it, he argues, is the conception 'If it be Thy Will'. Consequently, prayers 'may be regarded from one point of view as freeing the believer from dependence on what he is supplicating for'; but they 'cannot play this role if they are regarded as a means of influencing the outcome for in that case the one who prays is still dependent on the outcome'.[68] Thus it is certainly worth asking if Azande magic is actually trying to find out the truth – as opposed to expressing an attitude to the world. The fact remains that the answer given by Evans-Pritchard, who is after all Winch's sole source, makes it clear that the Azande were interested in outcomes. Evans-Pritchard's account does, however, support Winch's view in a crucial respect: in his view the Azande

---

[67] Winch, 'Understanding', 104–5.   [68] Ibid., 104.

notion of magic is not vulnerable to refutation by Western science. On this Evans-Pritchard is convincing and a solid support for Winch.

This forces us to face a little prematurely the question of whether culture goes 'all the way down'. ('Prematurely', because the theory underpinning the answer is not set out in detail until the next chapter.) If Azande magic could stand up so successfully to Western rationality, can there be any common rationality at all? Is there no firm point to provide logical leverage against an alien system? On the other hand, if there is no bedrock, how are we able to understand the alien system at all, as anthropologists routinely claim to do?

Peter Winch offers an answer: that certain fundamental notions 'are inescapably involved in the life of all known human societies' and that 'conceptions of good and evil in human life will necessarily be connected with such concepts';[69] also he thinks that when they seem to be simply wrong, we may be misunderstanding what is going on.

Problems with pluralism

Problems nevertheless arise with Winch's idea that rationalities are like language games; also with other theories gravitating towards the extreme edge of cultural relativism. If it is proposed that truth can't transcend all specific cultures, is that proposition a truth transcending all cultures? Relativists might be able to find ways around that.[70] But even if relativism is philosophically tenable, does it allow any kind of criticism of, say, Heinrich Himmler's world-view, which had its own coherence? Not many people in academic life today would want to accord his ideas the same kind of respect that Evans-Pritchard paid to the Azande or Sahlins to eighteenth-century Hawaiians. Given relativism, however, could one go beyond expressing a personal reaction to his views? One can say in emotivist mode that one hates them, but is this just a matter of emotion, not of reason?

There are other objections to the idea that each society has its own system of rules, like games or grammars. For one thing, cultures are not usually monolithic: there are usually several rationalities within them. In modern Britain a secular humanist and a believer in Islam have fundamentally different views of the world. In thirteenth-century Europe a Cathar 'Perfect' would have a different rationality from that of a friar, despite similarities in the externals of their way of life. Again, each individual can have his or her own 'culture' or value rationality. The range of possible non-conformity varies from society to society but there are

---

[69] *Ibid.*, 111   [70] Cf. Meiland, 'Bernard Williams' Relativism'.

probably always some who reject the dominant system, even if they don't dare say so.[71]

The kind of approach adopted by Winch is also ill equipped to explain the loss and gain of values, which will be discussed in a later chapter. Finally, the impossibility of refuting one value rationality from the standpoint of another does not logically prove that none of these rationalities is objectively right. Many may be radically wrong, even if there is no general method of identifying them. Thus the anthropological and philosophical theories treating each rationality as a self-contained world have their vulnerabilities. The foregoing is not a refutation of Winch but a suggestion that his approach is inadequate on its own, just as Rational Choice Theory is inadequate on its own at the opposite pole.

Antithetical approaches and possible syntheses

A pattern has emerged: a field of apparently incompatible views. We have seen that there are two poles in research on rationalities, tending to attract it in two contrary directions. At one end is the conviction that all humans share the same unitary rationality. In their different ways, Donald Davidson, Habermas, Obeyesekere, and Rational Choice theorists tend towards this theory. At the other end, many anthropologists and other scholars posit a plurality of rationalities.

The present study fits into a tradition of integrating the two apparently incompatible approaches with the help of a 'two rationalities' schema. Such an approach underpins de facto the account of Azande magic by Evans-Pritchard (a difference between him and Winch, who did not follow him here). The Azande system of oracles belonged to a world-view which is both coherent and utterly strange to Westerners, yet it does in fact use in its own different context a type of reasoning familiar to modern experimental scientists. Evans-Pritchard shows a system of 'cross-checks' at work. Once the poison oracle gave an answer, the question was reversed, so that the same physical outcome would give the opposite answer. If the oracle was asked whether a man would die if he moved to a government settlement, and the chicken survived, giving the answer 'no', the next question would be 'did the oracle speak truly', so that if the next chicken also survived, it would be clear that the oracle wasn't working properly for some reason. The 'cross-check' system is actually the same sort of reasoning as the use of control samples in modern Western science and medicine, but the activity as a whole seems rather different

---

[71] For the so-called 'Ages of Faith', for instance, see Murray, 'Piety and Impiety in Thirteenth Century Italy'; Reynolds, 'Social Mentalities'; Arnold, *Belief and Unbelief*.

because the convictions or axioms behind them are so different. This is best explained by examples. Here is one invented by Evans-Pritchard:

First Test. If X has committed adultery poison oracle kill the fowl.

If X is innocent poison oracle spare the fowl. The fowl dies.

Second Test. The poison oracle has declared X guilty of adultery by slaying the fowl. If its declaration is true let it spare this second fowl. The fowl survives.

Result. A valid verdict. X is guilty.[72]

What we see here is surely a logic no different from our own within the parameters of a very alien world-view. Azande oracles deserve the attention that they have received since Evans-Pritchard made them famous. They are a paradigm case of how rationality can be both particular and universal.

The Azande case fits neatly into Max Weber's distinction between *Wertrationalität* and *Zweckrationalität* – value and instrumental rationality. It may serve as a first illustration of how this crucial distinction works in practice. The Azande system of beliefs about oracles, witchcraft and magic is a value rationality; the 'cross-check' on the accuracy of the oracle's verdict is instrumental rationality ultimately identifiable with the logic of control samples.

Rational Choice Theory becomes much more convincing when integrated into this Weberian schema, as it can be. A good model is Dennis Chong's analysis of decision-making in a Texas community, in which the parameters of rational choices are set by values and convictions.[73] As Chong puts it: 'people may choose among alternatives based on the beliefs they hold about those alternatives in a manner that mimics rational [i.e. 'rational choice'] decision making, but the beliefs themselves may be immune to counterevidence'.[74] (To anticipate, it will be argued below that this immunity is compatible with 'value rationality'.) Chong explicitly acknowledges his debt to Weber's distinction between value rationality and instrumental rationality.[75]

---

[72] Evans-Pritchard, *Witchcraft, Oracles and Magic*, 139 (first example).

[73] Chong, *Rational Lives*, ch. 5, 'Economics Meets Morality in a Texas Community', 154–85.

[74] *Ibid.*, 183.

[75] 'To use the classic Weberian distinctions, the moral actions of the residents were not purely affective or habitual, but value-rational in the sense that their actions were calculated to defend their values; furthermore, their values were not merely value-rational, but arguably motivated by self-interested reasons. While defence of social values sometimes took the form of moral absolutes without regard to worldly benefits, they were also frequently couched in instrumental terms' (*ibid.*, 175).

At almost the opposite end of the social science spectrum from Rational Choice Theory, in anthropology, we can also see Weber's schema at work. Gananath Obeyesekere, an advocate of universal common-sense rationality, in practice proposes a two-rationalities model which more or less mirrors the Weberian schema. His common-sense rationality – 'pragmatic rationality' – can be equated with Weber's 'instrumental rationality',[76] while he uses the phrase 'symbolic formations' in a sense not very far from Weber's 'value rationality'.[77]

Max Weber's terminology

Max Weber's value–instrumental distinction was already briefly discussed in the Introduction. By instrumental rationality (*Zweckrationalität*) Weber clearly meant the ability to match causes and effects; one can extend this to include logical consequences: 'Being able to put two and two together' captures both the logical and the causal kinds of reckoning. *Zweckrationalität* could be translated as 'ends–means' or 'calculating' or 'instrumental' rationality.[78] 'Instrumental' seems the least unwieldy term and will be used most often. This word can cause misunderstanding since it is often used in current English to mean simply the choice of means to satisfy wants. Or again, it is taken to imply cynicism or manipulation, the use of things or people for something other than the ostensible purpose. These are serious drawbacks to adopting the word here but it is so current as the English for *Zweckrationalität* that there is not much choice but to use it. However, as I hope will become clear both from the analysis of Weber and from the application of the concept to such fields as devotion and monasticism, instrumental rationality can take many other forms. It is not just about manipulation, or indeed about rationalities associated with the modern West such as technological development, capitalism, or bureaucratic efficiency. The tendency to understand 'instrumental' as excluding any influence of values has a subtly warping influence on

---

[76] Obeyesekere, *The Apotheosis of Captain Cook* (1992), 19.

[77] 'for almost all later accounts are unanimous concerning the cult of Cook's bones . . . I must give an interpretation of how this cult developed, taking into account the interplay of rational pragmatics with powerful symbolic formations in Hawaiian society and consciousness' (*ibid.*, 89).

[78] Weber's distinction between value and instrumental rationality calls to mind Kant's distinction between 'Sittlichkeit' (easily translated as 'morality') and 'Geschicklichkeit' (somewhere between 'cleverness', 'ability', and 'skill'): see Kant, *Grundlegung zur Metaphysik der Sitten*, 59–61, but, at least in the *Grundlegung*, Kant seems to imply that a given action belongs to one category or the other, whereas Weber's pair of concepts is not really a dichotomy or a set of alternatives, in that most instrumental action is shaped by values.

interpretation: scholars assume that either instrumental rationality looks like modern Western secular instrumental rationality, or it isn't instrumental rationality at all. Against any such interpretation, it will be stressed here that instrumental rationality is a chameleon that takes the colour of the values in its mental milieu. These changes of colouring make it harder to realise that it is still the same animal in its different value contexts and that it transcends the specific domains of economics, technology, religion, etc.

Universality of instrumental rationality

The chameleon-like character of instrumental rationality explains why its universality is not patently obvious. In a combination of values and instrumental reasoning the instrumental element is hard to distinguish. The amalgams produced by combining it with various value systems look very different one from another – as with Azande magic and modern experimental science.

The distinction between the two rationalities together with awareness of their symbiosis solves the problem of whether human rationality is universal. Value rationalities are evidently not. This is the problem with Davidson's eirenic universalism, which may itself be a value rationality of a civilised modern academic who believed that reasonable people could reach consensus about basic things if they only understood each other. But very reasonable people, even modern academics, fail to reach consensus about, say, suicide, abortion, or eating meat, even when they really try. The next chapter will explain why they can fail without irrationality (stupidity, wilful ignorance) on anybody's part. To perceive its universality, one needs to abstract instrumental rationality from its various value contexts, and also to admit that it cannot solve these basic world-view problems.

We have defined instrumental rationality as the ability to put two and two together logically and causally (granted premises which may indeed vary enormously from culture to culture and person to person). Put like this, the onus of proof shifts to those who deny its universality: they need to find societies where this ability was or is altogether absent. Consider some basic aspects of human life: war, justice, medicine and language. Can the chances of winning a war be estimated without causal reasoning? One might indeed have religious reasons to believe that one has immunity from bullets, or that death will be followed by resurrection and happiness,[79] and one might adjust one's calculations accordingly;

---

[79] Cf. Ranger, 'Connexions between "Primary Resistance" Movements', 449–50.

these would be cause-and-effect calculations nonetheless. Legal practice, written and unwritten, can seldom, if ever, be conducted without
some investigation of causes, even if by oracles, as with the Azande. On
medicine, it is hard to disagree with Obeyesekere (however it may be with
his theses on Captain Cook):

> if I fall seriously ill in Sri Lanka, I might decide to consult a shaman or an M.D.,
> or my astrologer or a seer; or I might go see an Ayurvedic physician, or simply
> do nothing and blame my karma, or say it is my karma and then perversely
> perform some of the foregoing alternatives, or say there's a new type of medicine
> in a neighbouring country, so why not give it a try. Underlying these alternatives
> and the judgments I make is a form of reasoning I have labelled 'practical' or
> 'pragmatic rationality'.[80]

Implicit in this is that the person's choices will be affected by his world-
view. If one is dead against astrology or does not know what an Ayurvedic
physician is, those alternatives are unlikely to be considered. Taking for
granted any value premises, however, and suspending disbelief in their
rationality, the reasoning is of a universal sort.

The universality of instrumental reasoning, in the sense of 'putting two
and two together', seems to emerge also from consideration of general
linguistics. Languages have different grammars but these grammars all
share some features in common: it was Ferdinand Saussure's achievement
to elucidate them.[81] Distinction between arbitrary signs (words) to enable
them to label different classes of things and actions involves abstraction.
This is 'system', in Saussure's terms. Now, the classification of sets of
things as the same or as similar is heavily influenced by world-views and
values and is very variable in time and space.[82] Yet all societies seem to
do it in one way or another: at least one awaits counter-examples with
scepticism. Then there are sentences (under the rubric of 'syntagm' in
Saussure's terminology) – and again all spoken languages seem to have
them in one form or another. Sentences enable speakers to subsume one
class of things under another class of things.

Now, is there any language in which one cannot say in one form or
another that something is bad for children to eat or drink? Call the
whole set of things bad for children to consume y. Call a given subset
x. For a modern British housewife, y will include subsets like whisky,
gin, and disinfectant. For the Lele of Zaire, y will include among its

---

[80] Obeyesekere, *The Apotheosis of Captain Cook*, 19.
[81] Saussure, *Cours de linguistique générale*. Saussure is a household name in intellectual
    households as the putative ancestor of the 'linguistic turn' of social scientists, etc. in the
    1960s and 1970s, but the real nature of his fundamental intellectual contribution gets
    less attention.
[82] Cf. Douglas and Hull (eds.), *How Classification Works*.

subsets anything poisonous but also young animals.[83] Recognising that a particular piece of meat, call it *a*, was from a young animal, they could express the idea that this *a* is *x* (young animal), but young animals are *y* (dangerous for children to eat), so this is dangerous for children to eat – which is a perfectly logical syllogism:

all *x* are *y*, but *a* is *x*, so *a* is *y*

Languages will express this basic logical form in different ways, but they will all have some equivalent of *x*, *y* and *a* and some way to combine them – however much the content of *x* and *y* may differ. At least, one may challenge comparative linguists to find a counter-example, without too much anxiety about the outcome.

Arguments for any kind of universal rationality are unlikely to elicit assent from all quarters, as the opposite view can be almost an article of faith, an academic world-view – a value rationality in fact. This takes us to the problem of how 'value rationality' may most usefully be defined.

The meaning of value rationality

What Weber meant by 'values' is not pellucid, though they are central in his oeuvre. The concept will be refined and developed in the next chapter, but a preliminary delimitation of its scope should not be delayed. To start with Weber's own pregnant explanation of Value Rationality:

A person acts purely in accordance with value rationality (*wertrational*) when he or she acts without thought for the foreseeable consequences, in the service of his or her conviction of what seems to be demanded by duty, self-respect (*Würde*), beauty, religious teaching, piety, or the importance attached to a 'cause' of any sort whatsoever. In the sense attached to it by our terminology, value-rational action is always action in response to 'commandments' or 'demands' to which the person doing the action believes that they must respond. Only insofar as human action is orientated towards such demands – and this is the case only with a fraction that varies greatly in size and is mostly very small – do we wish to speak of Value Rationality. As will become apparent, it is important enough to be distinguished as a special type, although otherwise no attempt is being made here to give classification which is in any way exhaustive of the types of action.[84]

It seems to me that this can imply something more than a positive or negative judgement and that one can get the most out of his insights by extending his concept of value rationality to include all kinds of deeply

[83] Douglas, 'Rightness of Categories', 240.
[84] Weber, *Wirtschaft und Gesellschaft*, vol. 1, pp. 12–13, passage beginning 'Rein wertrational handelt, wer' and ending 'zu geben versucht wird'.

held convictions. Donald Davidson is relevant again here, in that he breaks down the wall between evaluations and other judgements:

> What makes our judgments of the 'descriptive' properties of things true or false is the fact that the same properties tend to cause the same beliefs in different observers, and when observers differ, we assume there is an explanation . . . My thesis is that the same holds for moral values.[85]

While I dissented above from Davidson's optimism about resolving disagreements about basic values, he is right in thinking that value judgements and 'is' judgements are the same kind of thinking. (I am pessimistic about resolving to every reasonable and well-informed person's satisfaction disagreements about basic facts, such as whether humans have a non-material mind, just as I am about resolving value differences, such as whether polygamy is good. So I agree with Davidson's assimilation but don't share his optimism.)

This extension of Weber's term 'value rationality' to cover convictions about how things are will be justified more fully in the following chapter. From now on 'value rationality' and 'conviction rationality' will be used practically as synonyms, and often almost interchangeably, with 'values' taken to mean more than purely 'ought'-type propositions. Even when we enlarge the category in this way, value rationality's influence on past and present must not be overstated. Emotion, unthinking tradition and free-wheeling, purely instrumental reasoning no doubt dominate much of the history of human actions and thoughts. Nonetheless, rational values or rather values and convictions shape the course of history in crucial respects, not least by setting the parameters of instrumental rationality, as we shall see that they often can.

The relation of instrumental to value rationality is not quite the same as the relation of means to ends, *pace* a distinguished sociologist.[86] That

---

[85] Davidson, 'Objectivity of Values', 47.

[86] This was suggested by the eminent sociologist W. G. Runciman, *A Critique of Max Weber's Philosophy of Social Science*, 14: 'The distinction between "value-rationality" and "purpose rationality", to which corresponds the distinction more common among English-speaking sociologists between "expressive" and "instrumental" action, continues to be widely used. But it can as well be expressed in terms of the traditional distinction between means and ends.' Quite apart from substantive objection that ends do not have to involve values – e.g. 'Girls just want to have fun' (Cindi Lauper) – Runciman's equation is unfortunate because it sows confusion on a verbal level. From the sense, he has to be equating 'value rationality' and 'ends' (I assume this despite the word order because the alternative would be a misunderstanding of Weber too total to be credible in the case of a scholar of Runciman's stature). But this leaves Runciman's 'instrumental' action, a.k.a. 'purpose-rationality', as the equivalent of 'Zweckrationalität', which could be literally translated as 'End-rationality'. The subject is complicated enough without this verbal complication. 'Homer nods' is the best commentary on these particular remarks by a sociologist to whom historians are greatly indebted.

equation does not do justice to the text of Weber, who makes it clear that instrumental behaviour can be an end in itself:

the person acting can arrange the competing and conflicting ends along a scale of urgency consciously estimated by himself, without any value-rational orientation towards 'commandments' and 'demands', but simply as felt subjective needs which present themselves as a given; and accordingly so to orientate his or her action that so far as possible they are satisfied in the same order (the principle of marginal utility).[87]

Ends–means rationality includes the weighing up of different ends against each other in terms of their power to satisfy needs that do not necessarily have anything to do with values.

In short: why should all 'ends' be values?[88] They may just be things enjoyed for their own sake, in an essentially instrumental way. If someone pursues pleasure just because they want to, not out of some Benthamite principle, their action seems more appropriately described as instrumental than as value rational. Actually, it is clear from experience, not to mention history, that people are often motivated by ends that have little to do with values (except that values ignored can be a source of inner guilt). Though this book concentrates on the interconnections of values and instrumental rationality, the existence of untrammelled instrumental calculation is in no way denied. It creates 'ends' which are unconnected with values and convictions.

Conversely, some values are not 'ends' but prohibitions or 'side-constraints'. To believe that torture is always wrong is a value: at least, there would be no reason to deny that except the circular one that a value

---

[87] 'Oder es kann der Handelnde die konkurrienden und kollidierenden Zwecke ohne wer-trationale Orientierung an "Geboten" und "Forderungen" einfach als gegebene subjektive Bedürfnisregungen in eine Skala ihrer von ihm bewußt abgewogenen Dringlichkeit bringen und darnach sein Handeln so orientieren, daß sie in dieser Reihenfolge nach Möglichkeit befriedigt werden (Prinzip des "Grenznutzens").' Weber, *Wirtschaft und Gesellschaft*, 13.

[88] Identification of 'values' with 'ends' *tout court* can work if ends are defined in the rather special sense we find in the Aristotelian tradition. A 'telos' in Aristotle's sense means more than just any old goal: it is close to G. E. Moore's idea of an intrinsic good. Cf. White, *Sovereign Virtue*, 12. Granted this rather special sense of end, one could translate Weber's concept of *Zweckrationalität* very approximately and perhaps rather temerariously into Aristotelian language by identifying 'instrumental rationality' with 'calculation': 'to logistokon'; or with deliberation: 'bouleuesthai'. See Aristotle, *Nicomachean Ethics*, 6.1, 1139^a Bekker, and cf. 6.7, 1141^b Bekker. The Aristotelian Thomas Aquinas also uses 'end' (*finis*) in a sense which goes well beyond the modern everyday English usage of 'end' and which approximates to Weber's idea of a value. Cf. Aquinas, *Summa Theologica*, 1–2, q. 1 art. 3: passage beginning: 'Dictum est autem supra' and ending 'quantum ad passionem' (*Sancti Thomae Aquinatis . . . opera omnia*, vol. 6, p. 10).

has to be an 'end'. With some considerable intellectual contortion one could perhaps define avoidance of torture as an 'end', but it is simpler to regard it as a passionately held negative principle or side-constraint to action.

A further point, only apparently recondite, and closely connected with the central arguments of this book, is that values are sometimes already internalised, and then manifest themselves through a variety of instrumental extensions, which reinforce them and reproduce them. A lot of ritual belongs to this interface between convictions and instrumental rationality: to describe this in terms of ends and means is possible but awkward. To call a bar mitzvah ceremony a means to an end seems strained. This is important for an argument to be developed later: that concrete ways of thinking are characteristic of 'values' and convictions and that instrumental rationality plays an integral role in the renewal and reproduction of such concrete ways of thinking.

Far from being dispensable, the value rationality/instrumental rationality distinction is crucial to Weber's thought and also to the present investigation. The book is in a sense a development, with applications, of this central idea in his sociology. A key thesis is that these two types of rationality are seldom if ever separated. They are complementary. They can hardly exist without each other. Weber says as much, though very succinctly.[89] Of course this is not the first study to make the point about Weber,[90] but the systematic use of these concepts to elucidate historical developments and causal connections may be new. The ideal-types of formal and substantive rationality are defined to be distinct from, but integrated with, and subordinate to, the value–instrumental distinction.

As the Introduction made clear, the methodology adopted here is also Weberian in its use of 'ideal-types'. The distinction between conviction rationality and instrumental rationality is itself of course an ideal-type. It is a schematic simplification serving as a tool for getting a grip on infinitely complicated past realities. It is hard if not impossible to find either value-rational or instrumentally rational thinking in a pure form. Ideal-types are not Platonic ideas but instruments of analysis.

---

[89] This is clear from Weber's text: 'Totally instrumental action is, however...a more or less artificial limiting case...Very rarely is action, particularly social action, oriented exclusively in only one of these two ways.' ('Absolute Zweckrationalität des Handelns ist aber...ein im wesentlichen konstruktiver Grenzfall...Sehr selten ist Handeln, insbesondere soziales Handeln, nur in der einen oder der andren Art orientiert.') Weber, *Wirtschaft und Gesellschaft*, 13.

[90] 'rational social arrangements cannot create values, they can only function as a means to the furtherance of pregiven values' (Boucock, *In the Grip of Freedom*, 185).

These considerations on method are preliminary to the main task, which is to clarify the sociology of rationality. The central question is: how does conviction rationality interact with instrumental rationality? It will be emphasised that modernity and instrumental rationality do not have some kind of special relationship. Making this point will lead on to a re-examination of our other pair of concepts: formal and substantive (or 'material') rationality, with an attempt to get more empirical mileage out of them.

2 The structure of values and convictions

In the previous chapter the failure of Rational Choice Theory to explain the constitution of values was included among the problems with that whole approach to rationalities. 'There's no accounting for tastes' may be an adequate response to the choice of Pepsi rather than Coke (or vice versa) but not to contrasting ideas in Islamabad and Ann Arbor about the relation between the sexes. Here the Rational Choice theorists need to listen to historians. Conversely, historians need to lift their empirical expertise up to a higher level of generality to understand why so many different value systems have such a tenacious purchase on different sets of minds. It can hardly be genetic! G. A. Cohen tries a thought experiment about identical twins separated at birth:

One was raised as, and remains, a devout Presbyterian. The other was raised as, and remains, a devout Roman Catholic. They argue against each other's views, but they've heard those arguments before, they've learned how to reply to them, and their opposed convictions consequently remain firm.[1]

The study of value systems is a field par excellence where the old discipline of History, if allowed to go beyond period specialisation to comparisons disciplined by clear concepts, can redress the imbalance in the relatively new field of Rational Choice.[2]

We know a conviction when we meet one. 'Some of Kant's views about sex are so extreme as to be either ridiculous or abhorrent to all enlightened people', says a distinguished philosopher in a book generally very sympathetic to Kant.[3] That certainly tells us what the modern philosopher in question believes to be beyond question. For him, it is obvious that Kant is mistaken: anyone who agrees with Kant is excluded from the set of all enlightened people. A feeling that a given conviction is self-evident is often combined with the notion that opponents cannot really

---

[1] Cohen, *If You're an Egalitarian*, 8.
[2] For detailed applications of the ideas set out in this chapter see d'Avray, *Medieval Religious Rationalities*, ch. 2.
[3] Wood, *Kantian Ethics*, 224.

think what they do for the weak reasons they allege, and must have other motives of which they are perhaps unaware:[4] they are wrong because of diminished rationality.

Perhaps Kant would have dismissed the modern philosopher's convictions no less summarily had he not been dead and unable to answer back. We need to remain open to the possibility that both these opposing sets of convictions about sex might be rational; we need to keep this possibility separate from our personal opinions of these convictions. This chapter does not just assume, but tries to explain, *how* exactly it is that contradictory convictions can in principle all be rational, though they cannot all be correct. It is about 'what different peoples at different times may have had good reasons by their lights for holding true, regardless of whether we ourselves believe that what they held was true was in fact the truth'.[5] The explanation will be twofold, invoking the force of antecedent probability within world-views, and of concrete as opposed to notional or abstract ways of thinking.

Recapitulation: convictions and values

To take up again a line of thought from the previous chapter: the word 'convictions' is used in such a way as to include 'values' without confining discussion to 'good/bad' 'ought/ought not' certitudes. The distinction between 'value rationality' and 'instrumental rationality' drawn by Max Weber has been a driving force in the research behind this book, but the problems with the word 'value' have already been discussed, and to avoid these it has been treated as a subset of the more general concept of a 'conviction'. The word 'value' will still be freely employed below for those convictions which involve 'ought' judgements. The phrase 'values and convictions', which will also be used from time to time, does not imply a disjunction between the two.

There is no point here in being drawn into a debate about 'What Weber meant' by values. As noted in the last chapter, Weber seems not to commit himself to a full-dress definition. I suspect that he knew what he wanted to do with the word but preferred not to tie himself down. A 'positivistic theory of value' has been attributed to him, for instance: that values are deliberate choices, individual rather than collective, and more to do with the will than the intellect.[6] My overall impression from Weber's

---

[4] Cf. *Ibid.*, 229–30, for an example.

[5] Skinner, 'Interpretation, Rationality and Truth', 52.

[6] Kronman, *Max Weber*, 21, 186, and *passim*. Note the words that I have italicised, which bring out the internal tension within Kronman's interpretation, in the following sentence

sociological and historical writings is that collective beliefs matter more than the 'positivistic' (deliberate individual choice) interpretation might suggest. However that may be, the present study is not an interpretation of Weber's insights (except perhaps quite secondarily) but an attempt to build on them by using them, as he intended, for fresh sociological and historical analyses.

Whatever Weber's views, the advantage of using 'values' loosely and interchangeably with 'convictions' is that it then becomes easier to include 'is' as well as 'ought' judgements.[7] It has already been suggested that the 'is/ought' distinction can be a source of confusion if it artificially segregates essentially similar ways of thinking. For instance, convictions about the basic nature of man are to do with 'is' beliefs rather than 'ought' beliefs. Is a human a highly evolved material animal, or a soul sojourning in a succession of bodies, or somewhere on a spectrum between these positions? The answer has implications for all sorts of ethical decisions: for what one eats (meat?); for whether rebellion is worth it if one has future lives to look forward to in which one may be better off; for whether newborn babies or comatose patients have rights – but the answer itself is not a judgement of how things *should* be, but of how they *are*. Similarly, belief in or scepticism about witchcraft in the first instance provides answers to an 'is' question rather than an 'ought' question.

Convictions such as 'witches don't exist', 'there is nothing after death', 'there is no such thing as "society"', 'humans are purely material', 'I will be reincarnated after death' seem phenomenologically similar to convictions like 'torture is never justified', 'turn the other cheek', 'treason is wrong', 'better to die on your feet than to live on your knees': that is to say, a close description of how people hold all such convictions, defend them against attack, build them into their decision-making, and so forth reveals similar patterns that are markedly different from other kinds of thinking. When people say 'all humans are equal' they mean something more than 'it would be nice if all humans were equal' or 'one should

from his book: 'What Weber's positivistic theory of value *does* imply is that the status of a value, the fact that a particular norm happens to be a value for someone, can be accounted for conceptually only if we view the value in question as the product of an act of choice, *no matter how unrealistic* this may be in any given case' (p. 21).
[7] Cf. the interesting comment by the *engagé* anthropologist David Graeber about the framework of the Harvard project, led by Clyde Kluckhohn, to study values comparatively: 'value orientations mixed ideas of the desirable with assumptions about the nature of the world in which one had to act' (Graeber, *Toward an Anthropological Theory of Value*, 4). Graeber goes on to point out that since the Kluckhohn project 'there has been next to nothing on "values" in general' (as opposed to the specific values of particular societies) in anthropology (*ibid.*, 5). He perceptively draws out the similarities between the Harvard project and Max Weber's comparative study of world religions. The interest of Graeber's book transcends his political perspective, though it does not enhance his appreciation of other approaches (see, for instance, p. 274 n. 9, on Mary Douglas).

treat all humans equally': they mean that in some sense humans actually are equal, and that entitlement to equal treatment is a consequence of that fact. Such 'factual' convictions seem very similar to values which use adjectives like 'good' or 'bad'.

As for non-factual values, it is useful to include not only ethical judgements but also those value judgements which are in a sense anti-ethical. Thus, Nietzsche's concept of value can be described as anti-ethical, if it is rightly understood to be something like the self-affirmation of the superior individual.[8] Similarly, some forms of nationalism could be non-ethical values – 'My country right or wrong'.

Values, traditions, and emotions

Most of these propositions appeal to the feelings as well as the intellect, but (following Weber) it is useful to distinguish conceptually between convictions (value rationality in his terminology) and emotions. Emotion and tradition were added to value rationality and instrumental rationality to make up the full complement of Weber's four determinants of social action.[9] The schema is thus as follows:

RATIONAL	NON-RATIONAL
value rationality + instrumental rationality	tradition + emotion

It is significant that he kept the ideal-types of 'tradition' and 'emotion' separate from values: this emphasised the rationality that he attributed to certitudes. Though the four determinants are intermingled in practice, conceptually speaking values are on the same side of the line between rational and non-rational as is instrumental calculation, while tradition and affect are on the non-rational side.

By traditional behaviour in a pure form can be meant nothing more than a habitual reaction to an accustomed stimulus.[10] A great deal of everyday behaviour approximates to this ideal-type. When a conscious effort is made to keep things as they are, traditional behaviour can move into the value-rational realm.[11]

---

[8] Joas, *The Genesis of Values*, 24.   [9] Weber, *Wirtschaft und Gesellschaft*, vol. 1, p. 12.

[10] 'Denn es ist sehr oft nur ein dumpfes, in der Richtung der einmal eingelebten Einstellung ablaufendes Reagieren auf gewohnte Reize' (*ibid.*).

[11] 'die Bindung an das Gewohnte in verschiedenem Grade und Sinne bewußt aufrecht erhalten werden kann: in diesem Fall nähert sich dieser Typus dem von Nr. 2 [i.e. to value rationality]' (*ibid.*).

Emotional behaviour can do so too. It may be a value that one needs to find an outlet for one's emotions.[12] On the other hand, it is common experience that emotions can operate independently of both convictions and instrumental calculation. Emotion is the category that would allow Weberian theory to accommodate the whole realm of irrational action, of which the briefest typology was sketched out in the Introduction. He left this sector of his theory relatively unexplored, as does the present study, without for a moment underrating its importance. Some of his ideas imply explanations in terms of non-rational motivations. Notably, the famous thesis about Calvinism and capitalism implies that the need to prove that their salvation and success were predetermined is what motivated Calvinist businessmen to choose to try harder. If he is right, the explanation for their efforts is one that they themselves could not have understood. A rapprochement between Weber and psychoanalytical insights would be possible thanks to this concept of affect, though this is not the place to attempt it.

Though emotions can operate without reference to values, there is a certain analogy between their modes of operating. Emotional action and value-rational action (or action dictated by convictions) have this in common: that the point of the action is the action itself rather than any consequences that may flow from it.[13]

On the other hand there is a crucial difference that distinguishes values and convictions from emotions (just as it does values from preferences, as argued in connection with Rational Choice Theory). With values and convictions, reference is made to general principles. With pure affect, however, that is not the case. Emotions *per se* do not embody general principles, though they frequently reinforce such principles. The distinction between values and emotions is analogous to the distinction between values and preferences in that the application of values can lead to un-desired conclusions. It is a fact that values or convictions can sometimes lead those who hold them into actions they find emotionally unappealing. The role of general principles in values does not, however, explain why they are so tenacious, the problem which must now be addressed.

Tenacity of convictions

There are many certitudes which are not obviously irrational but which are unscathed by counter-argument which cannot be answered

---

[12] 'Eine Sublimierung ist es, wenn das affektuell bedingte Handeln als bewußte Entladung der Gefühlslage auftritt: es befindet sich dann meist (nicht immer) schon auf dem Wege zur "Wertrationalisierung" oder zum Zweckhandeln oder zu beiden' (*ibid.*).

[13] 'der Sinn des Handelns nicht in dem jenseits seiner liegenden Erfolg, sondern in dem bestimmt gearteten Handeln als solchen' (*ibid.*).

immediately. One could short-circuit the problem by saying that such certitudes are by definition irrational. That is not so easy to do once one begins to consider examples.

If someone believes in the equality of men and women, they will not abandon their views just because a journal of psychology publishes a study purporting to show a systematic difference in IQ between the sexes. Rather, they will assume that further studies will correct the mistake, or reject IQ as an index of equality or inequality. If someone thinks imperialism is wrong, they will not abandon their view because someone demonstrates that it brought peace and prosperity whereas successor states lacked both: they may think of the new findings as a set of individual exceptions to a generalisation that remains valid, or, if that does not stand up, that independence under any circumstances is better than imperialism however benign. A believer in liberal democracy will not abandon his or her certitudes even if a great liberal democracy systematically uses torture, or if a prosperous majority puts through harsh legislation against a suffering minority. A real believer in state socialism would not switch his allegiance to capitalism just because capitalist countries seem to have more material goods. Values and convictions transcend the divide between secular and religious, left-wing and right-wing ideologies. Tenacity in the face of prima facie plausible objections characterises religious fundamentalists and die-hard communists, but also their opponents. An orthodox Muslim will know in advance that arguments against the historicity of Hadith (the oral source of revelation through the Prophet) must be mistaken; a literal-sense believer in biblical chronology will be able to explain away scientific evidence that the universe is fourteen billion years old; and a believer in the inviolability of scientific laws will not feel the need to examine the evidence for miracles collected (through a critical sieve[14]) in canonisation processes from the thirteenth century on.

Commonly, people have an instinct that it is not even worth looking at counter-arguments of others whose world-view they do not take seriously. Every now and again, however, people come face to face with objections to their own convictions. Yet when a person's values and convictions are confronted with counter-arguments, they are seldom seriously shaken. It is an inescapable fact that even intellectually honest people rarely suspend belief in their core convictions just because a plausible argument against them appears. The usual reaction, rather, is to maintain the conviction and assume that an answer to the objection will present itself sooner or later. Perhaps the answer will be found in the writings of some expert who shares the same framework of convictions.

---

[14] Cf. d'Avray, *Medieval Religious Rationalities*, index, *s.v.* 'canonisation'.

The problem in a nutshell is: if values are rational, why are they so resistant to attack by other people's logical arguments? A specious solution is that this obduracy is not rational after all. Though general principles may be invoked – one might cynically think – the real decision is at some different level of the mind, and the claim to rationality is self-deception. Some religious people think that unbelievers or adherents of different religions or churches do not see the truth because of some moral resistance or failure on their part. Some theological positions may be open to debate, they admit, but there are fundamentals to which everyone must subscribe or be damned. Much the same attitude is common among people with no religious beliefs, including intellectuals and academics. Most feel that there is a common core of values that every honest person must be capable of recognising.

It would be reassuring to believe that there were such a common core, about which most decent people agreed, so that divergences are secondary, or culpable, or uneducated or irrational: but to believe this is itself a faith-type position, hardly supported by empirical evidence. It would look more plausible if a specific set of core convictions could be identified in all the significant value systems of world history, but as soon as one attempts to establish such a list, counter-examples come to mind. Son–mother marriage might perhaps be a universal taboo, but to put together even a short list of key values consistently present within all the religious and secular belief systems of world history would be difficult. It is easy to find values that are very common – truthfulness, hospitality, fidelity – and that list would be extensive. Far from universal, though: non-trivial exceptions can nearly always be found.

Perhaps there are common 'norms' of the kind that Donald Davidson postulated to explain how communication is possible at all. 'With respect to the simplest and plainest logical matters, a sharing of norms of rationality is an inescapable artefact of interpretation',[15] he argues. Or again: 'the more basic a norm is to our making sense of an agent, the less content we can give to the idea that we disagree with respect to that norm'.

The problem is with the word 'basic'. If we understand 'basic' as Davidson would have to do for his argument to make sense, such questions as 'what is a human?' are secondary and superficial. For it is on just such problems as these that societies fundamentally disagree. Davidson's 'basic' norms may perhaps be identified with instrumental rationality or overlap with it. Perhaps they are on some more abstract plane. Whatever and wherever they are, we are unlikely to find them in the same sphere

---

[15] Davidson, 'The Objectivity of Values', 50.

as the concrete and tenacious values and convictions which concern us in this chapter.

One could imagine value systems as circles. Each one is interlinked with a number of others but there is no common ground within all the circles. Without a common territory to begin with, it is unlikely that all human societies will converge towards a consensus. This suggests too that self-deception and 'denial' are *not* enough to explain why people who are to all appearances well intentioned fail to convince one another. The failure is widespread, even normal. Some examples were mentioned briefly in the Introduction. For all the power of self-deception, it is not sufficient to explain the variety of world-views or their resistance to attack from one another.

This problem does not disturb believers in progress or cultural evolution. They can dismiss past values at odds with their own as literally primitive. Contemporary societies with alien values can be dismissed by proposing that Western societies are further advanced along the evolutionary or progressive path. But can a progressive evolution of values be demonstrated without a circular assumption, viz., that 'modern' values are better?

Modern people naturally tend to think so: they are brought up to believe in human rights, gender equality, and so on – as does the author! This takes us back to the paradox pinpointed by G. A. Cohen of identical twins separated at birth and brought up respectively as a pious Catholic and a pious Presbyterian, or again respectively as an uncompromising egalitarian and as a moderate liberal with an easy tolerance for inequality.[16] Cohen makes it clear that his imaginary twins are each familiar with each others' arguments and able to bat them back easily.[17] His thought-experiment can be generalised from the family to society as a whole. When values transcend particular families in a given society they will seem all the more persuasive – to people brought up in that society. People brought up in any of the modern Western families imagined in Cohen's thought-experiment might well agree that all humans have certain rights and that discrimination on grounds of race or gender is wrong. Societies in the past or in other cultures in which these values do not obtain seem obviously wrong – but people in those past societies might well feel the same about the modern West, and people in those other cultures definitely do. This chapter tries to explain how all concerned in these various disagreements can be rational.

The recurrent failure of honest and intelligent people to convince each other does not mean that they cannot understand each other or even

---

[16] Cohen, *If You're an Egalitarian*, 8.   [17] *Ibid.*

reach consensus after secondary disagreements. Any two people, any two subcultures, any two societies have enough in common to provide a basis for dialogue and communication, and to settle 'first decimal point' debates, even if not enough for either to win a debate about critical differences in world-views. Arguments can be won in academic life in areas where values overlap (as they thankfully do to a non-trivial extent), but when academics differ about values their debates too are inconclusive. In all these cases, common ground of the sort that can serve as the premise for a knock-down argument on one side or another is rare when it comes to radically different convictions. Common ground sufficient for mutual comprehension is much less rare.

The intersecting circles image is helpful here: even though there is no common area covered by all the circles, each value rationality overlaps with any other rationality enough for mutual communication to be possible. (Perhaps the shapes need to take contorted forms for the analogy to work out: it is an analogy, not an exercise in geometry.) It does indeed seem relatively easy to find a lot of common ground between any *pair* of value systems, and this is crucial to communication between cultures. Brahman Hinduism – using the word as a simplification for a complicated mass of religious phenomena – shares with Catholicism a tendency to treat marriage as indissoluble[18] and full of mystic significance, often expressed in elaborate religious rituals. Catholicism shares with the Church of Jesus Christ of the Latter-Day Saints (popularly known as Mormonism) the ideas of development of doctrine and of a leader with teaching authority (pope and prophet respectively). Catharism shared with Hinduism the idea of transmigration of souls, and with Zoroastrianism a dualist dichotomy between good and evil principles. Protestants, Catholics, and high-minded agnostics in nineteenth-century England shared an assumption that sexual promiscuity was wrong. The Soviet Union and the USA during the Cold War both took monogamy for granted. In early twenty-first-century Western controversy about same-sex marriage, the possibility of polygamy is not taken seriously. With all this common ground, value systems or rather the people who subscribe to them can certainly talk to each other, though the overlaps do not provide an arena for a knock-out conflict about which system is better overall.

Here too Donald Davidson's argument about 'shared norms' may finally come into its own. Though they cannot be 'basic', in the same

---

[18] See, however, Holden, *Hindu Divorce*, for the argument that divorce is a fact on the ground in Hinduism generally. But at the Brahman level there seems to be an ideology of indissolubility, which Holden is attacking as oppressive.

sense as questions like 'should we treat humans and animals the same?' or 'why should I be nice?' are basic, and though they are, frankly, difficult to identify if they mean more than 'putting two and two together', they would help to account for the possibility of communication, without persuasion, that concerns us here.

This chapter will try to spell out why there is nothing necessarily irrational about the failure to be persuaded, and to show why it actually makes sense for people to hold on to their convictions in this way. Values and convictions are psychological counterparts to logical premises. Their relative immunity to attack derives from their place in holistic systems of mutually supporting convictions, and their embeddedness in concrete thought.

Mutual protection of convictions in a system

Part of the solution is that values and convictions tend to be part of whole networks of interconnected reasons and certitudes that stand or fall together.[19] If one is attacked, the others provide reassurance. Conversely, the possibility that the whole network is a mistake seems hard (or dangerous) to take seriously, and motivation for being convinced is weak, since it would have far-reaching mental and practical consequences.

Ordinary 'stand-alone' logical arguments, by contrast, are linear; they are like old-fashioned Christmas lights: break one bulb, and the whole series of bulbs goes out.[20] Values and convictions are more like the electricity grid. If one source of power fails, other sources supply power while the fault in the system is repaired. Thus an argument directed against a real conviction may seem, to the assailant who wields it, to be fatal, but to the person holding the value it is just a difficulty which will surely be overcome after further thought on their own part or that of others within their community of convictions.

Values and convictions depart from the linear model of ordinary logic, without ceasing to be rational, partly because they tend to be formed by a convergence from all directions of perceived probabilities, a multiplicity

---

[19] Cf. e.g. Taylor, 'Rationality', 96. After the present work was completed, John Sabapathy drew my attention to the following passage from Wittgenstein (whose pervasive influence surely influenced subsequent philosophers and most notably Peter Winch and Alistair MacIntyre): '141. When we first begin to *believe* anything, what we believe is not a single proposition, it is a whole system of propositions. (Light dawns gradually over the whole.) 142. It is not single axioms that strike me as obvious, it is a system in which consequences and premises give one another *mutual* support.' Wittgenstein, *On Certainty*, p. 21e.

[20] My pupils tell me that Christmas lights are sturdier now, so the analogy is with the older sort.

of small bits of evidence that together make a person certain. This sort of certainty does not so easily lend itself to linear demonstration – or refutation. How do we know that the Americans really put men on the moon, and that it was not a brilliant propaganda illusion? How do you know that Hawaii exists? You are certain, but a logical proof would be difficult and leaky. Similarly, on a personal level, knowledge of someone's character, a knowledge made up of an infinite number of small experiences of it, may make one quite certain that they could not have committed certain crimes.

Now, this 'convergence of multiple probabilities and evidences' can also be found in much ordinary 'instrumental' reasoning – which can be either of this type, or more linear and logical. However, when one is absolutely sure on the basis of 'convergence', then reasoning becomes phenomenologically akin to a value or conviction. This may be because the convergence of many reasons seems to demonstrate not an isolated conclusion but rather a whole network of interconnected and mutually supporting or reinforcing principles. It may seem odd to extend the word 'value' to such cases, and common usage would make it difficult to do so, but in fact any certainty which is part of a whole web of thought is hard to distinguish objectively from a 'value': at least they behave in much the same way, especially if the certainty in question is concrete rather than abstract (a point to be discussed later in this chapter). These are of course reasons for expanding Weber's concept of value rationality and rechristening it 'conviction rationality'.

Values and convictions tend to be part of a general system of how things are and work. If one piece seems vulnerable to an objection, one assumes that the objection is probably fallacious even if it looks plausible on the surface. Rather than give up a complex general way of looking at things, one assumes the objection must be wrong. Nor is this necessarily irrational, or 'denial'. Even if ten able academic historians swore they had witnessed alien spacemen abducting a departmental secretary, I would not believe them. I would attribute it to alcohol, substance abuse, wishful thinking, collective dynamics, anything rather than alien spacemen, just because spacemen with a penchant for abducting earthlings do not have a place in my world-view.

The psychology of conviction can be translated to the logical level. The logic of conviction rationality is one of antecedent probabilities. (It has an affinity to Bayesian logic.[21]) If one element in a person's set of convictions is attacked, and all the other elements in the set fit with the disputed one

---

[21] Bayes is currently 'all the rage in philosophy' (Bovens and Hartmann, *Bayesian Episte-mology*, v). See e.g. Swinburne (ed.), *Bayes's Theorem*; Earman, *Bayes or Bust?*. Unfortunately, Bayesianism is too mathematical to be integrated into the argument here (if only

and create an antecedent probability in its favour, the arguments against it need to be strong enough to overcome that prior likelihood. If a person believes a, b and c, and these all combine to reinforce the prior likelihood of p, then p has a great advantage over any objections in the mind of the person whose views are attacked. It is not so for the attacker who does not accept a, b or c. This explains why an objection which seems powerful to one disputant often seems weak to the other.

To shake the convictions of the advocate of p, the critic would need to attack a, b and c at the same time. That is easier said than done. Argument normally progresses by isolating one specific issue and focusing only on that. To debate a whole series of issues simultaneously is hard. Thus the conviction p is protected either way: by the prior expectation that it is true generated by convictions a, b and c on the one hand, and by the difficulty of attacking all these propositions simultaneously on the other. The elements of a world-view can rely on each other's support.

Systems of convictions and social practice

This line of explanation may be extended to include social practice and the ideas that are implicit in it. Ideas are expressed in actions as well as in texts, and sometimes patterns of action amount to a 'general system' of thought in repeated and structured actions – a value rationality embodied in the practices. Social practices are shot through with meaning.[22] So when an idea links up with another idea thus embodied it becomes much more resistant to attack. A way of life is at stake. It will not be easily abandoned. The idea's roots stretch out in all sorts of directions. In the tradition which one can loosely name Hinduism, for example, three key ideas, Dharma, Karma and Samsara, all complement each other. Each makes the others so intrinsically plausible that an attack on any one of them individually will look like a mere attempt to be clever in the face of probability. Dharma is the cosmic order, which is also the ritual and ethical order. Karma is the law of consequences: deeds in accordance with Dharma produce good results eventually, deeds that violate Dharma eventually bring bad consequences. Now the principle of Karma would be easy to refute if it were not combined with the principle of Samsara, reincarnation. Because of this principle of rebirth, it can never be objected that evildoers flourish like the green bay tree. If their wrongdoing does not come back at them in this life it will do so in a future life. The social

because of my own limitations). It also seems difficult to attach numbers to probabilities in 'real-life' history and sociology.

[22] See e.g. Weber, *Wirtschaft und Gesellschaft*, vol. 1, p. 1; Winch, *The Idea of a Social Science*, 128; Geertz, 'Thick Description', 5.

system embodied this. Just as one could move up and down the scale between animals and humans by behaving well or badly in a given life, so one could move up and down the caste system within the human scale. For Hindus it may be all very well for a particular caste which represents one stage in the progress through lives to prosper materially or militarily as the case may be, but in the last analysis the material world and all its trappings are a sort of illusion. Ultimate escape is the extinction of individuality (an idea common to Hinduism and Buddhism despite their differences). So the material triumphs of the West did not subvert Hindu convictions (as they did belief in the Chinese imperial system). The ability of Westerners to win battles and industrialise production might impress the Westerners themselves, but cut no ice with a Hindu renouncer, the model of excellence. It is a striking instance of a more general feature of values and especially of value systems: their often amazing and genuine invulnerability to most attacks. As will be argued in the next chapter, this invulnerability is not absolute, but it is a widespread sociological phenomenon and cannot be relegated to the 'irrationality' file.

Competing systems within the same period

There can be a plurality of general systems within the same period. The idea that one world-view dominates each age is no longer widely held, even with the proviso 'in the last analysis'. Stuart Clark's study of early modern demonology is a model study of the network of interdependence between different parts of a world-view within the same period. He brings out the connections between belief that demons were active in the world and other lines of thought at the time:

in believing in witchcraft, writers of demonology took up positions in main areas of contemporary intellectual debate. In natural philosophy, they worked with a flexible amalgam of up-to-date Aristotelianism and natural magical theory; in history, they espoused an apocalyptic and prophetic understanding of the past and the events of their own times; their view of religious deviance derived from a providential interpretation of misfortune, a pastoral and evangelical conception of piety and conformity, and a preoccupation with sins against the first Commandment, notably idolatry; and their politics was built on a mystical and quasi-sacerdotal view of magistracy and on the working of charismatic ruler-ship . . . Mature and systematic witchcraft theory was possible because these ways of reflecting about science, history, religion, and politics (and, no doubt, ways of reflecting about other things too) were available as intellectual options during the early modern centuries.[23]

---

[23] Clark, *Thinking with Demons*, 684.

Although this network of alliances between doctrines was strongly present in the late medieval and early modern period (more so than either before or afterwards) it was not the only possible one:

> If demonology was congruent with some [doctrines], it was incongruent with others, with, again, important consequences for its fortunes and how we report them. Just as it comes to seem natural for some intellectuals to have taken witchcraft seriously . . . so it remains almost unthinkable in the cases of others – a Machiavelli, or a Montaigne, or a Henry Stubbe, perhaps. The sense of negative correlations here is just as important as my argument for the existence of positive ones; indeed, the first helps to confirm the second. Demonology's very kinship with various kinds of 'other beliefs' was matched by enmity, or indifference, or, simply, a less weighty construction of witchcraft from their competitors.[24]

It is a salutary reminder that several value rationalities can coexist and compete in the same society. The experience of living in the twenty-first century should make this obvious, but one can easily slip into the habit of talking about the rationality of 'a' culture because so much of the relevant background research and thought has been done by anthropologists working on small non-literate societies with one dominant world-view. The great virtue of such anthropological research on the other hand is that the fieldworker can live in the culture and become saturated with its values, suspending disbelief until it becomes evident how easily criticism of the system can be dealt with from within it.

Azande magic immune to empirical refutation

In the previous chapter the 'poison oracles' employed by the Azande of Central Africa as a decision-making mechanism were briefly discussed. They deserve further attention now as an instance of the immunity of value rationalities to criticisms that look powerful to an outsider. First let us return to a case discussed briefly in the previous chapter (p. 56). The oracle was supposed to tell someone whether or not to move into the government settlement. The question was put to the oracle twice, but it was reversed the second time around, in such a way that the same physical outcome would yield the opposite answer (as it did). This showed that the 'control experiment' principle is a type of calculation that transcends different value systems. Here the case illustrates a different point: the invulnerability of a value rationality to refutation.

The participants in the séance were not worried by the oracle's self-contradiction and had explanations at hand. To quote Evans-Pritchard's report:

---

[24] *Ibid.*, 685.

Someone suggested that the oracle was tired like a chief who has been sitting for hours listening to cases in his court and is weary. Another man said that the oracle saw some misfortune ahead, which was not death yet was a serious misfortune, and had taken this way of warning Bamina. In any case, the verdicts taken together were considered a bad augury and there was a short discussion about who was threatening the welfare of Bamina. Mbiri gave it as his opinion that the danger was from sorcery and not from witchcraft since witchcraft does not pursue a man from one place to another in this manner but ceases to trouble him if he leaves his homestead and goes to live elsewhere.[25]

Like meteorologists explaining a failed prediction, like historians accounting for conflicting evidence, like a finance minister presented with opposing economic forecasts, they discussed the problem rationally, weighing reasons why the data might be unreliable and asking whether the truth might not lie in between the two stark alternatives presented.

The very fact that the Azande conducted control tests indicates their capacity to cope with conflicting oracles. Still, for the average educated person today their whole system of magic and witchcraft must seem almost impossible to swallow. How did they fail to question it? Evans-Pritchard gives a series of explanations and by the end of his list Azande attitudes to magic seem much more rational.[26] It is worth quoting a few, singling out those which emphasise the mutual reinforcement of the different parts of the system.

Witchcraft, oracles and magic form an intellectually coherent system. Each explains and proves the others. Death is proof of witchcraft. It is avenged by magic. The achievement of vengeance-magic is proved by the poison oracle. The accuracy of the poison oracle is determined by the king's oracle, which is above suspicion . . . The failure of any rite is accounted for in advance by a variety of mystical notions – e.g. witchcraft, sorcery, and taboo. Hence the perception of error in one mystical notion in a particular situation merely proves the correctness of another and equally mystical notion . . . The place occupied by the more important medicines in a sequence of events protects them from exposure as frauds. Magic is made against unknown witches, adulterers, and thieves. On the death of a man the poison oracle determines whether he died as a victim to the magic. If the oracles were first consulted to discover the criminal, and then magic were made against him, the magic would soon be seen to be unsuccessful.[27]

---

[25] Evans-Pritchard, *Witchcraft, Oracles and Magic*, 141–2.   [26] *Ibid.*, 201–4.

[27] *Ibid.* A further reason (given *ibid.*, 204) is worth mentioning, though it does not come specifically under the 'mutual support of the parts' rubric: 'Zande beliefs are generally vaguely formulated. A belief to be easily contradicted by experience and to be easily shown to be out of harmony with other beliefs must be clearly stated and intellectually developed.'

Once within the system the objections to it seem to lose their power. The system has ways of dealing with them.

Motivation

Motivation has a lot to do with it, though by this I do *not* necessarily mean wilful ignorance (an important topic but not the present subject). Few people go to great lengths to destroy their own world-view. Once again Evans-Pritchard's study of the Azande points us to a more general truth: that people are not very interested in pursuing lines of enquiry that would be merely destructive of their universe.[28] The quality of being a witch was passed on by descent, male witches getting it from their fathers and female witches from their mothers. This means in principle that once a man had been uncovered as a witch, all his male relatives would be witches (the same with a woman, *mutatis mutandis*). The Azande did not draw this conclusion. At least in the case of a man they could evade it, if pushed, by inferring instead that the person revealed to be a witch must be a bastard, on the principle that it is a wise man who knows his own father (though presumably this line of reasoning would not work for a female witch if she was supposed to have inherited the quality from her mother). Conversely, if a man had been investigated and found to be free from the witchcraft substance, it would follow that none of his male relatives could be witches (and the same *mutatis mutandis* with a woman cleared of witchcraft). The Azande did not, however, draw this conclusion. Evans-Pritchard comments that 'Azande do not perceive the contradiction as we perceive it because they have no theoretical interest in the subject, and those situations in which they express their beliefs in witchcraft do not force the problem upon them'.[29]

Once again the modern West is not so far from the Azande as it might seem. In the last half-century notions of an immortal soul which all humans have in common and of a God who loves all humans equally have slipped away from a high proportion of the intelligentsia and others, and the idea of a human as wholly material has become quite general not only in philosophy but also in popular culture, as is suggested by the recurrent science fiction motif of a robot so sophisticated as to be indistinguishable from a man. At the same time, no society has felt so strongly the claims of human equality, rejecting racism, gender discrimination, ageism, and any other attitude that denies human equality. Yet there is tremendous tension between these two modern mentalities. Not many have the bleak clear-sightedness to point out the problem as starkly

[28] The lines that follow are derived from Evans-Pritchard, *Witchcraft*, 3–4.   [29] *Ibid.*, 4.

as Nietzsche did. Ingenious ways of resolving the tension can be found, as with the Azande.[30] In general there is more in common between the Azande and the world created by the Enlightenment than one might expect – a point that can be made without criticising either world.

Rationalism as a conviction rationality: miracles

Anthropologists are in the business of making sense of peculiar customs and historians of times and places distant from our own may feel the same way, but many other scholars will think in their heart of hearts that Western rationality is superior because it allows for refutation by empirical evidence. We should not too readily assume this is so or patronise the Azande for making their value rationality immune to empirical refutation. The limits of scientific empiricism were pointed out a generation ago by Thomas Kuhn. He argued that the psychology and sociology of science discourage assimilation of findings that undermine the very basic models dominant at a given time. Moreover, certain sorts of experiment are understood to be models of practice for the aspiring scientist and they tend to fit in with the current underlying model of the natural world. (My double sense of the word 'model' reflects Kuhn's double sense of the word 'paradigm'.) When a scientist does come up with a new model there may be a time-lag before it finds acceptance. His contemporaries and elders have to die off and be replaced by younger scientists who look at the new 'paradigm' without the old preconceptions.[31]

Kuhn's theory was controversial.[32] An approximate contemporary of his, Paul Feyerabend, was even more iconoclastic:

The assumption that there exist universally valid and binding standards of knowledge and action is a special case of a belief whose influence extends far beyond the domain of intellectual debate. This belief . . . may be formulated by saying that there exists a right way of living and that the world must be made to accept it . . . each movement filled the belief with its own particular content . . . But the

---

[30] Cf. *ibid.*, 6–7, for Azande explanations to meet the objection that the same person could be killed by vengeance magic employed by a dead man's kin for slaying the latter through witchcraft, and then avenged by his own kin as a victim of witchcraft (witchcraft killing and vengeance-magic killing being in principle totally distinct).

[31] Kuhn, *The Structure of Scientific Revolutions*. Kuhn's theory does not rule out scientific progress: see Tambiah, *Magic, Science, Religion*, 124.

[32] For a balanced assessment see Tambiah, *Magic*, 140–3, noting especially his wise comment that the professional scientist as such 'is in a special way open to the provisional nature of his knowledge . . . much more than he, as well as we non-scientists are open to, indeed resistant to, changing our social conventions and religious paradigms. This is so because the mode of acquiring scientific knowledge . . . is in some respects less ramified with all the other manifold features and values of our life' (p. 142).

idea that there is such a content, that it is universally valid and that it justifies intervention always played and is still playing an important role ... We may surmise that the idea is a leftover from times when important matters were run from a single centre, a king or a jealous god, supporting and giving authority to a single world view. And we may further surmise that Reason and Rationality are powers of a similar kind and are surrounded by the same aura as were gods, kings, tyrants and their merciless laws. The content has evaporated; the aura remains and makes the powers survive.

The absence of content is a tremendous advantage; it enables special groups to call themselves 'rationalists', to claim that widely recognised successes were the work of Reason and to use the strength thus gained to suppress developments contrary to their interests. Needless to say, most of these claims are spurious.[33]

There is no need to become embroiled in the debates about these assaults on the citadel of natural science and 'Rationalism'. A simpler way of correcting the sense that Western rationality is fundamentally different is to look at an immune system – one quite like that of the Azande, *mutatis mutandis* – which was created in the heart of Enlightenment Rationalism. The theories about miracles developed in different ways by Hume and Spinoza share with Azande mystical notions the capacity to repel any attack relying on specific empirical evidence. Both Spinoza and Hume worked out sophisticated logical arguments and in that sense they are worlds away from the Azande, but the crucial similarity is that they built systems (which had much in common) immune to refutation by concrete data. These two writers were among the most creative and the most formative of Enlightenment rationality. They influenced innumerable more ordinary men and women. Thus they stand for more than themselves. For all the differences between the two, furthermore, there is a certain affinity between their world-views, above all their rejection of revealed religion and supernatural intervention. Thus it is reasonable to classify them together and to treat them as representatives of a distinct value rationality, Rationalism.

Rationalism is often equated with Rationality *tout court*. One should not mock this position. Although the preceding pages might seem to have veered in the direction of denying objective truth, they were not in fact doing so. People believe what they believe and often with confidence. The fact that they do not convince each other does not prove that *none* of them has got it right. Confidence only becomes overweening if it is thought *self-evident* that Enlightenment Rationalism is superior to Hinduism, or even to the Azande world-view recorded by Evans-Pritchard. The Azande

---

[33] Feyerabend, *Farewell to Reason*, 10–11. Dr Jan Prelog pointed out to me the relevance of Feyerabend.

system too (let alone Hinduism) had intellectual coherence, consistency and invulnerability, the hallmarks of Spinoza, Hume and their followers.

Spinoza and Hume

Spinoza is near the origins of a new epoch in Western attitudes to the supernatural in general and miracles in particular: a real intellectual revolutionary,[34] despite the sporadic scepticisms discovered by historians of earlier periods.[35] His view of miracles has been summed up in a magisterial study:

Since 'the universal laws of Nature are God's decrees,' he argues, it follows from the necessity and perfection of the divine Nature that 'if anything were to happen in Nature contrary to her universal laws, it would also be necessarily contrary to the decree, intellect and Nature of God or, if anyone were to assert that God performs an act contrary to the laws of Nature, he would at the same time have to maintain that God acts contrary to His own Nature', which is absurd. From this it follows, argues Spinoza, that the notion of 'miracle' can only be understood with respect to men's beliefs 'and means simply an event whose natural cause we – or at any rate the writer or narrator of the miracle – cannot explain in terms of any other normal happening'. Hence, a 'miracle' is simply something the cause of which cannot be explained according to philosophical 'principles known to us by the natural light of reason'. Consequently, none of the 'miracles' or other supernatural happenings recounted in the Bible were, in fact, miracles or supernaturally caused.[36]

Logically, this framework would rule out of court not only biblical accounts of miracles but any evidence for supernatural suspension of the laws of nature.

Such views would have been much more normal by Hume's generation, in part because of Spinoza's influence.[37] Moreover, Hume did not publish his 'Essay on Miracles' until 1748.[38] Enlightenment Rationalism was by that time a widespread world-view which he reflected while reinforcing it. In his 'Essay on Miracles' he developed an argument designed to leave the rationalist untroubled by the empirical evidence for any religious miracle. His argument has a lot in common with Spinoza's, but Hume's

---

[34] 'in the entire history of modern thought, only Marx and Nietzsche have so openly and provocatively repudiated almost the entire belief-system of the society around them, as Spinoza does'; Israel, *Radical Enlightenment*, 220.

[35] Reynolds, 'Social Mentalities'; Arnold, *Belief and Unbelief*.

[36] Israel, *Radical Enlightenment*, 220.

[37] It is the achievement of Israel's *Radical Enlightenment* to show just how extensive that influence was.

[38] It formed part of his *Enquiry Concerning Human Understanding*: see Fogelin, *A Defence of Hume on Miracles*, 1–2.

task was complicated (as it seems to me) by his view that laws are just constant conjunctions rather than 'necessary' causal connections. I would suggest that one of the reasons why Hume's argument has proved difficult to understand is that he is trying to restate something like Spinoza's argument but in terms of his own rather special view of what scientific laws are – but this reading of Hume is not an essential component of the main argument being developed here. The essential thing is that he like Spinoza uses logic to inoculate his world-view against any future challenge in the form of evidence for a given miracle in the past, present, or future.

Hume's argument is still widely discussed and of course these discussions are not innocent of existential concern for the participants, whose own views of the world may often be at stake. The following analysis is not about the validity of the argument but to show its efficacy, if accepted, as an 'immune system' against hostile world-views.[39] It is worth quoting the summary by Robert Fogelin, a lucid modern philosophical supporter:

> Hume begins with a claim about testimony. On the one side we have *wide* and *unproblematic* testimony to the effect that when people step into water they do not remain on its surface. On the other side we have isolated reports of people walking across the surface of water. Given testimony of the first kind, how are we to evaluate testimony of the second sort? The testimony of the first sort does not show the testimony of the second sort is false; it does, however, create a strong presumption – unless countered, a decisively strong presumption – in favour of its falsehood.[40]

The second stage of Hume's argument is that testimony in favour of a religious miracle will always fail to outmatch the presumption that such things do not happen. Just as experience tells us that natural laws are constant, it tells us that when it comes to religion people are credulous and their testimony unreliable. The argument against miracles as restated by Fogelin has been purified of any suspicion of circularity.[41] The fact

---

[39] In a sense, though, the structure of Hume's miracle argument, transposed into a different register, helps underpin my own argument about value rationality. There are problems with Hume's essay: see below. Nonetheless Hume expresses with great clarity a crucial truth (which does in fact have a sort of affinity to Bayesianism): namely, that probative force depends not just on positive evidence or arguments relating to a specific case or issue, but also on the antecedent plausibility of the thing to be proved. The relevance of that idea to my ideal-type of conviction rationalities may be evident to alert readers.

[40] Fogelin, *A Defence of Hume on Miracles*, 20. For a less sympathetic presentation of Hume's argument, from a Bayesian perspective, see Earman, *Hume's Abject Failure*. Earman makes it clear that he is not a Christian but thinks Hume's argument is very vulnerable.

[41] Fogelin is anxious to counter the accusation that Hume's argument is circular. He denies that Hume meant anything like the following: '1. A miracle is a violation of a law of

is, however, that even in its purified form it gives the Humean rationalist absolute de facto immunity from the force of any evidence whatsoever for a religious miracle:

Through probabilistic reasoning, part 1 fixes the appropriate level of scrutiny for evaluating testimony with respect to miracles; part 2 considers the quality of the testimony that has hitherto been brought forth in support of religious miracles and concludes that it comes nowhere near to meeting the appropriate standards. More strongly, an examination of historical records shows such a consistent pattern of ignorance, deceit and credulity that the wise reasoner is fully justified in rejecting all testimony given in support of a miracle intended to serve as the foundation of a system of religion.[42]

The evidence in any particular case is ruled out of court in advance, leaving the rationalist conviction safe against any new concrete empirical threat. This kind of immunity is typical of value rationalities of all kinds, religious and non-religious.

Fogelin's clear and sympathetic exposition makes it easier to pin down an assumption in Hume's argument. Once it has been isolated it can help us to understand why a conviction can seem unassailable from within one value rationality and not from within another. It is taken for granted by Hume that the evidence for the regularity of nature and the evidence for any given individual miracle are in conflict.

In the later Middle Ages the idea of the regularity of nature was thought quite compatible with belief in miracles: from time to time in the course of salvation history God would suspend the uniform laws of nature, themselves divine in origin, in order to bring some point home to humans.[43] This line of thought holds no attraction for Hume. This may be because his conviction that miracles, including those attributed to Jesus Christ, were impossible constituted an insurmountable antecedent prior improbability of valid empirical evidence for a specific apparently miraculous event.

Hume addressed both of the following questions: (a) is there a God who is interested in human affairs? (b) Are miracles ever credible? The two questions were addressed in isolation from each other. One

nature. 2. A law of nature is an exceptionless (hence inviolate) regularity. Therefore: 3. No miracles ever occur.' (Fogelin, *A Defence of Hume on Miracles*, 17.) Revealingly, though, he admits that 'it is tempting to think, *as I once did* [my italics] that it or something like it lies in the background' (*ibid.*). In fact even in that form the argument is not necessarily circular (though it may be vulnerable on other grounds). It would be close to Spinoza's point of view, discussed above.

[42] *Ibid.*, 31.

[43] Cf. Thomas Aquinas, *Compendium theologiae*, 1–205, at 1.136, p. 133. See too *Medieval Religious Rationalities*, index, *s.v.* 'miracles'.

could call it 'analysis', dividing up an issue into its component elements and treating them separately; or again it could be described as the 'divide and rule' approach to Christian evidences. A third question, (c) Does the Judaeo-Christian salvation narrative make sense?, did not need to be discussed seriously because the answers to (a) and (b) were 'no'.

Tacitly, an answer to (b) is taken for granted when (a) is discussed, and an answer to (a) when (b) is discussed. The tacit assumption is in each case a 'prior' which diminishes to vanishing point the probability of an affirmative answer, more or less ruling it out. The outcome in turn makes the antecedent probability of a positive answer to (c) negligible.

Discussing (a), the possibility of intelligible actions by God (if there is a God[44]) is scrutinised and rejected as a projection of human characteristics onto the unknown. Writing in the person of a 'friend' – Hume is careful and cagey but this is probably his own 'voice' – he wrote *à propos* of speculations about God that

The great source of our mistake in this subject, and of the unbounded licence of conjecture, which we indulge in, is, that we tacitly consider ourselves, as in the place of the Supreme Being, and conclude, that he will, on every occasion, observe the same conduct, which we ourselves, in his situation, would have embraced as reasonable and eligible. But . . . it must evidently appear contrary to all rules of analogy to reason, from the intentions and projects of men, to those of a Being so different, and so much superior. In human nature, there is a certain experienced coherence of designs and inclinations; so that when, from any fact, we have discovered one intention of any man, it may often be reasonable, from experience, to infer another, and draw a long chain of conclusions concerning his past or future conduct. But this method of reasoning can never have a place with regard to a Being, so remote and incomprehensible, who bears much less analogy to any other being in the universe than the sun to a waxen taper, and who discovers himself only by some faint traces or outlines, beyond which we have no authority to ascribe to him any attribute or perfection. What we imagine to be a superior perfection may really be a defect. . . . All the philosophy, therefore, in the world, and all the religion, which is nothing but a species of philosophy, will never be able to carry us beyond the usual course of experience, or give us measures of conduct and behaviour different from those which are furnished by reflections on common life. No new fact can ever be inferred from the religious hypothesis; no event foreseen or foretold; no reward or punishment expected or dreaded, beyond what is already known by practice and observation.[45]

---

[44] It is hard to say whether Hume believed in any sort of God: he may have thought there was some kind of remote First Mover. He was understandably inexplicit on such subjects.

[45] Hume, *An Enquiry Concerning Human Understanding*, Section 11, paragraph 27, pp. 109–10.

It is not surprising that Hume did not try to refute in this context the possibility that Christ might reveal more about God and work miracles that authenticated this action. Quite apart from anything else, a frontal assault on revealed religion would have been impolitic at the least. But one can be sure that for him it was a given that Christ had not worked miracles or revealed anything about God. This prior assumption naturally affected the antecedent probability of humans ever being in a position to know about God.

The chance of understanding anything about God disposed of at this early stage, with a firm 'no' in answer to question (a), hypotheses relevant to question (b) could not even be considered: it became frivolous to ask why a divinity might want to work miracles. The possibility of miracles had to be assessed exclusively with reference to the (generic) plausibility of testimonies to them. The theory of divine signification that might make sense of miracles was implicitly eliminated by Ockham's razor, as was any consideration at all of question (c).

Thus there could not even be a contest between Rationalism and the theology of redemption. The possibilities of an interventionist God and of miracles were eliminated in an early round of a sort of knock-out competition. With that out of the way, the idea of divine communication of emphatic messages to humans through occasional suspensions of the natural order, in the context of the traditional history of salvation, would be highly implausible a priori.

Nisi fallor, Hume never considers (a) and (b) as a package, and does not take (c) seriously. The separation of (a) and (b) as problems to be treated in isolation – let alone as a triangle with (c) – and in logical succession – is part of his 'conviction rationality'.[46] The divide-and-rule approach is a unifying principle crucially different from that of Aquinas and his contemporaries, who held their ideas of God, miracles (including miracles investigated in canonisation processes) and salvation history together before their minds.[47] The implicit exclusion principle by which evidence for (a) and (b) are never considered within the same frame – and (c) not at all – provides Hume's world-view with a powerful defence mechanism against attack. It is a different kind of mechanism from those that made

---

[46] More banally, as has been pointed out before, it may also have been a way of avoiding dangerous confrontation with the religious establishment; he could attack miracles while seeming to accept the Christian scheme of things on faith, his irony not quite evident: 'we may conclude, that the Christian religion not only was at first attended with miracles, but even at this day cannot be believed by any reasonable person without one. Mere reason is insufficient to convince us of its veracity: And whoever is moved by *Faith* to assent to it, is conscious of a continued miracle in his own person...' (Hume, 'Of Miracles', in Fogelin, *A Defence of Hume on Miracles*, 84).
[47] See *Medieval Religious Rationalities*, index, *s.v.* 'miracles'.

Azande thought about witchcraft and oracles immune to attack, but both are very effective, as has to be the case, almost by definition, with a value rationality.

Hume, miracles and concrete thought

The thought-world of sceptical Enlightenment rationalists did not consist of rarefied abstractions. Far from it: the conviction rationality of Rationalism was embedded in experience and in vivid and concrete images. Awareness of the terrible effects of the wars of religion between Protestants and Catholics, wars that finally ended without either side winning, so that neither side could claim that God had vindicated them, would have been part of the general consciousness of society, just as the wars of the twentieth century are in the twenty-first. To many the outcome must have seemed a strong lesson in the pointlessness of intolerance. Vivid accounts of the supposedly tolerant regime in China and a rosy representation of the prosperity of the Chinese empire would have provided an alternative model to society based on the Christian (or any other) revelation. Again, many would have concrete experience of observing scientific experiments, relatively accessible to the intelligentsia as a whole in an age when a country gentleman could have his own laboratory. Once the model of natural causation's absolute regularity was assumed, everyday experience constantly made it vivid to the imagination. A nineteenth-century critic of Hume said that he and his school

discard the very supposition of miracles, and scornfully refuse to hear evidence in their behalf in given instances, from their intimate experience of the physical order and of the ever-recurring connexion of antecedent and consequent. Their imagination usurps the functions of reason; and they cannot bring themselves even to entertain as a hypothesis . . . a thought contrary to that vivid impression of which they are the victims, that the uniformity of nature, which they witness hour by hour, is equivalent to a necessary, inviolable law.[48]

Now the philosophical validity of Hume's argument about miracles is not the concern of the present study. Fogelin would certainly disagree with Newman's verdict. The passage deserves attention, however, even from those out of sympathy with its argument, because it points out the role of vivid concrete images in the formation of values. The passage quoted is actually more polemical than the context that surrounds it. Newman is attempting a phenomenology of religious conviction. Crucially, however, he extends it here to non-religious or even anti-religious

---

[48] Newman, *An Essay in Aid of a Grammar of Assent*, chapter 4.2, p. 81.

conviction. His analysis of 'real assents' is detachable from its confessional context and usable by sociologists and psychologists of conviction as an explanation of the staying power of values. There is a curious affinity between the Catholic Newman's thought about 'real assent' and the 'religiously quite unmusical' Weber's idea of 'values'.

Concrete thought and values

Thus a second element can be added here to our ideal-type: conviction rationality is not only holistic, a set of assumptions linked together in one way or another, but also concrete and thus more vivid. These two elements in the ideal-type – coherence and concreteness – are distinct in principle but tend to go together, and when they do the combination is a strong one. For the tenacity of conviction rationality becomes much easier to understand when one adverts to its concreteness. Logical argument is predominantly verbal, 'propositional'. Convictions or values tend to be bound up with images, experience (especially during youth), the memory of concrete decisions taken oneself, and ways of life that embody principles. This kind of concrete thought is much more vivid than logical argument, and more likely to inspire emotion, though it is at one remove from pure emotion.

Experiences are a powerful kind of concrete thought but not the only kind. Simulacra of experiences are obtainable through fictional representations, if they are powerful enough and strike a chord. Visual and other mental images work together with abstractions in the same kind of way that experiences do.

Examples of concrete thinking

Examples of 'concrete' thinking can be easily multiplied: we find it wherever we find value rationality. The Greek *polis* or city state had its own value rationality. It was concrete and visible in a way a nation state cannot easily be. One could see the city, not just symbols of the country. Religious ceremonies, temples, political decisions in open meetings, fighting in close formation together in war, all made devotion to the *polis* concrete. Tribes in traditional Africa, and clans in classical China, were the basis of a value system in the same kind of way. Here the concreteness has its basis in memories of innumerable small and large acts of mutual support, affection and solidarity, clans being like families writ large. In Judaism the reproduction of historical memories through ceremonies like Passover has helped to keep the identity of the Jewish people throughout the centuries; in general the family religious ceremonies that punctuate the week and the year will be powerful in the thinking of any orthodox Jew. In Hinduism, Catholicism and the Greek Orthodox Church vivid ceremonies go together with belief, communion being especially powerful in the last two. Icons and images too have played a central role in making religious belief concrete in traditions like these. There are other ways of making religious thought concrete: hymns in Protestant churches, the call of the faithful to prayer and the concrete language of gesture, prostration, in Islam. Nationalism has constantly been reinforced by memories of war, and strengthened by such symbols as flags and anthems. It feeds above all on repeated experiences of familiarity at home, and occasional experiences of strangeness abroad. Abstract convictions like patriotism or class struggle are bound up with concrete symbols that may become almost inseparable from them. The flag in the USA, or memories of singing the *Internationale* for old-style communists, are cases in point. The vivid images of the Holocaust have been important in the conviction of our own times that racism is an evil. 'Freedom' as a value feeds on negative images of oppression. Thought becomes concrete in many ways: powerful mental images, experiences, memories of critical decisions crystallising a personal view of life, embodiment in a social form of life.

This last clause may be the bridgehead to a reconciliation between the Weber-inspired idea of value developed here and the ideas of Mary Douglas. Her inspiration was Durkheim and her teacher was Evans-Pritchard; and she was well aware of Wittgenstein. Look at the following passage, about her teacher's thought, but informed by her Durkheimian allegiance and her philosophical alertness:

Then there is the distinction to be drawn between the core of fundamental assumptions (the total system of hypotheses) and, on the other hand, the inductive reasoning that it makes possible. Deep assumptions about the universe that arise from how people live together are unchallengeable and largely un-inspectable. Somewhere the reasoning has to come to an end; it stops at these assumptions. Why are the people so certain that they are right and the missionary's story is wrong? Because they have to live and act: action proceeds upon decisions and decisions upon assumptions, but the assumptions anticipate possibilities of action.[49]

Embodiment in social action and institutional life makes principles concrete and durable. Mary Douglas's own anthropological writings bring this out exceptionally well, though the kinds of models she prefers, in which patterns of thought and patterns of social action constantly reinforce each other, do not cover all eventualities – for instance, cases of

---

[49] Douglas, *Evans-Pritchard*, 36–7.

passionate conviction acquired in exceptional and contingent circumstances and held in isolation against the grain of social institutions.

A definition of value/conviction rationality

In all these cases the whole style of thought is different from purely verbal ratiocination and generally speaking more tenacious and resistant to attack. If we put this analysis together with the previous one of the way in which different values within a system provide one another with mutual support we are not far from a definition. *Value rationality is a system where each part gives support to any other part that is attacked and where values are concrete in the mind, rather than abstract.*

It should be stressed that this definition is a composite ideal-type to help us pin down and categorise certain forms of thinking. Parts of it can work on their own. Thus individual ideas may be concrete enough to be usefully defined as 'values' even if they are not part of a mutually supporting system; and parts of a mutually supporting system can be rather abstract in character. The definition is not like a biological species whose structure has been discovered. It is a useful piece of conceptual 'software' for analysing complex systems and behaviour. For instance, it will be argued below that illiterate societies (such as pre-Christian Anglo-Saxon England) may be easier to convert because their values are not crystallised in written formulae, which makes it easier to reshape them. Religious feeling which is not fixed in written texts can be redirected. Conversely, theories expressed in texts can often be easily altered in response to argument if they are not combined with religious feeling. But a combination of religious feeling with textual formulation, an amalgam of power and rigidity, can make society highly resistant to conversion.

What is truth?

The position outlined in this chapter is a long way short of real subjectivism. It leaves open the possibility that a number of value rationalities are true. Quite a lot of them may be true, except insofar as there are contradictions between them, in which case at least some must be wrong. In practice, however, there seems no universal yardstick, available to the historian or sociologist or any other kind of academic, capable of marking off true from false to the satisfaction of all sincere enquirers.

Consequently, changes in the history of values and convictions cannot be explained simply in terms of a battle between a universal rationality and irrational forces such as tradition, superstition or ignorance. It also leaves us with the problem of explaining how systems of values and convictions rise and fall, advance and retreat. Answering such questions means moving from analysis of structure to analysis of dynamics. In fact the distinction is misleading since even a system in an apparently steady state is in fact dynamically reproducing itself: if it does not do so actively it is likely to lose many of its adherents over a generation or two.[50] This and other dynamics of conviction rationalities are the next topic to consider.

---

[50] Cf. Giddens, *New Rules of Sociological Method*, 128–9: '*structuration*, as the reproduction of practices, refers abstractly to the dynamic process whereby structures come into being. By the *duality of structure* I mean that social structure is both constituted *by* human agency and yet is at the same time the very *medium* of this constitution.'

3   Dynamics of values and convictions

In the previous chapter it was argued that conviction rationalities have an intrinsic durability and tenacity, arising, first, from the logical and psychological support that the various elements of a value system provide for the others. Rational people do not easily allow themselves to be persuaded by other views when it comes to fundamentals. Frequently their views are fixed. Paradoxically, it is often rational for them to be unmoved by individual objections. For the convictions of such a person are interdependent. They form a coherent system. Each part supports the others. The motivation to abandon the whole framework of a person's mental world is understandably weak, and may not be even rational. It goes beyond sawing off the branch one is sitting on: it is to try to uproot the whole tree. Secondly, the abstract framework of conviction is embodied in concrete experiences direct or vicarious, or in strong mental images. The force that this kind of concrete thinking exerts on the mind (and on the emotions) increases the reluctance to change. When all this comes together one may usefully speak of a conviction rationality. This combination gave the Azande immunity from empirical evidence against their poison oracles, and it gave Hume immunity from empirical evidence in favour of any miracle.

Functionalism and the durability of values

This Weberian approach should be clearly distinguished from 'functionalism', ultimately compatible though these two approaches are. The distinction is not always drawn but it is important for clear analysis, in that some irrational attitudes may be functional – for instance an unfounded self-belief may be a practical asset in a politician, whose confidence in his chances may communicate itself to his followers and help his chances. An army that believes in its own invincibility beyond what objective facts warrant will fight with higher morale and greater success. Irrational (often manipulated) fears of another state or hidden enemy may reinforce social cohesion. We need to be able to say that an action or belief is both functional *and* irrational.

In a functionalist explanation of how a system maintains itself, the unintended consequence of habitual actions or attitudes is the preservation of a social order. Functionalism comes in various colours. A Durkheimian version has been illustrated by Mary Douglas through the example of how a social group with 'no coercive power and no individual selective benefits of a material kind' can flourish.[1] She envisages a sequence of unintended consequences which turn into a self-reinforcing loop. To simplify her not-uncomplicated presentation: when a group is marked out from the rest of society by clear boundaries (one imagines a religious or political sect), bad behaviour cannot be policed by authority, so the only way to do so is to accuse anyone who looks as if they are taking advantage of the rest of betraying basic principles, using expulsion as the sanction. This has the unintended consequence of creating a belief in a conspiracy of evil people in the midst of the group, a belief which in turn has the unintended consequence of keeping the community in being, and, what is more, since schism or expulsion do actually follow when treachery is suspected, and would-be leaders are consequently nervous of accusations, of preserving its character as clearly defined and weakly led. Thus the loop is completed.[2]

An elegant case has also been made by Gerry Cohen for the compatibility of functionalism with Marxism.[3] Cohen, incidentally, gives the best brief thought-experimental account of functionalist explanation that I know of: 'Imagine ten godless communities, each, because it lacks a religion, teetering on the brink of disintegration. A prophet visits all ten, but only one of them accepts his teaching. The other nine subsequently perish, and the single believing society survives. But they took up religion because they liked the prophet's looks, and not because they needed a religion (though they did need a religion).'[4]

Functionalism and social evolution

Cohen's example illustrates how functionalist explanations can be reconciled with social evolutionary models, because it is an example of

---

[1] Douglas, *How Institutions Think*, 39.   [2] For the full complicated version, *ibid.*, 38–41.
[3] Cohen, *Karl Marx's Theory of History*, ch. 10.
[4] *Ibid.*, 281–2. Incidentally, Cohen's thought-experiment brings out the elective affinity between functionalism and explanations in terms of 'cultural evolution': systems preserved by the mechanism functionalism describes are by the same token adapted for survival. He emphasises the compatibility of the two approaches: 'Darwin's theory is not a rival of functional explanation, but, among other things, a compelling account of why functional explanations apply in the biosphere' (*ibid.*, 271).

'dynamic functionalism': a functionalist explanation of change. The religion is new, the factors leading one tribe to accept it may be random, or the product of events rather than structures, waves of history rather than tides or currents, to use Annales-school language. Yet the functional efficacy of the new religion ensures its survival and that of the society. 'Dynamic functionalism' and social evolution are arguably almost the same thing,[5] if one recognises the radical discontinuity between biological and social evolution (for genetic make-up of humans remains identical throughout the vicissitudes of social evolution, and 'memes', though useful as an ideal-type,[6] are quite different from genes in that they have no clear boundaries or mathematical structure).

Values can change

This side-glance at dynamic functionalism and at social evolutionary theory reminds us that the values of a society or an individual always have a beginning and sometimes come to an end. This chapter will attempt to bring out the time-bound character of value systems and to give a more dynamic picture of how they interact with each other, and how they reproduce themselves. (The discourse of functionalism or social evolutionary theory would not add much to these particular lines of explanation, so the ordinary language of comparative historians will be the language of the following analysis.) Value systems put pressure on each other and the success of one is often a threat to another. The advance of one value system and the retreat of another can thus be a single process viewed from different ends.[7]

Apparent loss of values

The previous chapter shows how capable a system of values and convictions can be of resisting attack. When we do see what appears to be a change of values, furthermore, it can turn out to be a modification of less firmly held opinions. Some apparent changes of values may conceal an underlying continuity: the core of the value system may in fact have remained consistent throughout.[8] For instance, a person might well start

---

[5] It seems to me that Runciman, *A Treatise on Social Theory*, vol. 2: *Substantive Social Theory*, is in effect applying dynamic functionalism, to excellent effect.

[6] Richard Dawkins's well-known concept of a meme is itself a meme with good survival capacity.

[7] As general background, see Buckser and Glazier (eds.), *The Anthropology of Religious Conversion*, especially Austin-Broos, 'The Anthropology of Conversion', 1–12.

[8] Cf. the comment of Rebecca Sachs Norris that 'although a convert experiences conversion as a reorientation to a new religious belief system, the conversion occurs primarily

as an Anglican, try Roman Catholicism, and end up in the Greek Orthodox Church, without changing a fundamental religious value; the core
consistent conviction could be that a liturgy expressing religious mystery
is the crucial index of the right Church. Again, an underlying belief or
conviction might actually incorporate the option of changing external
affiliation and internal commitment, as a study of the Gwembe Tonga of
Zambia showed.[9] On the one hand, this study found 'a high degree of
mobility in changing religious affiliation'.[10] On the other hand, there is an
underlying consistency: 'Given that locally religious truth did not reside
permanently in any one religious institution – because the empowering
spirits were experienced as evanescent entities – occasionally changing
one's religious affiliation was considered inevitable' (p. 107).

> when people changed from denomination to denomination, they frequently
> claimed that the previous church had lost its association with the Holy Spirit
> and had instead started to employ evil powers...that merely resembled,
> though falsely, the true Holy Spirit. This strategy implied the existence of an
> Archimedean point, namely the Holy Spirit, to which were ascribed purely posi-
> tive qualities. Yet where to find this Archimedean point and how to identify these
> positive qualities were a matter of interpretation.[11]

Or again, an evangelical Christian might change Churches, retaining the
whole time a guiding belief in the literal inspiration of the Bible; the
changes are simply attempts to find out which sect is true to what the
Bible says.

Mutatis mutandis, it is the same with politics. A move from fascism
to communism or vice versa, without abandoning a core conviction that
salvation lies with the state, would have been perfectly conceivable. An
idealistic politician might change parties, always seeking the one that will
really help the poor. Free-market views might give way to protectionist
policies without touching the core conviction that the nation's interest
must be paramount. In the politics of the USA in the 1960s, Southern
Democrats could have switched to the Republican Party without inconsistency. When a society or at least many individuals are converted with
relative ease, this may be because the new religion or ideology contains
values close to some they hold already, whether or not that is immediately
apparent.

Nevertheless, real fundamental change of convictions is possible: they
can be lost and they can be gained, and the two processes cannot be
separated, since values may be lost because they are replaced by new
values.

---

because it corresponds with the convert's preexisting ideas or feelings about truth or
meaning' ('Converting to What?', 171).
[9] Kirsch, 'Restaging the Will to Believe'.   [10] *Ibid.*, 699.   [11] *Ibid.*, 706.

Individuals and systems

Individual stories of values gained or lost lie behind the advances and retreats of whole value systems. When Christianity 'retreated' before the radical Enlightenment, or Catholicism before the Reformation, this means that individuals gave up certitudes, or at least that a new generation grew up in which fewer people acquired those certitudes. When retreat turns into advance, that also means that individuals have changed their minds (or that more members of a new generation have internalised a conviction than in the previous one).

Experience and the change of values

For both individuals and groups, values can form when abstractions meet concrete experiences and emerge hardened and fixed one way or another:[12] a theory perhaps close to that of Hans Joas in his *Genesis of Values*.[13] A theoretical pacifist has to decide whether to use violence to defend someone he loves: after deciding, the abstract principle will never be the same again. Perhaps it will have been replaced by a modified conviction which will be much more intense than the previous view; or if the non-violent option was chosen the pacifist principle would take on a new force. A third possibility would be for violent action to be followed by violent guilt, so in this case too the former abstract principle would take on a new character. A sense of national identity may be cemented by war. Arguably, both England and France acquired such an identity in the course of the later medieval wars between them.[14] This was in effect the genesis of a new value system. The pacifist example, on the other hand, illustrates a way in which an individual comes to internalise an existing value system.

In extreme cases, collision with experience can also destroy existing values. A striking case is Confucian China. In a few decades one of the great cultural and religious systems of world history virtually ceased to exist as a living force (the sack of Peking in 1900 being a symbolic date).[15] To clarify: what disappeared was not Confucianism as a world-view

---

[12] Cf. *Medieval Religious Rationalities*, index, *s.v.* 'experience' and 'changing convictions'.

[13] I say 'perhaps' because the book's style and whole approach favours subtlety at some cost to clarity. Still, Joas's remark that 'values originate in experiences of self-formation and self-transcendence' (Joas, *The Genesis of Values*, 164) seems to be a strong insight, if I have understood it correctly. Cf. also *ibid.*, 12: 'values and value commitments arise in experiences of self-formation and self-transcendence'.

[14] Cf. Lewis, 'War Propaganda and Historiography'; Jones, 'The English Church'.

[15] Cf. the useful timeline for the 'The dismemberment of China' in Gernet, *A History of Chinese Civilisation*, 603.

(it is very much alive), but the system of thought and practice centred on the Emperor and administered by civil servants saturated with the Confucian classics. The Confucian-imperial system promised to deliver prosperity in this life. When the political structure began to fall apart under the attacks of Western countries, and when those Western countries appeared to enjoy material superiority, the Confucian-imperial value system was fatally undermined.[16] This suggests one explanation for the loss or change of values. The doubt, or the alternative value system, must be able to exert some leverage from within the old one. In this case, it was the belief in success and prosperity as legitimisation. Failure had not mattered before (say in the face of the Mongols or the Manchus) because the victors had accepted the system and the Mandate of Heaven and simply started a new dynasty. The successes of the West, however, and of Westernised Japan, led to attempts to emulate their educational system.[17] Idealisation of Western education was bound to subvert to some extent the imperial examination system,[18] which was a crucial carrier of the system's ideology. There was also the practical matter of competition for resources between the new schools and the old examination.[19] Even so it took a generation or two for the Mandarin class to abandon attempts to rationalise the collapse of their world.[20]

Military superiority underpinned by the industrial revolution brought this mighty value rationality low because the Confucian and Mandarin value system put such a high value on military and economic success. Defeat by the West both undermined the rationale of the system and then destroyed the social and political order in which the rationality was embedded. Strictly speaking, then, we have two distinct causal processes following on from the defeat: the logic of the system was undermined and then the form of life and thought which supported it fell apart around it.

[16] The classic study is Levenson, *Confucian China*.
[17] 'For... the reformers, Western schools and Westernised Japanese education were examples that the Ch'ing dynasty must emulate... Uncritical presentations of Western schools and Japanese education as success stories were widely accepted' (Elman, *A Cultural History of Civil Examinations*, 586).
[18] According to Elman the 'educational efficiency [of the imperial examination regime] was now, in the 1890s, suspect' (*ibid.*); cf. 603, and 617.
[19] 'competition between financial costs for maintaining an empirewide network of examinations and funds for new schools became keen' (*ibid.*, 586).
[20] This was the central theme of the first volume of Levenson's magnum opus. Elman's findings should not necessarily be regarded as incompatible with Levenson's, in terms of broad interpretation (although the advance in detailed scholarship is massive). He writes, for instance, that 'K'ang Yu-wei's efforts to reinvent "Confucianism" in 1898 represented a form of "symbolic compensation" paid to classical literati thought... by unilaterally declaring its eternal moral superiority as a reward for its historical failure' (Elman, *A Cultural History*, 594).

The West found a fatal weaknesses in the armour of the Mandarin value system.

Destruction of the social framework

Value systems bound up with a social or political order or framework can succumb when the latter is dismantled:[21] the Confucian-Mandarin state religion of imperial China could hardly survive the dismantling of the examination system, even though Confucianism itself could survive in a different form; it is hard to imagine the Azande system of witchcraft, sorcery and magic being continued outside the tribal society in which it flourished.

Crisis generated from within

As has been said of the Roman Empire, the Mandarin value system 'did not die of natural causes, it was assassinated'. Occasionally, on the other hand, a value system which has had a non-trivial impact on history collapses as a result of a crisis generated by its own logic. The interesting sect known as the 'Catholic Apostolic Church' eventually died out in Britain because its theology did not admit of an apostolic succession; the last of the twelve apostles died in 1901 and, unsurprisingly, this 'unexpected event caused a great deal of dejection and self-doubt in the ranks of the CAC community, since one of its cardinal assumptions had been that the Second Coming of Christ would immediately follow the conclusion of the apostles' latter-day work'.[22]

This is an extreme example of what Alasdair MacIntyre has called 'epistemological crises', which happen when a system seems to be found wanting by its own core criteria of rationality. MacIntyre's analysis is worth quoting (note that his concept of a 'tradition' is close to the concept of 'value rationality' or 'conviction rationality' as used in this book):

Every tradition, whether it recognises the fact or not, confronts the possibility that at some future time it will fall into a state of epistemological crisis, recognisable as such by its own standards of rational justification, which have themselves been vindicated up to that time as the best to emerge from the history of that particular tradition. All attempts to deploy the imaginative and inventive resources which the adherents of the tradition can provide may founder, either merely by doing nothing to remedy the condition of sterility and incoherence into which the

---

21 Cf. *Medieval Religious Rationalities*, index, *s.v.* 'social framework'.
22 Ruotsila, 'The Catholic Apostolic Church in British Politics', 81. Ruotsila notes, p. 90, that small pockets remained and that a new schismatic movement, the 'New Apostolic Church', emerged.

enquiry has fallen or by also revealing or creating new problems, and revealing new flaws and new limitations. Time may elapse, and no further resources or solutions emerge.

That particular tradition's claims to truth can at some point in this process no longer be sustained. And this by itself is enough to show that if part of the relativist's thesis is that each tradition, since it provides its own standards of rational justification, must always be vindicated in the light of those standards, then on this at least the relativist is mistaken.[23]

MacIntyre argues that epistemological crises are sometimes surmounted by 'the invention or discovery of new concepts and the framing of some new type or types of theory'.[24]

This is exactly what happened with the Catholic Apostolic Church, in the short term, at any rate:

A new corpus of theological interpretation was... quickly fashioned by the remaining coadjutors of the apostles, men whose intimate collaboration with the apostles was believed to have given them special insight into the further unfolding of the divine eschatological plan. The concept of 'the time of silence' was now put forward, denoting the interlude between the restored apostolate and the Second Coming, during which no apostolic guidance was given and when it was up to each believer to hold fast and to prepare to be raptured.[25]

In the longer term, admittedly, the mainstream of the church dried up in Great Britain.[26]

Leverage

Systems of conviction are also more likely to be undermined and replaced when their critics are able to use elements of the system itself as intellectual leverage, so that they argue against some of their opponents' certitudes on the basis of other convictions which they also hold.

The chances of new values being accepted depend not only on their own power but also on the character of the system under attack: for all the differences between Hinduism and Buddhism, there are common assumptions which make movement from one to the other easier; pre-modern Chinese influences with very deep roots permeated

---

[23] MacIntyre, *Whose Justice? Which Rationality?*, 364. MacIntyre does not think the crises have necessarily to come from within: he argues that 'it is... untrue... that traditions, understood as each possessing its own account of and practices of rational justifica-tion... cannot defeat or be defeated by other traditions' (p. 366).
[24] *Ibid.*, 362.   [25] Ruotsila, 'The Catholic Apostolic Church', 81.
[26] I believe that a version of the movement survives in Germany.

pre-modernised (pre-Meiji) Japan,[27] and it is possible that awareness of this earlier willingness to borrow from another culture may have made the Meiji restoration and a kind of 'Westernisation' easier than in China itself.

Literacy and orality

The spread of Christianity into Germanic lands in late Antiquity and after, or more recently the conquests of both Christianity and Islam in Africa at the expense of indigenous religions, may suggest that conversion is easier when the values under attack have not been crystallised in written texts. (An 'other things being equal' proviso must immediately be added, together with a disclaimer that this is only a rough schema for investigation and correction.) Apart from the practical advantages of literacy and the prestige that accrues to those who transmit it,[28] the logic of this ideal-type is that the precision of the textual formulation fixes the feeling that permeates the values into a more rigid form, resistant to being assimilated into another system. When a society's values are not fixed in written formulae, they may presumably mutate more easily into a different value system. Resistance to other people's systems is enhanced when abstract and concrete thinking are combined. Fixed words, reinforced by strong emotions generated by rituals which also use specified words, would seem to constitute an amalgam with stronger powers of resistance than ritual actions that might be replaced by similar actions with a different inner meaning. Religious emotions and experience-based perceptions on their own may be able to slide into a new system. Once the intuitions have been embedded in texts they may be in too precise a form for broad similarities with values in other systems to be apparent. Furthermore, the intellectuals or prophets who explain value systems in texts often tend to contrast them with rival systems, so that common elements are pushed into the background. Shared assumptions about monogamy were not going to open the door to dialogue between Russia and the USA in the 1950s or to facilitate conversion of individuals from one system to another. Judaism and Islam naturally share many values (if only because of the latter's acknowledged debt to the former), but the affirmation in sacred texts of Muhammad's prophetic role on the one hand, and of the unique status of the chosen people on the other, makes conversion rare in either direction. Obviously this is not to say that

---

[27] Jansen, *China in the Tokugawa World*; Gernet, *A History of Chinese Civilisation*, 290–1, for the deep roots.

[28] Duncan, 'Untangling Conversion', 311; Bartlett, 'Reflections on Paganism and Christianity', 56.

literate value systems are immune to the conversion process. Even when they lose a lot of ground, however, they sometimes regain it a generation or two later, provided that the infrastructure survives.

Convergence

The dechristianisation of the intellectual elite in mid- to late Victorian England was due in part to the essentially accidental convergence of two independent lines of intellectual development:[29] from natural science on the one hand and German biblical criticism on the other.[30] Attacks on a rationality by rival ideas are much more likely to succeed if they come from different directions at once, even if the attacking ideas are not intrinsically related, so that the besieged rationality cannot concentrate on one threat at a time and there is a sense that probabilities are converging from different directions against the set of values in question. We have noted that the coherence of related values within a world-view creates an antecedent probability in favour of any one of them when it is under attack. But the converse is also true. When different doctrines within the value system are simultaneously attacked by different antagonistic ideas, the latter enhance each other's antecedent probability.

Timing

The timing of exposure to ideas can make a difference both to individuals and to social groups. If an objection to a value system is raised from outside it can often respond given time and reflection. Thus, for instance, Protestant Christianity, then Catholic Christianity (a good deal later), found in 'Form criticism'[31] and in a nuanced appreciation of literary genres, a way of assimilating the results of academic biblical criticism which had once looked like an outright threat. At first the alternatives had seemed to be: the Bible as History *or* the Bible as Myth. Gradually, a view evolved that the Bible was history presented through fictional devices of various sorts. The time-lag before these responses matured was long enough for massive dechristianisation to take place. The same pattern

---

[29] Cf. *Medieval Religious Rationalities*, index, *s.v.* 'miracles'.

[30] Cf. Chadwick, *The Victorian Church*, vol. 1, ch. 8, esp. p. 551 (adding another force): 'Three forces were driving Christianity to restate doctrine: natural science shattered assumptions about Genesis and about miracles. Criticism questioned whether all history in the Bible was true. Moral feeling found the love of God hard to reconcile with hellfire or scapegoat-atonement'; for general background, see Larsen, *Contested Christianity*. Larsen argues that 'the nineteenth-century story is really one of contested Christianity rather than the ebbing of the sea of faith' (*ibid.*, 4).

[31] For a summary of its development see Mihelic, 'The Influence of Form Criticism'.

is played out repeatedly on the individual level, whenever the challenge is known before the response. At the individual but especially at the social level the question of timing is crucial, because developments in biblical criticism are unlikely to interest agnostics, unless they happen to be academics. This holds good especially for second- or third-generation agnostics.

Timing has been important in the history of the 'Science v. Religion' debate in another way. As just noted, the combination of evolutionary biology and German Bible criticism had alienated a large part of the intellectual elite by the end of the nineteenth century. If the quantum mechanics revolution had occurred half a century earlier and the Darwinian revolution a century later things might have been different. Darwinism destroyed the arguments from biological design. Heisenberg revealed a subatomic universe governed by mathematics, the ultimate elegant science.[32] In itself, this was not going to reconvert anyone to Christianity. A central argument of this book is that arguments do not stand or fall alone, but in networks. Still, in an intellectual milieu already unquestioningly Christian, the mathematical micro-universe of Heisenberg might have been a powerful argument for a designed universe.

Genesis of values: charisma

So far the focus has been on loss and gain of values. A more fundamental question is: where do values come from? How do new values and value systems begin and first catch on? A classic answer is: they can start with a charismatic leader.[33]

New values may appear in history through the influence of a charismatic leader (such as Muhammad, Buddha or Freud); or of a writer regarded as a genius (and so a sort of charismatic) such as Adam Smith or Marx, who did not lead movements but whose writings influenced actions as well as minds. That is Weber's straightforward suggestion, not exhaustive but valid for some movements central in world history. He puts it thus:

Charisma is the great revolutionary power in epochs that are in the grip of tradition. By contrast with the no less revolutionary power of 'ratio'[34] . . . charisma

---

[32] Heisenberg, *Physics and Beyond*, 14 together with 245.

[33] Cf. *Medieval Religious Rationalities*, index, *s.v.* 'charisma'.

[34] Here Weber means bureaucratic *Zweckrationalität*, instrumental or 'ends–means' rationality: see the parallel treatment of the topic later in the book: 'As we have seen, bureaucratic rationalisation too can be and often has been a revolutionary force of the first order. But this is revolution effected by technical means, in principle, as with every transformation of the economy, "from outside": starting with objects and structures,

can be a transformation from the inside, which, born of necessity or enthusiasm, means a fundamental change in the direction of central convictions and actions with a completely new orientation of all attitudes to all specific forms of life and to 'the World' generally.[35]

Or again:

For all the enormous differences between the spheres in which they move, religious, artistic, ethical, scientific or scholarly and all other ideas, in particular those to do with political or social organisation, arise in essentially the same way . . . The mathematical imagination of, say, a Weierstrass is intuition in exactly the same sense as that of any artist, prophet and – demagogue . . . [The difference] in no way lies . . . in the person or in the psychological 'experiences' of the creator of ideas or 'works', but in the way in which those who are being ruled or led appropriate, internalise and experience them. We saw above that the process of Rationalisation is such that the great majority of those who are led appropriate or adapt to only the external and technical outcomes which are in their practical interest . . . while the ideas in the mind of their creators remain irrelevant to this majority. This is the meaning of the formula that rationalisation and rational 'order' bring about revolution 'from outside', while charisma, when it does succeed in bringing about the effects that are specific to it, makes its revolutionary power manifest from within, by means of a fundamental 'conversion' of the whole way in which the people ruled think.[36]

This important explanation of how values take hold of social groups deserves a gloss, especially since 'charisma' is nowadays mostly used in a sense very different from Weber's. He does not mean a special gift of personal magnetism (the common current sense of the word). He does not apply the word to any quality that the charismatic leader actually possesses, but only to the way in which the leader's ideas are received by the followers. The head of a bureaucracy may have inspired ideas in the same way that a charismatic leader does, but they are accepted for different reasons by the members of the organisation: because he is the boss, because those are the rules, etc. Only if they are accepted because the subordinates think that their leader has some extraordinary gift can one talk of charismatic leadership (in combination with bureaucratic authority, in that case). Weber is not saying anything one way or another

then on to people, in the sense of rearranging the conditions to which they have to adapt, and in some cases increasing their capacity to adapt to the external world through the rational arrangement of ends and means' (Weber, *Wirtschaft und Gesellschaft*, vol. 2, p. 657, passage beginning 'Auch die bürokratische Rationalisierung' and ending 'durch rationale Zweck- und Mittelsetzung').

[35] *Ibid.*, vol. 1, p. 142; Cf. the translation in their different style of G. Roth and C. Wittich, *Economy and Society*, vol. 1, p. 245.
[36] Weber, *Wirtschaft und Gesellschaft*, vol. 2, p. 658, passage beginning: 'Bei aller abgrundtiefen Verschiedenheit' and ending 'seine revolutionäre Gewalt manifestiert'.

about the real powers that a leader might or might not possess. As a historian and sociologist he does not feel he should express a view on whether (say) Muhammad was truly inspired by God – but he can be sure that Muhammad's followers thought so and it is the transformation of the values of the group, rather a large one over the course of time in the case of Islam, that comes within his remit.

Weber is thus at pains to make it clear that he is only explaining group behaviour. It is possible in principle for a 'charismatic leader' to be without inspiration of any kind and even without any personal magnetism, provided it is projected on him or her by the media, collective desires, or through some other mechanism. Statements about 'charisma' in Weber are statements about the image of the leader in the minds of the followers.[37]

Nevertheless, a certain approximate correlation might be expected between the acceptance of individuals as charismatic leaders and the personal qualities of the leader. They are likely to be marked out by the intensity of their convictions or by belief in their own destiny. So where does the intensity come from? Believers will think that it can come from God, but even believers will not find that a sufficient explanation because it is clear that leaders like Lenin and Hitler possessed it to a high degree.

Whatever the source of the intensity, it is not so very often combined with radically new ideas in such a way as to initiate an entirely new movement, but when it does happen the consequences are far reaching, the Reformation started by Martin Luther being a notable case in point.

The Continental Reformation as a case study

Though no one case study can exemplify all the foregoing points about the dynamics of values and convictions, many of them are well illustrated by the history of the Reformation: notably the continuities that can underlie apparent loss of values, the fissures within a system that can create an 'epistemological crisis', charismatic leadership, the role of experience in the formation of values, and techniques for making ideas concrete in the minds of masses of people.[38]

---

[37] Weber speaks of the 'extraordinary dedication to the holiness or the heroism or the exemplary character of a person and of the orders [structures?] that they reveal or create' ('außeralläglichen Hingabe an die Heiligkeit oder die Heldenkraft oder die Vorbildlichkeit einer Person und der durch sie offenbarten oder geschaffenen Ordnungen') (*ibid.*, vol. 1, p. 124).

[38] I am grateful to Diarmaid MacCulloch for reading my comments on the Reformation. The pages that follow owe a great deal to Pettegree, *The Reformation and the Culture of Persuasion* and the recent works whose findings it draws together into its powerful argument.

Underlying continuities between medieval and Protestant Christianity

If one breaks away from the crude and implausible stereotype of the Middle Ages as an age of monolithic Catholic faith, it is likely that many of those whom Luther won over had never held with real conviction the doctrines he attacked. For instance, for many, belief in papal authority would have been undermined by the collective memory of the Schism, the Conciliarist critiques of papal monarchy, and awareness of the political preoccupations of a Julius II or the moral notoriety of an Alexander VI. This is not to deny the continuing hold of the papal idea.[39] But it can hardly have been a firm conviction of all Luther's contemporaries. Conversely, many core convictions of medieval religion continued on into Lutheranism, ensuring psychological continuity: for instance, belief in the Trinity, the Incarnation, and in the Redemption and in Grace.

Leverage from within: the Bible in the Reformation

Luther was able to use the general acceptance by everyone in his world of the sanctity and inspiration of the Bible as an axiom on the basis of which he could attack other doctrines. The absolute authority of the Bible was a widespread medieval assumption.[40] 'In his early works, which according to Luther himself belonged to his "papist" phase, he already presupposed the Scriptures to be the obvious sole source of faith.'[41] Popular preaching was peppered with scriptural texts,[42] so that the authority of the Bible must have become taken for granted and integrated into popular religious mentalities. Movements such as the Waldensians and the Lollards had already attempted to out-trump Church authority by appealing to the Bible. Since they had been more or less successfully repressed by persecution, the problem of how to reach consensus about the meaning of the Bible would not have been so apparent at the start of the Reformation.

Timing and 'Scripture alone'

By the seventeenth century the proliferation of interpretations of the Bible's meaning provided ammunition for Catholic apologetics.[43] The divergences on such subjects as the eucharist, baptism and religious

---

[39] d'Avray, 'Papal Authority and Religious Sentiment'.
[40] On the Bible in the Middle Ages see e.g. Dahan, *L'Exégèse chrétienne*; Lobrichon, *La Bible au Moyen Age*; or B. Smalley's still valuable *Study of the Bible*.
[41] Oberman, *Luther*, 223.
[42] See e.g. d'Avray, *The Preaching of the Friars*, 172–3, 194–5.
[43] Cf. Rébelliau, *Bossuet* (he argues that Bossuet's polemic did not have the intended effect); Pelikan, *The Christian Tradition*, vol. 4: *Reformation of Church and Dogma*, 265–6.

images did indeed become unmistakable in the first century of Reformation history. After the initial dramatic successes, however, there was no turning back: the horse had bolted. The various Protestant churches were firmly established, and belief in the authority of the Bible had hardened into a strong doctrine of the verbal inspiration of the Scripture.[44]

Luther's charismatic leadership

Not only did Luther believe that he had received 'an overwhelming enlightenment of the mind' – he was able to communicate this conviction to a mass public through published works: his autobiography and the preface to the first volume of his collected works.[45] He fits the Weberian ideal-type of the charismatic leader who sends a new value system into the world. His ability to communicate vivid, intense and emotionally charged conviction through his published writings[46] is evident to anyone who takes them up.

Experience and Luther's doctrines

Luther had personal experience of what looks like obsessive guilt, a persistent fear that he had committed sins; the doctrine of justification by faith alone will have enabled him to discard this anxiety. A famous passage from a Bible commentary written much later speaks volumes – especially the passages I have italicised:

When I was a monk I used to think straightaway that my salvation was at stake, if ever I felt the concupiscence of the flesh, that is, an evil urge, desire, anger, hatred, envy, etc. against some brother. I tried many things, *I confessed every day*, etc. But this got me nowhere at all. As the concupiscence of the flesh always came back, consequently *I could have no peace of mind, but I was constantly tormented by this thought: You have committed this sin or that sin, again you are tormented by envy, impatience, etc.*[47]

---

[44] Pelikan, *Reformation*, 343–7.

[45] Chadwick, *The Early Reformation*, 125; cf. Pettegree, *Reformation*, 4.

[46] This is part of the core of truth within the much overblown argument that printing was a cause of the Reformation: for reservations about the argument see d'Avray, 'Printing, Mass Communication, and Religious Reformation'.

[47] 'Ego monachus putabam statim actum esse de salute mea, si quando sentiebam concupiscentiam carnis, hoc est, malum motum, libidinem, iram, odium, invidiam etc. adversus aliquem fratrem. Tentabam multa, confitebar quotidie etc. Sed nihil prorsus proficiebam. Quio [*sic* in Scheel] semper redibat concupiscentia carnis, ideo non poteram acquiescere, sed perpetuo cruciabar his cogitationibus: Hoc et illum peccatum commisisti, item laboras invidia, impatientia, etc.' (*Dokumente zu Luthers Entwicklung*, ed. Scheel, Doc. no. 52, p. 33. Stephen Ozment, while agreeing that 'Luther was extremely anxious and behaved neurotically in the monastery', explains all this by

This matches the description of a state of mind known as 'scruples', described thus in a standard reference work:

Scrupulosity may be the result of much ascetic reading of a rigorist tendency, but more often is the outcome of nervous disturbances. It usually manifests itself in the fear of having consented to sinful imaginations and desires, or having made incomplete confessions, and of being unworthy of the reception of the sacraments.[48]

The condition seems to be a counterpart in the religious conscience to a secular state of anxiety in which one groundless fear is replaced by another as soon as it is allayed. Luther's personal experience of it would help to explain how theological reflection became passionate conviction.[49] The idea of justification by faith alone was not brought about by his agonising over whether he had left a sin off his list or been inadequately sorry, but it did release him from the agony, by making such anxieties irrelevant. The experience and the abstract theory coalesced: no doubt this was part of the secret of Luther's extraordinary force.

The first generation of convinced Protestants must also have seen their convictions crystallised in the course of a more or less traumatic experience of conversion:

For the first years of the Reformation we have plentiful evidence that the decision to adhere to it involved conscious choice . . . For many in the first generation the choice was a lonely one, made individually or with a small group of fellows who thus excluded themselves from the fellowship of societies not yet ready to accept the evangelical message. For these men and women, to embrace the Gospel was to court calamity. Religious divisions ended friendship, caused division between neighbours and kin, damaged relations with parents beyond repair, sometimes even caused rejection by spouse or children.[50]

Reformation values and concrete modes of thought

Personal experience is one kind of concrete thought. Recent research on the Reformation has drawn attention to other kinds of concrete thought that have usually been interpreted less sensitively simply in terms of their message. Andrew Pettegree shows how the reformers 'grew adept

---

'subjection to medieval religious culture in its purest form, the monastic regimen' (Ozment, The Age of Reform, 229). The obvious problem with this is that such obsessive anxiety was not the norm for medieval monks or friars at any level of fervour: the daily confession is the giveaway that Luther fits the scrupulosity syndrome.

[48] Oxford Dictionary of the Christian Church, 1475.
[49] See Chadwick, The Reformation, 45, economically on the mark as usual.
[50] Pettegree, Reformation, 2–3.

at manipulating symbols[51] by which supporters expressed their loyalty to
new communities of protest or belief[52] – symbols that made their convictions more concrete. Medals were one sort of symbol: carrying portraits
of Luther or other heroes of the Reformation, or biblical themes favoured
in the new movement, like Abraham and Isaac or Christ and the Samar-
itan woman.[53] Less obviously, but convincingly, Pettegree argues that a
woodcut or a pamphlet could function in the same way as a medal: 'as a
badge of identity, a tangible symbol of allegiance for those who wished
to affirm the general programme of the Gospel preachers'.[54] Convictions
were strengthened by being embedded in these concrete things, quite
apart from the message. Here we see both a key feature of value or conviction rationality, and an instrumental technique by which it was kept
alive.

The two rationalities again

It is clear that the dynamics of values cannot be brought under a single
heading. The explanations that account for their rise, fall, and reproduction over generations are heterogeneous. The case study of the Reformation illustrates only some of the dynamics of change. Notably, one needs
to add transformations of the economic and social setting as potent causes
of value change – a kind of cause not obviously operative in the Reformation. Cities and sophisticated commerce were hardly new, and the importance of printing has been greatly overrated.[55] However it may be with
the Reformation, social transformations have been central to overturning
some systems of convictions, such as that of China's elite in the late nineteenth and early twentieth centuries. Still, the Reformation encapsulates
most of the dynamics discussed above. Change of values is easier when
the systems overlap, and we have seen how many core doctrines Protestantism retained from the tradition it left. Medieval belief in the authority
of the Bible, interpreted to the letter, gave Luther leverage in winning
converts through his passionate exegesis of passages from St Paul. The
timing was good in that literacy was widespread enough for the Bible to
be accessible to many, while it was still widely viewed as historically accu-
rate on a literal level, unambiguous as to essentials, and unproblematic
as to the authorship and composition of the different books. Luther was
a charismatic leader in both the modern and the Weberian sense. The

---

[51] I would distinguish between manipulating symbols and manipulating people, who are
not necessarily manipulated when they willingly and consciously make symbols their
own.
[52] Pettegree, *Reformation*, 215.   [53] *Ibid.*
[54] *Ibid.*, 216.   [55] d'Avray, 'Printing, Mass Communication'.

intensity which made so many trust him as an extraordinary religious
leader came out of the crucible of experience. Techniques of propagation
(as opposed to propaganda in the sense of mass manipulation) such as
songs and tangible symbols helped his followers to internalise his message
as their own value system. In this last case we have moved into the realm
of instrumental rationality – not intended here as a pejorative description.
These instrumental techniques in turn helped to give the thinking that
holds systems of values and convictions together its 'concrete' character.
The next chapter will therefore focus on a theme which is central to
the book as a whole: the interdependence of the two rationalities – their
symbiotic relationship.

4   The instrumental–conviction rationality interface

Starting from Weber's key distinction between value and instrumental rationality, the concept of value and conviction rationality was defined to make it more precise and serviceable for research, and then some of the factors affecting the ebb and flow of values and convictions were analysed. The dynamics of value systems depend perhaps more than anything else, however, on the relation of those systems to instrumental technique. The interactions on the interface between Weber's two main types of rationality are important in that and in a series of other ways: Weber's distinction between these two types should not be treated as a simple dichotomy: they are an invitation to causal analysis.

Accordingly we must turn to the interface between value and instrumental rationality. The aim is to get a purchase on the infinite variety of historical cases by articulating some causal schemas that help us make sense of the complexity. The following ideal-types of the relation between the two rationalities may usefully be distinguished.

(a) Instrumental techniques reproduce values, both extrinsically by making them widely known, and intrinsically by enabling people to internalise them as concrete and vivid.

(b) There is an instrumental rationality of spirituality just as much as of the phenomena grouped under the heading of 'modernity'.

(c) Since values mould instrumental rationality, the degree to which instrumental rationality in different cultures coincides depends on the degree of overlap between their value rationalities. To expand this schema: sometimes two or more sets of instrumental rationalities from different cultures seem remarkably alike, and sometimes so dissimilar that it is hard to remember that they are the same kind of rationality: so is instrumental rationality homogeneous or heterogeneous? The key is the causal dependence of instrumental technique on values. Similar values generate similar instrumental techniques. To complicate matters, some apparently similar instrumental techniques can be actually different 'on the inside', because different values lie behind them and affect their social meaning. Finally, differences in underlying values can cause the whole character of the instrumental rationalities they generate to look entirely different, as vodka changes its taste with different mixers.

(A) INSTRUMENTAL TECHNIQUE AND THE REPRODUCTION OF VALUES

The psychological concreteness of values and convictions (by contrast with verbal, propositional or purely abstract thought) was part of the ideal-type worked out in Chapter 2. It is related to the techniques of reproducing values because successful techniques can create concrete mental images. A skilful sermon on the Passion can make it real to the audience. A well-designed Holocaust museum can impart the 'Never Again' message to new generations of children in a way that dry propositions cannot. At the same time, technique can sometimes be easily distinguishable from content: the organisation of mass meetings or the use of music in television programmes may have a purely extrinsic connection with the values being propagated. Even so it is simpler to treat extrinsic and intrinsic reproduction of values together, since they merge into each other in so many cases. The uses of imagery in speaking, ritual enactment, appeals to emotion and appeals to sense imagination (etc.) are hard to pigeonhole as 'extrinsic' or' intrinsic' propagation of convictions and it is simpler to group them under the same heading.

Appeals to senses and emotions

The techniques used to make Reformation ideas more concrete, discussed at the end of the previous chapter, are by the same token excellent illustrations of successful appeals to the senses in the propagation of ideas. Another powerful tool both for inculcating core Protestant doctrines and for stimulating emotions to match was singing. Luther gave great attention to this crucial technology of devotion. He built singing into his new order of service in such a way as to involve the congregation systematically. Early Protestants also used singing outside the context of church services as a polemical instrument. Both functions were combined in Luther's hymn 'Ein feste Burg', 'always clearly intended for liturgical use' but 'with its militaristic language . . . a battle song, the "Marseillaise of the Reformation"'.[1]

Techniques similar to those used by religions – notably songs[2] – have been employed as well by secular workers' movements. This 'technology'

---

[1] Pettegree, *Reformation and the Culture of Persuasion*, 50.
[2] Cf. Körner, *Das Lied von einer anderen Welt*, and 'Antiklerikale Ideen und religiöse Formen'.

for the emotions is not manipulative unless those whose emotions are
aroused intended no such thing. It is on the contrary quite normal for
the adherents of value systems to use such instrumental technologies
quite deliberately to bring their feelings into line with principles.

Preaching, Buddhist and Christian

One of the most crucial forms of instrumental rationality in religious
history is preaching. The extraordinary diffusion of Buddhism could not
be explained without it. Preaching per se is quite close to the core of
Buddhist convictions, though the particular techniques examined are
not actually entailed by the core value. The early Buddhist text known
as the Mahâvagga presents the Buddha as undecided whether he should
preach the enlightenment he had just attained. 'Now if I proclaim the
doctrine, and other men are not able to understand my preaching, there
would result but weariness and annoyance to me';

Enough! Why should I now proclaim it? This doctrine will not be easy to understand to beings that are lost in love and hatred . . . When the Blessed One pon-
dered over this matter, his mind became inclined to remain in quiet, and not to
preach the doctrine. Then Brahmâ Sahampati, understanding by the power of
his mind the reflection which had arisen in the mind of the Blessed One, thought:
'Alas! The world perishes!'[3]

So the Brahmâ Sahampati went to the Buddha and persuaded him to
preach the doctrine.[4]

Thus the idea of preaching is part of the system of Buddhism.[5] Its
history seems to have been neglected until recently.[6] Preaching the doctrine is part of the doctrine. This is not the place to trace the long history
of Buddhist preaching back into the distant past,[7] but a few techniques
deserve mention as examples of instrumental rationality in this domain.

One such technique was the 'two-pulpit ritual drama in which both Pali
(the sacred language of Theravada) and Sinhala (the vernacular language
in Sri Lanka) were used to inspire and inform Buddhist audiences'.[8] This
technique seems to have originated in the eighteenth century (p. 18). In
addition to the two preachers, a non-monastic member of the audience
played a part as respondent. He sat between the pulpits and the audience

---

[3] Mahâvagga, I.5.2–4, in *Vinaya Texts, Part I*, 85–6.   [4] *Ibid.*, 86–8.
[5] Cf. Deegalle, *Popularising Buddhism*, ch. 2: 'Buddha as the Best Preacher'; Freiberger,
Der Orden, 195–6.
[6] Deegalle, *Popularising Buddhism*, 3–6; but see pp. 10–16 for some recent studies. Deegalle's book should put the subject on the map.
[7] On which see *ibid.*, chs. 3–4.
[8] *Ibid.*, 18; and cf. 107. Further references are given in the text.

(p. 105). His job was to say 'It is so, Lord', after important statements by the preacher, and to ask for clarification on his own account or at the request of a member of the congregation.[9] The venue was elaborately decorated or even constructed from scratch (pp. 103, 116). A two-pulpit event might last all night, with large numbers present (p. 102); it must have been a powerful technique for transmitting religious fervour to the laity.

Western technology put more familiar instruments to work in the preaching of Buddhism in Sri Lanka. From the later nineteenth century the printing press was combined with preaching in ways that the West had anticipated: 'Most popular preachers began to print their sermons as pamphlets; this method eventually made the preachers even more popular, and their sermons became readily available to a wider audience.'[10] In the twentieth century, radio 'enabled the Buddhist preacher to go beyond his own temple and locality and enter a much broader and larger national scene' (p. 147; see also 165–6). In due course television became a medium for Buddhist preaching (pp. 166–7). There are strong similarities between these techniques and those of Christian preaching, with convergence especially striking when one comes to the twentieth century.

The instrumental rationality of Christian preaching

Preaching transcends different religions and churches. One common value is required: the belief that the message should be impressed on the minds of others. While not a universal religious value – one does not associate preaching in the normal sense with the mainstream Quaker movement for instance – it is extremely widespread, with the expected consequences at the instrumental level. At this level historians can ask questions that transcend most of the differences in religious content.

For instance, the core beliefs may leave much room for manoeuvre in the techniques of selecting and structuring material for preaching: within the same religion or church the same core convictions can be expressed in quite different forms. But the instrumental rationality involved in structuring the content of preaching is too large a field to enter into here.

Leaving aside the forms into which the content is shaped (and thus avoiding the tricky question of how far the medium is the message), one can still ask about the 'delivery' systems of preaching in different times

---

[9] *Ibid.* In a personal communication, Prof. Gombrich tells me that the non-monastic interlocutor continues to play his role in the traditional preaching that remains common at least in a village setting to this day. His interventions can be compared to the ejaculations of 'Amen' during sermons in some Christian traditions.

[10] *Ibid.*, 134; for twentieth-century volumes of Buddhist sermons see *ibid.*, 161–3.

and places. Preachers need audiences to hear them. There is a comparative history of how that was managed. That leads on to further questions about the relation between preaching and other forms of communication with which it was combined.

Reformation preaching

Of the early Reformation, for instance, it has been argued that preaching 'was the bedrock around which the churches harnessed other communication media'.[11] It was not that popular vernacular preaching was new: it had been central to religious life at least in the towns for some three centuries and there is a massive scholarly literature on its medieval history.[12] In the Reformation communication through preaching was combined more systematically than before with the use of hymns, which were a complementary method of communicating core theological ideas.[13] The result was a highly effective propaganda machine for the new convictions.[14]

The rationalisation of revivalism: George Whitefield and Oral Roberts

The sixteenth-century reformers knew how to combine the impact of preaching and print. A new way of doing so was pioneered by George Whitefield (1714–70), whose career brings together the history of Methodism and of the first of the 'Great Awakenings' that have punctuated American religious life. Whitefield belonged to the Wesleys' group at Oxford and like the Wesleys he went to America to spread the gospel. His preaching campaigns there were wildly successful. The technical advance that he pioneered, and which enabled him to collect large audiences even when Church of England pulpits were closed to him, was the use of the newspapers to promote his revivalist preaching:

Before Whitefield, the newspapers did not include religion in their subject matter . . . To traditional churchmen it represented an alien presence, at best

---

[11] Pettegree, *Reformation*, 39.
[12] For example: Longère, *La Prédication médiévale*; d'Avray, *The Preaching of the Friars*; Bériou, *L'Avènement des maîtres de la parole*; Bataillon, *La Prédication au XIIIᵉ siècle*; Kienzle (ed.), *The Sermon*. There is a journal devoted to *Medieval Sermon Studies* (formerly this was the *Medieval Sermon Studies Newsletter*). For medieval revivalism see now d'Avray, *Medieval Religious Rationalities*, index, *s.v.* 'preaching'.
[13] Pettegree, *Reformation*, 49.
[14] Particularly since the reformers' message was also put over by the religious stage and through the printing press – by prints, pamphlets and books – though the role of these as visible signs of adherence to the Protestant faith may have been as important as the content they communicated. See Pettegree, *ibid.*, 216; cf. chs. 4–9 *passim*.

indifferent and at worst a threat to traditional religious print. But to Whitefield it represented the perfect form of public outreach, for it reached precisely the 'customers' who eluded the nets of printed sermons and settled churches. Acting more instinctively than methodically, Whitefield eagerly embraced the popular press as an essential ally for his own pursuit of mass audiences.[15]

Newspaper coverage prepared the way for Whitefield's part in the 'Great Awakening', which began in 1740 in Philadelphia. The *Pennsylvania Gazette* and the *American Weekly Mercury* gave him plenty of publicity (p. 117). 'Soon American news printers throughout the colonies learned to pick up on any Whitefield materials that came to their attention' (*ibid.*). Whitefield kept them supplied with material. He appears to have had at his disposal 'a primitive publicity department' (*ibid.*).

Several supplementary techniques helped keep the public's eye on his preaching. He engaged in high-profile controversies, notably against Southern slave owners, for not doing enough for the spiritual welfare of their slaves (*ibid*). He wrote letters on an amazing scale (p. 118). He kept on the move – eventually back across the Atlantic to Scotland, where another amazing revival campaign followed (pp. 119–20). He controlled a religious magazine, 'filled with news of his revivals', selling it cheap and employing an efficient distribution network (p. 120). Other magazines imitated it (p. 121).

Whitefield had developed a rationalised method of evangelisation that would have a long and successful history ahead of it:

His mass revivals were not really a church, nor were they connected to local communities and congregations. The audiences changed with every meeting, evidencing no permanent structure or leaders aside from Whitefield's own charismatic ministry and his network of media promoters. In addition, the audiences were routinely enjoined to support their local congregations and parishes . . . In reality, Whitefield's audiences, publishers, and loyal supporters represented powerful new 'parachurches' – groups of otherwise disconnected individuals bound in voluntary religious associations based on a marketplace organisation . . . What had initially been a convulsive and mysterious force upsetting ordinary life and catching participants by surprise had become, after 1745, something different – a familiar event that could be planned in advance, executed flawlessly, and then repeated at the next stop. (p. 122)

Plus ça change, plus c'est la même chose: in the twentieth century new techniques and technologies were employed but the underlying structure was the same. The career of Oral Roberts (b. 1918) is remarkably reminiscent of Whitefield's.[16] It is true that for much of his career he was a Pentecostal (he became a Methodist in 1968; p. 326) and healing played

---

[15] Stout, 'Religion, Communications', 112. Further references are given in the text.
[16] Harrell, 'Oral Roberts'. Further references are given in the text.

a central part in his preaching, even via the mass media.[17] What White-field would have recognised was the rationalisation and coordination of means to maximise the impact of the preaching.

Like Whitefield, Roberts kept on the move, at least in the decades when he was establishing himself. He travelled all over America and preached in dozens of other countries (p. 322). He preached in vast tents (*ibid.*) but also over the radio, using this medium as skilfully as White-field had used the newspapers: by 1953 he was on 200 radio stations (pp. 322–3); then a contract with ABC enabled him to raise the number to 500. 'His radio programs meshed well with his crusade ministry, providing advance advertisement and continued contact with the people who attended his crusades' (p. 324). Like Whitefield (but on a far larger scale) he used postal correspondence to reinforce the impact: 'By the mid-1980s, the ministry received over 5,000,000 letters a year, about half of them including contributions. In return, the organisation mailed around 50,000,000 pieces per year at a cost of over two million dollars. A letter received by the association would usually be answered within three days' (*ibid.*).

The rational next step was television. The first experiment was unsuccessful, but then he tried filming tent services, both the healing and the preaching. This worked. By 1957 Roberts's programme 'was being shown on 135 of the nation's 500 television stations' (p. 325). The healing and the Pentecostal style annoyed a lot of people and efforts were made to restrict this kind of broadcasting (p. 326).

Though they came to nothing, Roberts himself was changing his approach. As noted above, he converted to Methodism. He also stopped his programme and his tent preaching and healing. Instead he pioneered a new kind of programme, more like a variety show, featuring the 'World Action Singers' and celebrity guests; in the first programme the sermon and prayer by Roberts took up only seven minutes (pp. 327–9). The new format was, once again, dramatically successful: 'In 1973, the spring special attracted an estimated audience of over 37,000,000 viewers; in its wake, the ministry's mail reached an astonishing all-time monthly high of about 76,000 letters' (p. 329).

The moral of the stories of Whitefield and Roberts is that charisma is not just followed by organisational routinisation, but accompanied by it and dependent on it. In both these cases and of course in many others such as Billy Graham we see a rationalisation of charismatic preaching

---

[17] In his radio days, Roberts put his hand on the microphone, told his listeners to touch their radios, and said: 'I lay my hand over this microphone, and, lo, I am laying it upon you there in your home': quoted *ibid.*, 323.

missions to produce the maximum impact, creating an efficient administration, adapting rapidly to social change, and using new media. Oral Roberts unwittingly put his finger on something not far from the distinction between value and instrumental rationality when he said: 'I'm married to principles but I'm not married to methods. I'd change my method tomorrow if I could find a better one. But I'll never change a principle' (p. 331).

Individual magnetism and the crowd

The chemistry which enables a magnetic speaker to react with the emotions of a crowd is a thread which runs through the history of revivalist preaching, as important in the age of Oral Roberts as in the age of George Whitefield. There is nothing specifically Christian about this chemistry. Here is a description of a Sunni Islamic sermon delivered in Baghdad in 580/1184:

> he gave a tender and graceful sermon . . . causing the hearts of those present to pass swiftly into a state of ardent desire . . . Souls melted as though consumed by fire so that cries rang out and sobs rose up, and they fell on him like moths on a lamp. Each offered him his forelock which he cut off [a symbolic expression of remorse for sins], and placing his hand on the head of each, he prayed for them. Some fainted, and he raised them to himself in his arms.
>
> What we witnessed at this meeting was a terrifying sight which filled those present with penitence and remorse, and forcefully brought to mind the terrors of the day of the resurrection.[18]

The comparison with eighteenth-century (and one might add later) Christian revivalism in the USA has already been drawn.[19] It is easy to dismiss this kind of reaction as irrational, but not necessarily fair. The real or perceived intensity of the revivalist preacher's convictions is communicated to the crowd. If the religious belief system involves an antecedent expectation that God's power may be channelled through one individual to many there is nothing irrational in open-mindedness to the possibility that this or that preacher may indeed be such a conduit of divine force, however far from the mark the judgement may be in particular cases.

---

[18] Swartz, 'The Rules of the [sic] Popular Preaching in Twelfth-Century Baghdad', 233. Ideally, further comparisons should have been drawn with the Islamic popular preaching tradition or traditions, a field which deserves more Western scholarly attention. See, however, Antoun, *Muslim Preacher in the Modern World*, esp. 101–3.

[19] Cf. the comments by Swartz, 'The Rules', 234–5.

Mass education

Revivalist preaching's effects can be transient, as readers of Mark Twain's *Huckleberry Finn* will remember. More routine techniques are indispensable for keeping convictions steady and strong. For this reason, no doubt, the inculcation of values as part of the formation of youth can be and often is consciously and intentionally orchestrated by political, religious or other institutions. (Does this make it manipulation? Not necessarily. Manipulation (as the word is used here) involves persuading others to believe something that the persuaders do not personally believe, using reasons that do not convince the persuaders themselves.)

The German Reformation is a case in point. Luther's right-hand man Melanchthon made it his business to educate Protestant Germany by 'creating schools, making schools better, creating universities, making universities better; all of which meant making teachers more able to communicate knowledge, and pastors better equipped for their pulpits, and professors more likely to look for truth'.[20] This educational programme was propagandistic rather than 'manipulative'. It was certainly a successful technique for consolidating the Reformation.

'Lay' education in France is another good example. A 'lay' (i.e. anti-clerical) schoolmaster was described thus by a writer whom he taught before the First World War:

He lived through and for his class; he was, like many of the schoolteachers before 1914, a true priest of knowledge. He had been formed with the same rigour as my Jesuit uncles, but he embodied the Republic rather than the Church... He was one of those forty thousand anticlerical missionaries who were installed at that time in the most remote French villages to run the school, to lay the foundations, through the Secretariat of the Mairie, of the Republican commune.[21]

The following passage is from a book – on the sociology of values as it happens – based on lectures given at the Sorbonne to future schoolteachers. The cards are on the table: it would be a misnomer to describe such an open policy as 'manipulation':

The secularisation (*laïcisation*) of morality (*la morale*) is not only – as people usually suggest – a particular case of the differentiation of values... however tightly tangled up together religious ideas and the practice of morality seem to be originally, a process of dissociation is at work, with a dynamic which gathers pace with the increasing complexity of civilisation. The final end of virtues becomes the good that they do to men rather than the pleasure they give to the gods. An increasing number of human values win their autonomy in this way. It is natural

[20] Chadwick, *The Early Reformation*, 249.
[21] Guitton, *Écrire comme on se souvient*, 85 (my translation).

that, in a state where religion is no longer the principle of unity, the decision should be made that national schooling will insist on those particular values.[22]

The French Third Republic is a good example of the conscious and undisguised effort to instil values, the secular values of citizenship.[23] It is just one case of the commonest phenomenon: propagation and reinforcement of values without any particular effort to disguise what is going on, and often, especially in the case of voluntary organisations, with the willing participation of those who are the object of the exercises. There is much in common between methods used by religious and secular organisations (a point to which we must return). The impact of such techniques will be uneven, but it is safe to assume that in some cases they help to turn theoretical views perhaps mildly held into values as defined above.

Social and legal structures

It was argued earlier that social and legal structures embody convictions. They also communicate the values implicit in them to those who grow up within them. When people grow up in a society where the law and social practice on the one hand, and commonplace discourse on the other, converge to send much the same message, the values thus transmitted are hard to resist. This is a kind of education that continues throughout life.

Most children are hermeneutic anthropologists without knowing it and understand the meaning of the institutions and social practices they grow up in. As their values continue to be reinforced, they pass them on to their children. Millions of people internalise value systems as far apart as Islam and liberalism in this practical way, by living in institutions drenched by the value system in question.

In modern Western societies very many are brought up to think that the state's legitimacy derives from some kind of social contract which democratic elections renew; that the state has a monopoly of legitimate

---

[22] Bouglé, *Leçons de sociologie*, 285–6 (my translation).

[23] 'Few have indulged in the rhetoric of education more than the politicians and notables of the Third Republic. Ceaselessly they broadcast its merits as a universal panacea...Whereas in 1848 a Republic had been founded among people lacking the virtue to sustain it, and their ignorance had played into the hand of feudalism, despotism, and the government of priests, now a Jacobin alliance of democratic bourgeoisie and people would be...educated in their rights and duties as citizens of the Republic' (Gildea, *Education in Provincial France*, 254; 'A study of the social ideology of the Third Republic must take into account not only the evidence of the class-room but also...that of a whole congeries of post-school institutions that made up a veritable Republican Church' (*ibid.*, 269).

violence outside situations of extreme self-defence; and that its powers can run up against limits set by human rights. Social practice tells the same story. Elections are held and people take the trouble to vote (causing headaches for rational choice theorists). Murder and grievous bodily harm are punished and people approve of the state's retributive violence. Television programmes send the same message. States that violate human rights are presented by the news in negative terms. The precise boundaries of human rights are debated but few doubt that there are such rights. There are some heretics (criminals, neo-Nazis, Colonel Blimps) who dissent from this rational consensus, but they come up against a wall of disapproval. Laws governing marriage or 'partner' relationships in the West (benefits, inheritance rights, etc.) take it for granted that only two people are involved in a legitimate sexual partnership at one time, and social events (even if broad-minded about the marital or gender status of the partners) make the same assumption. Both social pressure and the law take values about incest for granted in virtually all societies, though the lines are drawn in different places. In this way a value rationality can be acquired just by growing up in a certain sort of society, in this instance our own.[24] It is not brainwashing. The certitudes thus produced are not infallible but they are rational.

Logical arguments and 'apologetics'

Logical arguments may be regarded as 'instrumental' reasoning when they are not part of the core axiomatic structure of the value system, though they extend and protect it. Systems unable to defend themselves this way may be vulnerable to other systems. Even if the convinced remain convinced, their children are less likely to acquire their convictions, and outsiders will tend not to sign up to the movement. 'Apologetics' as the word is commonly used refers to the argumentative defence of religions.

---

[24] Here Durkheimian comments of Bouglé are worth quoting: 'How do [value judgements] acquire the compelling prestige with which, in various degrees, they seem to us to be clothed, if not from this special force emanating from the convergence of many people's consciousness? . . . to understand the type of authority peculiar to values, we need to understand first how the *collective consciousness* is constituted and how it functions . . . We could begin by using the phrase collective consciousness to describe a common set of ideas. A set? It would be better to speak of a system, one which is itself the result of a synthesis.' ('D'où peut leur [i.e. to value judgements] venir le prestige contraignant dont, à des degrés divers, ils nous paraissent revêtus, sinon de cette force spéciale qui émane de la réunion des consciences? . . . pour comprendre le genre d'autorité propre aux valeurs, il importe de comprendre d'abord comment se constitue et comment agit la *conscience collective*. . . Un lot commun d'idées, c'est d'abord ce que nous pourrions appeler une conscience collective. Un lot? Il faudrait dire plutôt un système, et qui est lui-même le résultat d'une synthèse') (Bouglé, *Leçons*, 27–9).

The development of a vigorous argumentative apologetic can ensure that a religion survives and flourishes even in a critical environment. Thus, for instance, Hinduism seems to have developed its own apologetics in the nineteenth century in reaction to criticisms by Christian missionaries; in the same period it became an actively proselytising religion.[25] Similarly, early modern Catholicism developed a forceful apologetics against Protestantism in the aftermath of the Reformation.[26]

Argumentation, education, organisation and unconcealed appeals to emotion – in all these ways instrumental technique has reproduced the values it serves. Clearly they can transcend the divide between secular values. Even preaching has its secular counterparts – speeches in well-organised political campaigns, for instance. The instrumental techniques to which we must now turn are more specifically associated with religious devotion.

(B) THE INSTRUMENTAL RATIONALITY OF SPIRITUALITY

The introductory chapter briefly discussed the tendency to associate instrumental rationality too closely with modernity, capitalism, bureaucracy and technology.[27] As a corrective, it is worth devoting especial attention to the instrumental rationality of spirituality – the rationalisation of asceticism, forms of piety, etc., in the service of religious values and convictions. Religious techniques constitute instrumental rationalities which are shaped by values quite different from those associated with 'modernity': yet they can be described as 'rationalisation' within their value systems, just as much as technology or bureaucracy can within the value systems of capitalist firms or modern states.

Jewish spirituality

Weber's analyses of religious spiritualities bring out their instrumental character – without separating it from the underlying values. The instrumental techniques identified in the following passage are yeshiva training, wakeful self-discipline, constant study of the Jewish Law, and control, so far as external behaviour is concerned, of the passionately felt resentment of the merciless and powerful enemies of the Jewish people. The dependence of these techniques on value premises is evident:

---

[25] King, 'Some Reflections on Sociological Approaches', 87.
[26] See e.g. Rébelliau, *Bossuet* (discussed above, p. 107 note 43).
[27] See Introduction, section on *Weber and 'Modernity'*, pp. 19–21.

Living out the consequences of the Law[28] and of the intellectualism of yeshiva training in the Law constitute the 'Method of Life' of the Jew and his 'Rationalism'... The 'rationalising' effect of anxiety about the Law is exceedingly pervasive, but wholly indirect. The wakeful self-discipline... of the Jew whose piety is of the traditional sort derives from poring over the Law, which has been the school of his mind, and from the necessity to be constantly alert to make sure it is fulfilled with exactitude. This, however, acquired its specific tone and efficacy from the pious Jew's consciousness that only he and his people have this Law, and for the sake of it they are persecuted by all the world and vilified, that it is binding nonetheless and that eventually, through a deed accomplished overnight, at a time no one can know, and which no one can do anything to hasten either, God will turn the social hierarchy of the earth upside down, and into a messianic kingdom for those who have remained true in all things to the Law. The pious Jew knew that uncounted generations by now have already waited and wait in this way however much they have been derided for it; and with the feeling, to which this knowledge gave rise, of a certain sense of as it were extreme watchfulness,[29] was combined in his mind the necessity to nourish his sense of self-worth from the Law and the precise observance of it, as an end in itself, to a degree in direct proportion to the length of time during which he might, so far as he could tell, be obliged to go on waiting in vain. Last and not least the need to be on guard all the time and never to give free rein to his passionate indignation against the enemies who were as merciless as they were superior in strength: combined with the effect, discussed above, of *Ressentiment*, as an unavoidable factor, deriving from Yahweh's promises and the fateful destinies of his people, unparalleled in the whole of history, that those promises entailed. These are the circumstances which, essentially, underlie the rationality of Judaism. Not, though, asceticism.[30]

In the preceding passage Weber is talking about only one kind of Judaism and he is sketching an ideal-type, a simplified schema to help grasp the infinite particularities of history. Anyone reading a work by a German intellectual of Weber's period will be on the *qui vive* for signs of anti-Semitism, but I do not think there is any of that here, the method and tone being the same in his treatment of the ascetics and mystics to be discussed below. The point is that he sees Orthodox Judaism as a rationality, and its method of life as a rationalised one. We also see how the value rationality and reasoning which is not in itself part of the core rationality merge together, a reminder that the 'two rationalities' are to be distinguished analytically rather than separated in empirical investigation and that the values tend to colour all other reasoning.

---

[28] 'Die Wirkung des Gesetzes' is hard to translate more economically.

[29] I have translated 'Überwachheit' thus, rather than as 'sense of being watched over', because the latter would be 'Überwachtheit' and emendation is not required by the sense.

[30] Weber, *Wirtschaft und Gesellschaft*, vol. 1, p. 372, passage beginning 'Die Wirkung des Gesetzes' and ending 'Nicht aber "Askese".' My thanks to Axel Körner for correcting a crucial mistake in my translation and for other suggestions.

This-worldly asceticism

For 'asceticism' as Weber understands it here,[31] the key to salvation is 'a specific gift of active ethical action with the consciousness that this action is guided by God: that one is a tool of God'.[32] Asceticism involves 'the exclusive concentration on active achievements leading to salvation'.[33] One path is to live the ascetic life within the world.[34] This is the path that Weber rightly or wrongly associated with the Protestant ethos.

Weber describes the way in which the organisation of life is coloured by the value of asceticism when it is lived 'in the world'. The instrumental rationality of this-worldly asceticism includes making money ethically and legally, procreating children in a sober spirit within marriage, the rationally organised repression, through state institutions, of wrongdoing, the exercise of legal authority without enjoyment of power, and, generally, a disciplined life. In short, the things of this world provide the matter to be formed by the ascetic's style of life:

The world persists in its creaturely worthlessness: to give oneself over to its good things and enjoy them threatens the concentration on the good of salvation and the possession of it, and would indicate an impious frame of mind and that one had not been reborn. Nevertheless the world, as the creation of God . . . is the only material available on which one's own religious charisma has to prove itself through rational ethical action, in order to become and remain certain of one's own state of grace. As the object of this proving of oneself through action, the structures of the world take the shape, for the ascetic who finds himself put into them, of a 'vocation' and the task is to 'fulfil' it rationally. Thus the enjoyment of wealth is regarded as evil, but it is a 'vocation' to conduct economic activity within a rational ethical order and within strict respect for the law, the result of which – profit, that is – makes visible God's blessing on the work of the God-fearing man and thus the acceptability to God of the way he runs his economic life . . . Eroticism, which idolises creatures, is regarded as evil, but 'the begetting of children in a spirit of sobriety' (as the Puritans put it) within marriage is a vocation willed by God. Violence on the part of an individual directed against humans, deriving from passion or desire for revenge,

---

[31] 'For our purposes we would like to call this kind of attitude, which is conditioned by a religious methodology for achieving salvation, a "religously-"ascetic"" one – without in any way denying that the expression can be, and is, quite properly used in another, broader sense' ('Wir wollen für unsere Zwecke diese Art der durch religiöse Heilsmethodik bedingten Stellungnahme eine religiös-"asketische" nennen, – ohne irgendwie zu bestreiten, daß man den Ausdruck sehr wohl auch in anderem, weiteren Sinn brauchen kann and braucht') (*ibid.*, 328).

[32] 'Entweder ist dies [the 'Heilsgut'] eine spezifische Gabe aktiv ethischen Handelns mit dem Bewußtsein, daß Gott dies Handeln lenke: daß man Gottes Werkzeug sei' (*ibid.*).

[33] 'der alleinigen Konzentration des Handelns auf die aktiven Erlösungsleistungen' (*ibid.*, 329).

[34] *Ibid.*

or from any personal motive, is regarded as evil, but the rational suppression and punishment of sin and rebelliousness, in a functionally ordered state, is willed by God. The personal and worldly enjoyment of power is held to be evil, as being an idolatry of created things, but the rule of the rational order of the law is God's will. The 'ascetic within the world' is a rationalist both in the sense of rationally systematising the personal conduct of his own life, and in the sense of rejecting anything that is irrational from an ethical point of view, whether it is artistic or the result of personal emotion, within the world and its structures.[35]

In this passage most readers will of course recognise Weber's ideal-type of the Puritan ascetic, but his concept of asceticism as a value, with methods of life distinct but derived from it, is a lot broader, and includes the kind of asceticism that rejects the world and actively works for perfection outside its framework of economic, sexual and political relations:

This concentration [on active achievements leading to salvation] can make a formal renunciation of 'the World', of the social and psychological bonds of the family, of possessions, of political, economic, artistic, erotic and in general any kind of preoccupation with creaturely things seem necessary, and any involvement in them seem like an acceptance of the world that alienates one from God: this is world-rejecting asceticism.[36]

The essential point is that all this is rational in Weber's eyes, which relativises all that he says on rationalisation in the West in modern times.

Hindu asceticism as the most rationalised

A possible riposte would be: surely Weber thought that the West carried technical rationalisation much further than these other civilisations? Though he seems to say so in some places it is not so clear that he really thought so: at any rate any generalisation about his views needs to be hedged in with qualifications. Granted the values of capitalism and the modern state, their level of technique is incomparable. Still, a different value rationality can generate a different kind of ends–means rationality which may surpass the rest technically, though of course the techniques are very different because drenched in the values from which they derive. In another work we find the following passage, which should give pause

---

[35] Weber, *Wirtschaft und Gesellschaft*, 329: passage beginning 'Die [Welt] verharrt in ihrer kreatürlichen Entwertetheit:' and ending 'innerhalb der Welt und ihrer Ordnungen' (*ibid.*, 329).

[36] *Ibid.*, 329, passage beginning 'Diese Konzentration [des Handelns auf die aktiven Erlösunsleistungen] kann ein förmliches Ausscheiden' and ending 'weltablehnende Askese'.

for thought to anyone who imposes on Weber an evolutionary schema culminating in modern Western rationality:

> Indian asceticism was technically probably the rationally most highly developed in the world. There is hardly any ascetic method which was not exercised in virtuoso fashion in India and very often rationalised into a theoretical technical science, and many forms were only here carried all the way to their ultimate logical conclusions, which are often simply grotesque for us.[37]

The 'for us' is crucial. Weber means that they are grotesque given *our* value rationality, not theirs, and not *tout court*.

Mysticism

There are other major forms of instrumental rationalisation too. The methods of life derived from the values of mysticism then are contrasted with those of asceticism. The core value of mysticism is not the translation of God's will into human action but illumination, absorption into the one essential thing to the exclusion of all distraction:

> the specific good which constitutes salvation is not an active quality characterising behaviour, so: not the consciousness of the fulfilment of a divine will, but a state of being of a particular sort. In its pre-eminent form: 'mystical enlightenment'. This too can be achieved only by a minority of specially qualified persons and only through a systematic activity of a particular sort: Contemplation. To achieve its goal, contemplation always needs to eliminate day-to-day preoccupations. Only when everything that is creaturely in man falls altogether silent can God speak inside the soul, as the experience of the Quakers has it, and all contemplative mysticism from Lao-Tsu and Buddha to Tauler is probably in agreement with this experience in substance though not in their verbal formulations.[38]

Contemplation is thus a peculiar kind of ends–means rationality. It consists in large part in simply avoiding things.

> Abstinence from action, abstinence from thought if one follows the logic to its ultimate conclusion, emptying oneself of everything which in any way reminds one of the world, at any rate to do the absolute minimum, externally and internally – these are the ways to attain that inner state which is enjoyed as the possession of the Divine, as unio mystica with it . . .[39]

---

[37] Weber, *Die Wirtschaftsethik der Weltreligionen: II. Hinduismus und Buddhismus*, repr. in *Gesammelte Aufsätze zur Religionssoziologie*, vol. 2, p. 149, passage beginning 'Die indische Askese war technisch wohl die rational entwickelste' and ending 'grotesken Konsequenzen hineingesteigert worden'.

[38] Weber, *Wirtschaft und Gesellschaft*, 330, passage beginning 'das spezifische Heilsgut' and ending 'von Laotse und Buddha bis zu Tauler, übereinstimmt'.

[39] 'Nichthandeln, in letzter Konsequenz Nichtdenken, Entleerung von allem, was irgendwie an die "Welt" erinnert, jedenfalls absolutes Minimisierung alles äußeren und

Thus Weber did not present 'rationalisation' and 'instrumental rationality' as somehow peculiar to the secular West of recent times, or as uniquely developed by 'Modernity'. Different values generate different kinds of rationalisation. Religious values create spiritualities which are sometimes instrumentally rationalised to a high degree.

The instrumental rationality of Buddhist monasticism

The instrumental character of religious practices and techniques may well be explicitly recognised by religious leaders.[40] This seems to have been the case with Buddhist monasticism in its formative period. Monks were 'technicians' of asceticism in the sense that many of their austerities were not actually imposed by their core values, but were techniques developed to serve them. As Richard Gombrich has pointed out with reference to Theravada Buddhism, monks could choose from a 'list of ascetic options in what one ate or wore or where one lived', but 'they are only worth while if they are undertaken to cultivate "being content with little"'.[41] That is, to be content with little was a value, and the ascetic options are techniques for attaining it, techniques which are distinct from the value itself and which may backfire. In the Introduction a brief mention was made of the (real or invented) schismatic Buddhist monk who maintained that 'subsisting on alms, vegetarianism, wearing only rags, living only in the jungle, and living only at the foot of a tree' were absolute obligations. The rejection of this view attributed to the Buddha in effect classified these practices as instrumental decisions, however much shaped by the value system.[42]

A generation ago an anthropologist who did fieldwork on Buddhism in Burma captured rather effectively the instrumentality of the attitude to the rules of monastic life:

in reading the longer interview protocols it is evident, so far as the monks are concerned, that the main basis for these [monastic] rules (and for monastic asceticism in general) is to decrease the passions and the attachment to worldly things, and hence purify the mind (thereby freeing it for meditation and other nirvana-pursuing activities). As one monk put it, the various desires are 'like wild elephants which, enclosed in a stockade, must be tamed. Only after they are tamed is a person psychologically prepared for meditation. They can be tamed only through observing the precepts, especially abstinence from food, sex, and so on.'[43]

---

inneren Tuns sind der Weg, denjenigen inneren Zustand zu erreichen, der als Besitz des Göttlichen, als unio mystica mit ihm, genossen wird' (*ibid.*).

[40] The sections on Buddhism owe much to the advice of Professor Richard Gombrich, who is, obviously, not responsible for any shortcomings.

[41] Gombrich, *Theravada Buddhism*, 96.   [42] See above, pp. 23–4.

[43] Spiro, *Buddhism and Society*, 299. Cf. Harvey, *An Introduction to Buddhism*, 218: 'The Buddha felt that the life of a householder was somewhat spiritually cramping, such

Thus the rules and regulations of Buddhist monasticism could be regarded by practitioners as instruments to be used in the service of a value rather than as values in themselves. The following features of Buddhist monastic life could all be brought under the rubric of instrumental rationality:[44]

1. There was a ritual rite of passage into the monastic life. There could in fact be two rituals: in boyhood and at or after adolescence.[45]
2. Monks were allowed only minimal private possessions.[46]
3. Buddhist monasteries accumulated collective property which was presented to them by lay donors; theoretically this left them free to concentrate on their religious functions (practical realities are another matter).[47]
4. In the Theravada Buddhist tradition there is an aversion to physical money.[48]
5. Monks had a disciplined eating day, following rules about when they could eat and when they could not.[49]
6. The pattern of the day was regulated and it began early.[50]
7. After the early period,[51] chanting played a central role in the lives of Buddhist monks. 'The chants are usually in ancient languages . . . thus giving them an added air of sanctity. This, plus their sound-quality and accompanying thoughts, generates a mixture of uplifting joy . . . and contemplative calm. Thus monks and nuns can transmit something of the tranquillity of their way of life when chanting for the laity.'[52]
8. Visualisation techniques to aid contemplation were highly developed in Buddhism. To mention two examples: one could visualise the heavenly Amitabha Buddha in a simple way by 'contemplating an image . . . till it can be seen in great detail with the eyes closed', or in far more elaborate ways;[53] or one could pray with the help of a

that it was difficult for a layperson to perfect the "holy-life" . . . As the monastic life of one "gone forth from home into homelessness" lacks many of the attachments and limiting involvements found in lay life, it is seen as having fewer obstacles to, and more opportunities for, persistent and consistent spiritual practice.'

[44] Compare here the list of seven practices in Buddhism, in Aitken, 'Formal Practice: Buddhist or Christian'. This list too fits under the heading of 'instrumental rationality'.
[45] Gombrich, *Theravada Buddhism*, 108–9; Spiro, *Buddhism*, 290–2.
[46] Gombrich, *Theravada Buddhism*, 95.
[47] *Ibid.*, 97, 161–5; Harvey, *Introduction*, 230; Gernet, *Les Aspects*; Gunawardana, *Robe and Plough*.
[48] Gombrich, *Theravada Buddhism*, 104–5.
[49] *Ibid.*; Spiro, *Buddhism*, 307; Harvey, *Introduction*, 238.
[50] Spiro, *Buddhism*, 306–7.
[51] The Buddha 'actually forbade what we'd call "chanting" in reciting his words: the texts were to be spoken, not chanted "like the Veda". The meaning was what counted.' (R. Gombrich, pers. comm.; he surmises that the drift into chanting was not long delayed.)
[52] Harvey, *Introduction*, 175–6.
[53] *Ibid.*, 258–9.

mandala: a schematic representation of 'the luminous world, or Pure Land, of a specific holy being, with other holy beings particularly associated with it arrayed about it'.[54]

9. Confession of faults to the community played an important role in monastic life. Originally it would seem that the Buddhist *Patimokkha* ceremony included public confession of faults. Subsequently the opportunity to confess at the ceremony became a formality: monks would not reply when asked if they were pure and this would be taken to show that they were. They would in fact have confessed beforehand. In some parts of the Buddhist world at least the more serious offences are confessed before several monks and a penance is attached.[55]

Where offences are concerned the universal values and the conventional rules are imperfectly distinct and cannot be neatly segregated: 'all universal offences are also included in one way or another in the Community's code of Discipline, as conventional offences'.[56] Still, there are other conventional offences that are not intrinsically wrong: thus there is a ban on swimming though 'swimming as such does not constitute a demeritorious act in Buddhism'.[57] Pali vocabulary in Buddhist texts differentiates 'demeritorious actions' and 'universal offences' from 'conventional offences', which may or may not also be universal offences.[58]

All these various methodologies of spiritual development seem a long way from instrumental rationality as commonly conceived in modern interpretations of Max Weber. We have explored rationalities that are instrumental but neither modern nor secular. They bring home the adaptability of instrumental rationality, which changes its livery with every master it serves.

(C) SPECIFIC AND UNIVERSAL RATIONALITY IN HISTORY

We have circled around the question of how far rationalisation is culture-specific. For this purpose call 'rationalisation' the effective

---

[54] *Ibid.*, 264. I have seen a mandala made in the Ashmolean Museum by visiting Tibetan Buddhist monks out of coloured sands. At the end they demolished it. 'Demolition is essential to the ritual, which must have a formal end' (R. Gombrich, pers. comm.).

[55] Spiro, *Buddhism*, 302–4; Gombrich, *Theravada Buddhism*, 110, Harvey, *Introduction*, 225.

[56] Wijayaratna, *Buddhist Monastic Life*, 154 n. 5.   [57] *Ibid.*, 149.

[58] 'there exists in Buddhism a difference between a "sin" and an offense; the Buddhist equivalent of the notion of sin seems to be *papa kamma*, "demeritorious action," . . . and so Buddhist texts refer to demeritorious actions as *loka vajja*, "universal offenses." On the other hand, the term *apatti* denotes the transgression by monks of codified institutional rules; they are called *sammuti vajja*, "conventional offense," and are not necessarily all included in the class of universal offenses' (*ibid.*).

implementation of values by instrumental rationality. It was argued in Chapter 1 that instrumental rationality is universal, but that its appearance is radically affected by the values and convictions on which it builds. Some of the subtler implications must now be explored, viz., that when two systems of conviction have overlapping values (however different their overall structures may be) they can generate remarkable similar instrumental rationalities; that similarities at this instrumental level can sometimes nonetheless be merely superficial, when the 'inner side' or thoughts behind the practices are different; that differences in values create sharply differing forms of instrumental reasoning – notably in ethics, where different 'interface values' in different systems define 'arenas' for instrumental reasoning that differ enormously in size and shape.

The section ends with a case study of a particular 'interface value' relevant above all to law, *epieikeia* or equity. On the one hand, this transcends cultures, creating similar instrumental rationalities in widely different settings. On the other hand, it is no universal. This will take us on (in the final two chapters) to the principal topics still to be considered: substantive and formal legal rationality.

Instrumental rationality in spirituality: cross-cultural resemblances

The close correlation between the nine features of Buddhist monasticism listed above and characteristics of Christian monasticism will not have escaped notice. It is not that one could find an exact match between any one version of Buddhist monasticism and any one Christian religious order. The two traditions are like two branches of a family: no one individual on either side shares all the features of any one individual on the other side of it, but the total repertory of features and combinations of features on either side is strikingly similar.[59] Buddhist and Christian revivalist preaching discussed earlier in this chapter have much in common at the level of instrumental rationality. Different though the two religions are, there is a distinct family resemblance between their instrumental techniques for reaching a mass public, notably the use of the press and the radio.

The same holds good for Catholic and Hindu devotional styles. It is striking, for example, how many of the elements of a traditional Catholic

---

[59] A review of a book on Zen Buddhism makes the following perceptive comment: 'While Jesuits are vowed cenobites living in a closed community, they ... do not communally recite the Holy Office nor do they take vows of stability. Benedictine, Cistercian and Trappist monks and nuns, on the other hand, do parallel Buddhist monks and nuns in their use of meditation, communal prayer, and periodic retreats, but they take vows of stability, which their Zen Buddhist counterparts do not' (Goulde, reviewing Buswell, *The Zen Monastic Experience*, 188).

devotion have parallels in the following description of a Hindu service for the Goddess Mariammam (and similar parallels could be drawn with, say, Jain rituals).

he pushes through the crowd to enter the temple itself. Inside it is dark and cool, filled with the thick, sweet smell of incense . . . He reaches up to ring a bell suspended from the stone ceiling. Its strong tone clears his brain of extraneous thought and allows him to focus on the deity. By craning his neck he can just get a glimpse of the blackened stone image of the Goddess. She is dressed in a brilliant red sari, her neck covered with jewels and garlands of flowers, her head crowned with a diadem. The priest comes down the line of devotees collecting their offerings and returns to the sanctum. A curtain is drawn across the shrine for a few minutes of eager anticipation. Then, amid the clamour of bells, it is opened. The image of Mariammam is radiantly beautiful to him, newly adorned with fresh flowers . . . The priest waves a brass lamp lit with seven flames in a circular motion in front of the Goddess . . . The priest then brings out a tray of lighted camphor. All the worshippers place their hands quickly into the cool flame before touching them to their closed eyelids, symbolically opening their souls to communion with the Divine. On the same tray are little mounds of white sacred ash and red vermilion powder. With the fourth finger of his right hand, Ramachandran puts a dot of each in the centre of his forehead between his eyebrows, the ash symbolising purification through worship and the red symbolising Shakti, the power of the Goddess. Then each person's basket of offerings is returned, some of its contents remaining as a donation to the temple, the rest blessed by the Goddess to be shared by the devotees. Ramachandran will take this *prashad* ['newly blessed food'[60]] back to his family, so that they may partake in Mariammam's blessing.[61]

We have here incense, bells, flowers,[62] a sanctum in the place of worship,[63] lights, ash on the forehead (cf. Ash Wednesday). Footnotes are hardly required to prove that these techniques for heightening devotion are commonplace in Catholicism past and present. The list of devotional 'techniques' which Catholicism shares with Hinduism can easily be extended. Thus the technique of punctuating prayer with rosary beads is found in both;[64] both used and use hymns;[65] pilgrimages are

---

[60] Huyler, *Meeting God*, 63.   [61] *Ibid.*, 49–50.

[62] For incense, bells and flowers in Jainism cf. C. Humphrey and J. Laidlaw, *The Archetypal Actions of Ritual*, 24–5.

[63] Central sanctuary in a Jain temple: *ibid.*, 22.

[64] For Hindu rosaries see Blackman, 'The Rosary in Magic and Religion', 258–63; see 260 for Jain rosaries. For the rosary in Western Christendom see Winston-Allen, *Stories of the Rose*. She points out (p. 14) that prayer beads in the West antedate the Crusades, so that they are probably not a borrowing from the Islamic world.

[65] Note, however, that the association between hymns and formal religious services familiar in the West cannot necessarily be transferred to Hinduism: cf. Michaels, *Der Hinduismus*, 251: 'These hymns and poems were recited alone or in a group, but not, however, in a communal service' ('Diese Hymnen und Dichtungen werden, allein oder in einer Gruppe, nicht aber in einem gemeinschaftlichen Gottesdienst rezitiert'). Cf., however,

firmly rooted in both;[66] and festivals and processions give a dramatic and colourful aspect to devotion in both.[67]

Thus techniques for arousing devotion, monastic practices, and revivalist organisational methods transcend particular religious systems. On the other hand, the passages from Weber bring out the differences between different kinds of religious rationalisation: mystical contemplative techniques, ascetic techniques for escaping the world, ascetic techniques to be practised in the world, and so forth – let alone the differences between all the above and the instrumental techniques of modern capitalist firms and bureaucratic states.

The apparent contradictions here can be resolved if one bears in mind not only the distinction between the specificity of value rationality and the universality of instrumental rationality, but also the action of the values on technique: the symbiosis of the two kinds of rationality.

The parallels between Buddhist and Christian preaching or monasticism make sense if one posits underlying common elements shared by the value systems in question. Christianity, Buddhism and Islam share the conviction that the truths they hold should be propagated to non-believers by preaching, so the development of similar revivalist techniques is not surprising. Nor is this a universal value. It seems not to go with Orthodox Judaism. Again, revivalist preaching, or indeed any sort of sense that systematic preaching was a religious imperative, does not seem to have been a prominent feature of pre-colonial Hinduism.

Buddhism and Christianity (or at least the largest Christian churches) also share a rejection of the individual's selfish cravings, especially for money and sex. Hinduism and Catholicism share a sense that it is right to express love and devotion to holy beings, and find similar techniques for channelling those emotions. Even if there is not much common ground shared by all value systems, any two value systems are likely to overlap

Huyler, *Meeting God*, 36: 'The closest parallel to Judeo-Christian services are *bhajanas*, in which followers of the Bhakti movement join to sing hymns and praises to their Lord Krishna.' For hymns in Jainism see Humphrey and Laidlaw, *Archetypal Actions*, 26.

[66] Cf. Jha, 'The Origin, Type, Spread and Nature of Hindu Pilgrimage'. He comments that 'The merit of pilgrimage ranges from immediate relief from mundane troubles to the expiation of sins and gaining the ultimate reality, i.e., the *moksha* (salvation)' (p. 14). One could say much the same, *mutatis mutandis*, about pilgrimage in the medieval West, and Webb, *Medieval European Pilgrimage*, practically does: 'On the one hand, there were physical and practical problems from which the suppliant sought relief; on the other there were spiritual objectives, including the forgiveness of sin . . . there was a lot of common ground between pilgrimages of different types, including the all-pervasive conviction of the need to make reparation for the basic sinfulness and imperfection of man' (p. 77).

[67] Huyler, *Meeting God*, 169–73. For a wide-ranging study of a late medieval festival involving processions see Rubin, *Corpus Christi*.

significantly, and thus to generate similar instrumental techniques. The overlap between underlying values may often be less obvious than the convergences at the level of instrumental technique, because the differing overall 'Gestalt' structures of the systems distract attention from the individual elements that are bound together in those structures. It is the Gestalt structures of value rationalities that give them their specificity.

Deceptive similarities at the instrumental level

In parenthesis, it should be remembered that apparent convergences at the instrumental level can be deceptive. There may be differences, ultimately traceable back to differences at the value level, on the 'inner side' of the apparently similar practices that meet the eye.[68] Though the convergences at the level of instrumental rationality are not illusory, they can be overstated if the different thought-worlds behind the techniques are not remembered.

Visualisation is a case in point. It is important in both Christian and Buddhist meditation. The *Spiritual Exercises*[69] of St Ignatius Loyola and the mandala method of meditation, focused on an often temporary image of concentric circles with a pure palace in the middle,[70] both systematised and rationalised visualisation techniques to a high degree. The underlying purposes are very different, however: in the case of the mandala technique,

By visualizing his physical body as the mandala, the yogin sees the universe contained within himself as microcosm, and by identifying with the central deity the yogin places himself in the ultimate state... In absorbing the compassion, wisdom, and skilful means... of that deity, the yogin effects a transmutation of his own mundane personality.[71]

The Jesuit taking the *Exercises* also no doubt wanted to transform his personality, but the contemplation of the incarnated Christ and the framework of a human history stretching from the original sin to the Last Judgement give a non-trivially different 'inner side' meaning to the meditation. A short extract from the 'First Contemplation' for the 'First Day' will give a sense of the difference: notably, the transcendent importance

---

[68] For a discussion of the concept of 'inner-side' differences see d'Avray, *Medieval Marriage*, 148–50 (with further references to the ideas of Max Weber, Peter Winch, and Clifford Geertz).
[69] For a substantial bibliography see *The Oxford Dictionary of the Christian Church*, 1530–1, s.v. *Spiritual Exercises*.
[70] For a good description of mandala visualisation see Harvey, *An Introduction to Buddhism*, 264–5; also *The Oxford Dictionary of World Religions*, 610, s.v. Mandala.
[71] *Ibid.*

of historical events and the significance in its own right of the specific and particular moment in time and space:

First preliminary. The story. Here it is how the Three Divine persons look down on the entire round of the earth's surface, filled with human beings. Seeing them all going to Hell, they decree in their eternity that the Second Person shall become man to save mankind. When the fullness of time comes they send the angel Gabriel to our Lady.

Second preliminary. The picture. Here it means seeing the great extent of the round earth, containing so many different races: then I must look at the room in our Lady's house at Nazareth in Galilee.[72]

The meaning attached to statues may also differ more than meets the eye. It would be easy to assimilate statues of Buddhist deities with images of Christian saints, *mutatis mutandis*. Some particularly interesting sixth-century Chinese Buddhist statues have been reinterpreted, however, to mean 'not Buddhist deities in a traditional sense, but rather the actual *devotees* of the Maitreya cult . . . these devotees indicated that they adopted an existing iconography and assigned to the image a new meaning relevant to their own spiritual quest'.[73] The statues 'were intended to represent the followers of the Maitreya cult enjoying their successful rebirths as bodhisattvas in Tusita. To get there, they visualized themselves as already there.'[74] The thoughts behind this practice clearly put it in a completely different category from devotion to a divine or saintly figure represented by a statute, however great the similarity from the outside.

Contrasting convictions create contrasting instrumental rationalities

We have moved from genuine similarities to deceptive ones, and must now turn to value rationalities that differ so much that the instrumental techniques they generate are hard to recognise as specimens of a common rationality. Heterogeneous value rationalities shape instrumental reasoning in such a way that it seems to lose its universal character and tends to appear value-specific.

Instrumental rationality is like the water added to different kinds of dehydrated foods: the outcome conceals the common component. Or it is like an adroit speech-writer, who can promote almost any kind of conviction. It wears the livery of the values it serves. Thus instrumental rationality is universal, but it is shaped by value rationalities.[75] When

---

[72] Ignatius of Loyola, *The Spiritual Exercises*, trans. Corbishley, paras. 102–3, p. 45
[73] Hsiang-Ling Hsu, 'Visualisation Meditation', 8.   [74] *Ibid.*, 30.
[75] See above, Ch. 1, p. 59.

anthropologists say that 'culture goes all the way down', they mean that there is no 'trunk' of 'human nature' below the level where the different cultural 'branches' separate; to change the spatial metaphor, they are attacking the idea that cultural differences are built on an underlying bedrock of common rationality. The assumption (shared by both sides of the debate about universal rationality) is that a common rationality if there is one will be at the base of culture. The argument is whether such a foundation exists at all. It is useful to reverse the metaphor, and to think of the different rationalities as the foundation, and the common rationality as building on top of them.

Thus one could say: 'culture goes all the way down' but not all the way up. What this reversal of the metaphor means is that different rationalities or different cultures are like different sets of premises. The logic used to draw inferences from them is common to all concerned. Still the conclusions will be radically different because the premises are different. Consequently, the difference at the base affects reasoning right up to the top, even though there is only one way of reasoning above the axiomatic level – the reasoning of rudimentary logic and practical calculations about causes and effects. In developing beliefs, instrumental rationality comes into play when people draw inferences from their premises.

The same world-view can accommodate different inferences, but debates about which is correct are much more likely to be conclusive than debates between people with different sets of premises. As for action, instrumental rationality comes into play when values and convictions can be embodied in more than one way. Choosing which way then becomes the business of instrumental reasoning. Again, people can argue about what to do and convince each other, if they are in a rational mode, because they share common premises. They are premises logically; psychologically they are convictions. When argument is a form of instrumental rationality in which people engage on the basis of common convictions it can lead to consensus; if the convictions which serve as premises are not shared, the disputants will not reach common conclusions even though they are using the same logic.

Early on in this book it was suggested that value rationalities per se are specific and heterogeneous, while instrumental rationality per se is universal and homogeneous. That still holds good, but we have seen that there is more to it. Differences in underlying values affect instrumental rationality, so that different world-views can generate instrumental rationalities which seem to have nothing in common unless one looks very closely – as when one notices that Azande poison oracles have mechanisms akin to a modern scientist's control sample. On the other hand, any two value rationalities are bound in practice to overlap to a greater or lesser degree, and insofar as they do so the instrumental rationalities generated may after all look strikingly similar.

Values relating to instrumental rationality ('interface values')

All this is especially true when the underlying values or convictions concern the actual role of instrumental rationality. Some value systems allow instrumental reasoning more room for manoeuvre than others do. Let us call values that regulate the exercise of instrumental rationality and define its scope 'interface values'.

Value systems which differ a great deal overall may happen to have similar 'interface values', but when they do not – when different value systems have radically different conceptions of the role of instrumental reasoning – this naturally tends to produce different-looking instrumental rationalities. Ethical systems are a case in point.

At one extreme, we have emotivism, according to which all ethical judgements are expressions of preferences and therefore instrumental.[76] Already some way from that position is utilitarianism in its Benthamite form. That does indeed create a large area for instrumental calculation, but the shape of the boundaries is set by a few core values. Good is pleasure and the absence of pain; actions should serve the greatest good of the greatest number; and therefore each individual counts equally towards calculating that number (as opposed to being merged into a larger whole, such as a class). Granted these values – for values they are – everything else is consequentialist instrumental calculation. For G. E. Moore, on the other hand, the core values are duty and friendship, which leaves room for many intricate calculations about the right course of action in individual cases. At the other extreme are ethical schemes which assume that there is an ethical principle for every concrete case. Perhaps rather curiously, in the pluralist secular world of modern academe, this view is widely held by contemporary moral philosophers.[77] That would imply

---

[76] There is thus an affinity between this school of ethics and Rational Choice Theory, but there are differences also. Emotivism, as its name suggests, emphasises the emotional character of preferences, not stressed in RCT. The theories come out of very different 'stables'. Emotivists in England were reacting to theories of moral value as perceptible to the discerning of aesthetic value, like good music (cf. MacIntyre, *After Virtue*, 16–17), though emotivist ethics also has deeper roots in nineteenth-century German and Austrian philosophy of value (cf. Satris, 'The Theory of Value'). RCT, by contrast, comes out of economics and game theory. Neither RCT nor Emotivism was a decisive influence on the other, yet the resemblance is non-trivial.

[77] According to Wood, *Kantian Ethics*, 46–7: 'another of the distinctive characteristics of the dominant theory is the way it conceives of moral principles, the kinds of demands

that all ethical decisions should ideally be the expression of a general value.[78] Aristotle's view is different again: there is a realm of particular decisions which no principles can reach. His language in the *Nicomachean Ethics* implies that this is a realm where instrumental reasoning rules:

the whole account of matters of conduct must be given in outline and not precisely, as we said at the very beginning that the accounts we demand must be in accordance with the subject-matter; matters concerned with conduct and questions of what is good for us have no fixity, any more than matters of health. The general account being of this nature, the account of particular cases is yet more lacking in exactness; for they do not fall under any art or set of precepts, but the agents themselves must in each case consider what is appropriate to the occasion, as happens also in the art of medicine or navigation.[79]

The value system cannot tell people 'what is appropriate to the occasion' in such cases.[80] It has been argued throughout that value systems impart something of themselves to the instrumental rationality that serves them. One can think of instrumental rationality as reasoning in the spaces not occupied by values and convictions. In this sense, instrumental rationality has a crucial role in ethical judgement according to Aristotle.

The idea of law and 'equity'

The passage of Aristotle just cited takes us on to the related idea in the legal domain of *epieikeia*, which may be used as a case study of how far common 'interface values' can create mutually analogous instrumental rationalities across cultures. (This section also marks the transition to the themes in the history and sociology of law with which the remainder of the book is primarily concerned.) *Epieikeia*, usually translated as 'equity', is a value that sets the tone of a certain sort of instrumental reasoning in the implementation of laws: an interface value par excellence. It is not unique to the society in which the word was coined, but it is far from

---

it places on them, and the way it thinks they apply to actions. On this conception, the aim of moral theory will be to settle all moral questions and make all moral decisions, as far as possible, by a rigorous derivation from precisely stated principles . . . Where there is unclarity or indeterminacy in our principles, or a threat of conflict between them, or any uncertainty about how they apply to particular cases, we should try to remove these deficiencies by formulating the principles more precisely, testing these formulations against overall coherence with our moral intuitions.'

[78] This kind of theory is also attributed to Kant, but Wood, *Kantian Ethics*, contrasts it to Kant's approach, which allows for *Spielraum*. Wood has a point but he would appear to be grinding a massive axe.

[79] Aristotle, *Nicomachean Ethics*, 2.2, Bekker 1104ᵃ; *The Complete Works of Aristotle*, ed. Barnes, vol. 2, pp. 1743–4.

[80] As a theoretical possibility, one could imagine a system of ethics which included 'one-off' values, not subsumable under any generality, but this is not what Aristotle seems to be saying.

being a sociological universal: in most modern legal systems it tends to be crowded out by another legal value, certainty. It thus illustrates both the homogeneity and the heterogeneity of instrumental rationality, viewed comparatively.

Epieikeia is the principle that the letter of city state (*polis*) law does not always reflect the legislator's true intentions.[81] The basic idea was not Aristotle's invention. Plato had a similar concept though he had expressed it differently.[82] But Aristotle puts it thus:

[Equity] makes up for the defects of a community's written code of law. For equity is regarded as just; it is, in fact, the sort of justice which goes beyond the written law. Its existence partly is and partly is not intended by legislators; not intended, where they have noticed no defect in the law; intended, where they find themselves unable to define things exactly, and are obliged to legislate universally where matters hold only for the most part; or where it is not easy to be complete owing to the endless possible cases presented, such as the kinds and sizes of weapons that may be used to inflict wounds – a lifetime would be too short to make out a complete list of these.[83]

Or again, in the *Nicomachean Ethics*:

And this is then the nature of the equitable, a correction of law where it is defective owing to its universality. And in fact this is the reason why all things are not determined by law, viz. that about some things it is impossible to lay down a law, so that a decree is needed.[84]

As with his observation of the limits of precepts when it comes to speci-ficities, these passages are in effect about a value defining the space for the exercise of instrumental rationality, this time in the administration of the law of the city state or *polis*.

Aristotle's theory is set in the world of the Greek city states, with their various law codes. Filling in gaps when these laws were silent was not a problem in Greek city states,[85] but Aristotle proposes a similar approach if the letter of the law, when applied to a particular case, went beyond what

---

[81] On *epieikeia* my principle guide is Triantaphyllopoulos, *Das Rechtsdenken der Griechen*; for an older treatment, see J. W. Jones, *The Law and Legal Theory of the Greeks*, ch. 3 on 'Law and Nature'; for more recent work on law in the *polis*, Foxhall and Lewis (eds.), *Greek Law in its Political Setting*; for a debatable but stimulating attempt to set Aristotle's ethical theory in its political and social context, see MacIntyre, *After Virtue*, chs. 11 and 12.

[82] Triantaphyllopoulos, *Das Rechtsdenken der Griechen*, 19.

[83] Aristotle, *Rhetoric*, 1.13, Bekker 1374ᵃ; *Complete Works of Aristotle*, ed. Barnes, vol. 2, p. 2188.

[84] Aristotle, *Nicomachean Ethics*, 5.10, Bekker 1137ᵇ, *Complete Works of Aristotle*, ed. Barnes, vol. 2, p. 1796.

[85] 'All Greek legal systems assumed that there were lacunae in the law and had rules to make them good' ('Alle griechischen Rechtsordnungen gingen von der Existenz von

the original legislator intended,[86] with the difference that with *epieikeia* the putative intention of the legislator was the criterion, rather than the judge's own assessment of what justice demanded.[87] Aristotle knew the harshness of Athenian law at first hand.[88]

Whether Aristotle's version corresponded to practice in Greek city states is impossible to say – the reasoning behind judicial decisions was not recorded.[89] These passages from Aristotle (and the similar views of Plato) do, however, show us that such an approach was perfectly conceivable in the *polis* context. The laws and judges of the city where he lived and others of his time are the setting in life for Aristotle's *epieikeia* concept.

The doctrine of *epieikeia* fits within a coherent system of values and convictions, involving the natural and the man-made, ethics and the law. Aristotle distinguished between natural (*physikon*) and legal (*nomikon*) justice. He also thought that the law of the *polis*, legal justice, should be a framework for the virtuous life;[90] as a modern scholar has put it: 'in prescribing conduct the legal system encourages the exercise and completion of the growth of virtue in the social and political sphere'.[91]

Though it belongs to a specific value system set in a specific culture, close equivalents to or descendants of Aristotle's *epieikeia* doctrine can be found in other value systems too. For instance, it has a place in English legal history, above all at the end of the Middle Ages and in the early modern period, after which it gave ground to formal legal rationality, on which more in Chapters 5 and 6. There was a not dissimilar value in an important strand of classical Chinese legal thought. The Dispensation system of the Catholic Church is yet another parallel, one of the best-developed systems of equity in world history. These instances of systematised equity must be discussed more fully in Chapter 6, in the context of the distinction between formal and substantive rationality (the pre-modern history of the Dispensation system is analysed in *Medieval*

Gesetzeslücken aus und besaßen Regeln zu ihrer Beseitigung.') (Triantaphyllopoulos, *Das Rechtsdenken der Griechen*, 21).
[86] *Ibid.*, 20–1.   [87] *Ibid.*, 21–2.
[88] 'Besides, Aristotle had personal experience of the harshness of Athenian public law, which knew no limits in the imposition of strict and extreme punishments, and had attempted, through his *epieikeia*, to limit rather than to extend such an inhumane state of affairs' ('Außerdem hat Aristoteles persönlich die Härten des athenischen öffentlichen Rechts erlebt, das keine Schranken in der Verhängung strenger und extremer Strafen kannte, und er hat versucht, durch seine *epieikeia* eine solch unmenschliche Situation eher einzuschränken als auszuweiten') (*ibid.*, 21).
[89] See Triantaphyllopoulos, *Das Rechtsdenken der Griechen*, 20.
[90] For the reception of these ideas in the Middle Ages, see d'Avray, *Death and the Prince*, 139–40.
[91] Rosen, 'The Political Context', 228.

Religious Rationalities, Chapter 6). Closer to home, the clause 'normally' in regulations governing British university departments embodies a similar approach.

Where this interface value obtained or obtains, judges and authorities, not to mention departmental tutors or chairs of examination boards, generally regard the rules with respect, but as tools of values rather than values per se – as the products of instrumental rationality attempting to implement those values. Consequently the law or the rules may be suspended when circumstances demand it. The decision to suspend them is also an instrumental calculation. In principle both the rules and the discretion to suspend them serve the same values. The instrumental reasoning is neither identifiable with, nor separable from, the values served. The two kinds of instrumental reasoning – making the rules and suspending them – are symbiotic too, precisely because they serve the same values. But this is to anticipate the argument of the next two chapters, about formal and substantive rationality.

Epieikeia-type values do not in fact seem to be very common in the philosophy of law or in the legal practice of sophisticated states in modern times. As something close to the opposite pole from Aristotle's attitude it is worth looking briefly at Kant's attitude to equity (*Billigkeit*). It seems to be uncompromisingly negative. A court of equity is a contradiction in terms, he thinks. Only where the judge's own rights are concerned can they be waived: Kant gives the example of the Crown granting a plea to make good losses suffered in its service when it had no legal liability to do so. The law of the State should not be confused with a court of conscience.[92]

Kant's attitude to equity seems to be more typical in the post-medieval Western tradition than Aristotle's. The historical mainstream of the civil law (i.e. Roman law) tradition has tended to reject at least in principle the idea of judges correcting the letter of the law. The principle underlying this rejection is that the law should all be contained in the code in force in that country, so the judge's job is simply to find the rule in that code which covers the case in hand.

The following characterisation is a caricature: an ideal-type or simplification. But it does pinpoint some widespread attitudes within the tradition. The civil law tradition does assume that law is 'positive' – made by man not by God. The civil law tradition's watchword is certainty – the

---

[92] Kant, *Die Metaphysik der Sitten*, ed. Ebeling, 'Anhang zur Einleitung in die Rechtslehre' I, p. 72, passage beginnning 'Hieraus folgt auch, daß ein Gerichtshof der Billigkeit' and ending 'dagegen jede Frage Rechtens vor das bürgerliche Recht . . . gezogen werden muß'.

predictability and consistency of the law.[93] If equity is allowed, it is explicitly built into the law by legislators, for carefully circumscribed types of case.[94] De facto things are different: judges have a great deal of equitable jurisdiction because some formal rules are defined so abstractly as to leave much room for discretion.[95] But this is not how the law is regarded in principle (or used to be, for the civil law tradition has undergone many changes over the last generation or so). In principle, too, the principles of the law should cover all but the most extraordinary cases. The judge's function 'is merely to find the right legislative provision, couple it with the fact situation, and bless the solution that is more or less automatically produced from the union'.[96] Common law theory allows for much more judicial discretion than civil law theory of the traditional mould.

Even the common law, however, circumscribes the power of the judge in principle. The experiment of a court of equity was in effect abandoned,[97] and the degree of discretion allowed to judges in the system operating in England is essentially different from Aristotle's *epieikeia*, which allowed the judge to depart from the letter of existing law as well as to make good the gaps in it. The common law makes a principle out of precedents in effect set by judicial decisions, but few English common lawyers think that it is the judges' job to override existing precedents or statutes in individual cases.

Evidence of this is an argument between Herbert Hart and Ronald Dworkin: when two disputants silently take some common ground for granted, those silent assumptions tend to be generally held convictions in their world. Hart wrote in a 'Postscript' to the second edition of his influential *Idea of Law*:

The sharpest direct conflict between the legal theory of this book and Dworkin's theory arises from my contention that in any legal system there will always be certain legally unregulated cases in which on some point no decision either way is dictated by the law and the law is accordingly partly indeterminate or incomplete. If in such cases the judge is to reach a decision and is not, as Bentham once advocated, to disclaim jurisdiction or to refer the points not regulated by the existing law to the legislature to decide, he must exercise his *discretion* and *make* law for the case instead of merely applying already pre-existing settled law.[98]

---

[93] Merryman, *The Civil Law Tradition*, 49–50 and ch. 8 *passim*.
[94] Merryman gives as an example 'Article 1226 of the Italian civil code, which tells the judge that if the precise amount of the damage to the plaintiff resulting from a breach of the defendant's obligation cannot be proved, the judge shall fix the amount according to equitable principles' (*ibid.*, 52).
[95] *Ibid.*, 52–3.   [96] *Ibid.*, 36.   [97] See above, p. 14 and below, pp. 170–1.
[98] Hart, *The Concept of Law*, 272.

This view is contrasted with Dworkin's claim that

> what is incomplete is not the law but the positivist's picture of it, and that this is so will emerge from his own 'interpretive' account of the law as including besides the *explicit* settled law identified by reference to its social sources, *implicit* legal principles which are those principles which both best fit or cohere with the explicit law and also provide the best moral justification for it. On this interpretive view, the law is never incomplete or indeterminate, so the judge never has occasion to step outside the law and exercise a law-creating power in order to reach a decision.[99]

What this passage shows is that Hart, Dworkin – and incidentally also Jeremy Bentham – did not even consider *epieikeia* à la Aristotle as a serious possibility.

Something superficially similar to Aristotelian *epieikeia* does seem to operate much more freely in another common law jurisdiction, that of the USA.[100] For example, in Michigan in the 1960s there was a law imposing a twenty-year prison sentence for selling drugs. The letter of the law left judges with no discretion, but they simply took it when the defendant did not seem to be a real drug dealer. As one judge commented in private: '"This is ridiculous law, passed in the heat of passion without any thought of its real consequences. I absolutely refuse to send to prison for twenty years a young boy who has done nothing more than sell a single marijuana cigarette to a buddy. The law was not intended for such a case."'[101] This looks like classic *epieikeia*. It 'seems to be an example of a fairly widespread phenomenon' in the USA.[102]

The attitudes behind this willingness to nullify the letter of the law are not necessarily the same as those of Aristotle. According to one scholarly study: 'the American position is significantly influenced by the existence of ill-conceived, badly drafted and obsolete legislation which it is very difficult to reform by legislative means'.[103] This is a more negative rationale than we found Aristotle's language suggests and it partly changes the 'inner side' meaning of judicial practice.

Equity outside the Western tradition is too vast a topic to be tackled here: one can only indicate very approximately the degrees to which anything like *epieikeia* or equity can be found. Islamic law would an obvious starting point because of its enormous influence. It has ruled so many and such diverse societies, however, that one can do little more than mention it here. According to some, the idea of equity is embodied

---

[99] *Ibid.*
[100] I follow Atiyah and Summers, *Form and Substance in Anglo-American Law*, 178–85.
[101] Quoted *ibid.*, 184–5.   [102] *Ibid.*, 185, and cf. ch. 11 *passim*.   [103] *Ibid.*

in the notion of *Ihstisan* (literally, 'to deem something good').[104] It has been strongly argued, however, that any similarity between the concept of equity or *epieikeia* and the *Ihstisan* would appear to be misleading: 'the concept of equity as we know it in the West is the antithesis of the Islamic view that all law is derived from God through the Koran and the sunna'.[105] Since the Sharia'h law is God's law, it makes no sense to seek tensions between it and 'natural right'.[106] In theory, too, the Sharia'h law is sufficient as well as necessary.

When one looks closer to the ground things are not so simple: the practice of Islamic law does seem to be compatible with something recognisable as equity. Lawrence Rosen makes the point through analysis of a concrete case from modern Morocco, one in which 'as a matter of strict law the qadi [Islamic judge] could only grant the plaintiff a revocable form of divorce' – but went ahead to grant the irrevocable kind, to prevent the husband availing himself of the option of revoking the divorce in the next three months; the judge 'clearly felt that it would be unfair to the plaintiff to subject her to this possibility'.[107] 'Although no formal confrontation of the rule of law and the role of equity was joined in this case, it appears that by using his powers of consultation and utilitarian reasoning [*istislah*], the present-day qadi may indeed be able to render an essentially lawless decision justified in terms of countervailing equities.'[108] It is true the direct conflict would seem to be with the Moroccan code rather than its Sharia'h sources, but the fact remains that the system allowed for rational instrumental calculation guided by equity. Historically, moreover, Sharia'h law has usually existed alongside a pragmatic law (perhaps not conceptualised as law in the same sense but doing the work done by law in the West) which fills in the practical gaps. Perhaps, well aware that it is a simplification, one might risk the formula that instrumental reasoning is not part of the theoretical self-image of Islamic law – at least not nearly so much as it is with Catholic canon law, as will become clear in the final chapter – but it is certainly an option in practice, and without any serious violation of the ethos of the system.

The core of Jewish law is also identified with the will of God. Thus there is so to speak no space between ethics and the divine written law. It is true that the law can be suspended, say in matters of life and death. Sabbath rules can be broken to save a life, for example. Arguably, however, the suspension of the law in such cases is itself a value-rational imperative, not a matter for instrumental calculation.

---

[104] Makdisi, 'Legal Logic and Equity in Islamic Law', 67.
[105] *Ibid.*   [106] *Ibid.*
[107] L. Rosen, *The Justice of Islam*, 19 (the whole of ch. 1, pp. 2–23, is relevant).
[108] *Ibid.*, 20.

On the other hand, rabbinic law may add extra obligations that are not as such a part of divine law. The imposition of monogamy on northern European Jews by Gershom ben Yehudah of Mainz would be a case in point.[109] There seems no reason in principle why such provisions should not be suspended on grounds of equity and for extreme situations there is a mechanism for lifting the ban on polygamy.[110] This we can classify as a form of equity.

Hindu law differs radically from the Aristotelian scheme sketched out above, in which equity is set against a backcloth of relatively strict positive law. In the Aristotelian schema, exceptions, dispensations, applications to concrete cases, *epieikeia*, etc., are set against the background of a set of rules which is 'normally' clear-cut, binding, predictable and therefore fixed. As a leading expert describes it,

> The most striking element of Hindu law throughout has been its unlimited diversity and flexibility... Hindu law strongly emphasises the rhetoric and practice of plurality and of relative justice, displaying tolerance almost to the point of selfless extinction. Legal diversity forms such an essential part of Hindu legal philosophy that uniformity of legal rules is often portrayed as a manifestation of injustice.[111]

One could perhaps characterise the Aristotelian position (and its classical Chinese analogues, on which more below) as a halfway house between the ultra-flexible legal attitudes of Hindu law and of the 'certainty' of Western civil law tradition. In this middle position we find definite rules on the one hand, but a rationale for some exceptions on the other. It is doubly hard for universal instrumental rationality to escape the influence of values when they define the limits within which instrumental calculation is permissible or desirable.

This chapter has examined a variety of different ways in which values and convictions interact with instrumental rationality. Summarised at the start, they need not be restated here. One general point applies to them all. The distinction between value rationality and instrumental rationality should never be taken to imply segregation. On the contrary, the two rationalities are hardly imaginable without one another. What we have seen in this chapter is the symbiosis of the two main types of rationality distinguished in the introductory chapter. Symbiosis is also a good rubric under which to analyse two secondary sorts of reasoning: substantive and formal rationality.

---

[109] Novak, 'The Structure of Halakhah', 225.

[110] 'it must be understood that the ban of Rabbenu Gershom does not have the status of an immutable law and in very special circumstances may be revoked' (Biale, *Women and Jewish Law*, 51).

[111] Menski, *Comparative Law in a Global Context*, 202.

5 Formal rationality

Formal rationality and the law

Here the phrase 'formal rationality' is taken to mean 'decision-making within a set of rules constructed to govern an aspect of life abstracted or demarcated from all other aspects, in such a way that the latter are not allowed to affect the decision-making process'.[1] The distinction between formal and substantive rationality works in various domains. In economic terms[2] it may be formally rational to let an industry or firm go under, but substantive considerations may force the government to subsidise it. The considerations might be humanitarian – the social cost to the workers. They do not have to be value-driven, however: it might be a cynical political calculation that a key constituency would be lost to the party if purely economic judgement prevailed. Or again, a war strategy may make no sense in purely military terms – making it formally irrational – yet it may be rational substantively because it is required by public opinion. Rather than try to keep all these thematic balls in the air simultaneously, however, the remainder of the book will focus on one key area that particularly lends itself to comparative sociological history: law.[3] Furthermore, the comparative history of law provides good data with which to make the central point of this chapter, viz., that formal rationality, which is most often a species of instrumental rationality,[4] is generally shaped by conviction rationality.

---

[1] I use the same definition in *Medieval Religious Rationalities*, ch. 5, which deals with the same themes in the medieval period.

[2] For Weber on formal and substantive (or material) economic rationality, see notably *Wirtschaft und Gesellschaft*, vol. 1, pp. 44–5 (definitions), and 78 (formal rationality and substantive irrationality of Capitalism).

[3] For Weber on formal and substantive legal rationality, see notably *Wirtschaft und Gesellschaft*, vol. 2, pp. 396–7, 462, 468–82, 507, 563. Curiously enough, Atiyah and Summers, *Form and Substance in Anglo-American Law*, seem to be unaware that they are writing in a very Weberian tradition. Nonetheless their own contribution does mark an advance on his highly compressed treatment of the dichotomy.

[4] To anticipate, the final chapter will argue that substantive legal rationality can also be a species of instrumental rationality: it cuts across the 'value–instrumental' distinction.

Dependence of formal rationalities on values

This argument grows out of a point made in the previous chapter: that one way in which values shape instrumental reasoning is by defining its scope and mode. Law was taken as an example, and Aristotle's idea of its role was set against the different approaches of other value systems. Aristotle saw the law of the *polis* as an instrument for making citizens virtuous, a tool of ethics but not identifiable with ethics, binding normally but not invariably. This was contrasted at one end of the spectrum with the modern civil (i.e. Roman) law tradition, where the values of certainty and predictability are so dominant that there is little place for the suspension of the rules; and at the other end with Hindu law, where there is much greater flexibility than even Aristotle's *epieikeia* would allow.

In Aristotle's theory of law the binding rules and the judge's right to depart from them do indeed both fall into the category here called instrumental rationality, but they are different sorts. Weber captured the difference by a further distinction: between formal and material legal rationality. He used 'material' and 'substantive' synonymously in this connection, and so they will be used here.

First, however, a verbal confusion with one common modern usage needs to be averted. It is common to speak of substantive law in a different sense: to mean laws about contracts, crime, and the like. Used like this, substantive law is distinguished from procedural law, in the sense of rules about proof and the conduct of courts. This is not what Weber is getting at: in fact his distinction cuts right across this usage. In what follows, 'substantive' will be used to mean 'non-formal' in this sense rather than 'non-procedural', unless otherwise stated.

This chapter and the next attempt to integrate Weber's formal/substantive distinction into his overarching conceptual framework of value and instrumental rationality. The present chapter will concentrate on formal rationality, the next on the interface between formal and substantive legal reasoning. The general theme of the current chapter is that formal rationality tends to be drenched in values, and helps them to get a grip on social practice. Formal rationality can indeed even become a value system in its own right: when adherence to the positive laws or the rulebook acquires a morally binding force, anchored in working practice and linked with a view of the world. This is especially likely with minor bureaucrats who tend to treat the rules as a given and treat them as absolute. For them, it is not just a value that one should go by the rulebook: the actual rules become values in their own right. It is probably more normal,

however, for a body of formal legal rules to serve as an instrument calculated to implement or reinforce convictions of one sort or another.
As with techniques of devotion and asceticism, formal law can be char-
acterised *grosso modo* as a type of instrumental rationality generated by
and serving conviction rationality.[5] The aims of value systems may be
served by systems of rules which go beyond the content of the values and
convictions themselves, but do so in order to implement them the more
effectively, by providing discipline and predictability or legal certainty.

Formally rational law in this sense is not a peculiarly modern development in a 'demystified' world. It can serve religious as well as secular
values. It was around long before 'modernity'. This theme was already
adumbrated in the introduction, but it needs to be stressed because
legal formality does seem to have been associated by some writers with
modernity and/or with the absence of values.[6] As a corrective this chapter will pay special attention to formal rationality as an instrument of
specifically religious values, as with the 'Congregation of the Council',
a body established to implement the reform decrees of the Council of
Trent.

'A Law [i.e. legal system] is "formal" insofar as only unambiguous
general legally relevant elements [*Tatbestandsmerkmale* – a technical term
in the legal domain] are taken into account, in substantive or in procedural law' – so Weber.[7] There would seem an implicit assumption in
this compressed sentence: that the general elements embodied in the
concrete situation are legally defined concepts or rules. The important
modern study by P. S. Atiyah and Robert Summers explains the concept
of legal formality thus:

[5] Thus I feel that the schema formulated in Uecker, *Die Rationalisierung des Rechts*, 18, of 'a
sequence of increasing rationality from traditional, through value rational, to instrumentally rational' ('eine Reihe *zunehmender* [my italics] Rationalität von traditionalem über
wertrationales hin zu zweckrationalem Handeln'), is misconceived even as an ideal-type,
whether or not it represents Weber's thinking. (Uecker's book is, however, in general a
valuable survey and its substantial bibliography obviates the need for a list in the present
study of books about Weber and law.
[6] See Introduction, at pp. 19–20, and also the following comment by Immanuel Wallerstein: 'liberals who seek the good society, who seek the realization of a rational world,
must bear in mind Max Weber's distinction between formal and substantive rationality.
Formal rationality is problem-solving but lacks a soul, and is therefore ultimately self-
destructive. Substantive rationality is extraordinarily difficult to define, lends itself to
much arbitrary distortion, but is ultimately what the good society is all about.' (Wallerstein, 'Liberalism and Democracy', 101 – a view which has been associated with the 'old
Frankfurt school': van den Berg, review of Wallerstein, 327).
[7] '"Formal" aber ist ein Recht insoweit, als ausschließlich eindeutige generelle Tatbestandsmerkmale materiell-rechtlich und prozessual beachtet werden' (Weber, *Wirtschaft
und Gesellschaft*, vol. 2, p. 396); cf. above, p. 146 n. 3.

A formal reason is a legally authoritative reason on which judges and others are empowered or required to base a decision and action, and such a reason usually excludes from consideration, overrides, or at least diminishes the weight of, any countervailing substantive reason arising at the point of decision or action. For example, it is a formal reason for making a decision that *there is a valid legal rule that*, in the given circumstances, D ought to be made to pay damages to P. Unlike a substantive reason, a formal reason necessarily presupposes a valid law or other valid legal phenomenon, such as a contract or a verdict. Indeed, the very existence of this law or other legal phenomenon, as interpreted, is a formal reason, or generates a formal reason for deciding an issue ... a formal reason usually operates as a sort of barrier which insulates the decision-making process from the reasons of substance not incorporated in the rule, either explicitly or implicitly.[8]

Statutory minimum sentences for certain crimes illustrate the point: they do not allow the hearts of judges to be softened by the circumstances of individual cases.

Rational and irrational legal formality: Roman forms of action

The association of formal rationality with 'modernity' does not fit very comfortably with the well-established view that classical Roman law achieved a high degree of formal rationality after the development of the 'formulary system'.[9] This system replaced one by which a plaintiff had expressed his case in rigid and constricting traditional formulas. That older system made it hard for the defendant to raise an objection and did not respond readily to new situations.

It was probably at some point in the second half of the second century BC that the new and much more flexible system of forms was introduced. What both the old and the new Roman systems had in common was that they channelled the *content* of the law – the kind of thing that modern states deal with through statutes or codes[10] – through procedural law. They also kept at bay substantive considerations in the Weberian sense of considerations falling outside the system of rules, in that a legal suit had to be framed in a standard form.

---

[8] Atiyah and Summers, *Form and Substance in Anglo-American Law*, 2. For an important older (rather critical) account of legal formality see Kennedy, 'Legal Formality'.

[9] Crook, 'The Development of Roman Private Law', 545–6; Wieacker, *Römische Rechtsgeschichte*, vol. 1, pp. 447–61; D. Walker, *The Oxford Companion to Law*, entry under 'Formulary System', p. 484.

[10] I.e. 'substantive' law in the other sense: 'non-procedural' (or in this context: 'not purely procedural'), rather than 'substantive' in the sense of 'non-formal'.

But the new 'formula' system enabled the rules to accommodate new needs, because a new form could be created by the praetor when required.[11] The praetor could avail himself of advice from expert jurists.[12] The Praetorian Edict contained the standard formulas used to start a legal action. Like standardised writs in English law, these are halfway between procedural and substantive law. In fact the similarity between the formulary system and the writ system developed by the common law is striking. In the normal course of the common law system, if you wanted to sue somebody you would look for a form of action, a writ, among the set of standard forms; at least early on in the development of the system new writs were rapidly multiplied, so that there would be enough forms for types of cases. 'As far as the courts were concerned, rights were only significant, and remedies were only available, to the extent that appropriate procedures existed to give them form.'[13] The resemblance to the Roman formulary system is striking.

The Roman formulary system has been admired for its instrumental efficacy. It embodies to a high degree 'the art of isolating the elements which were decisive from a legal point of view'.[14] It is this quality that makes the formulary system so close to Weber's ideal-type of formal legal rationality. As he said: 'The decisive turn of legal thought towards the rational was first prepared through the technical character of the direction of legal proceedings by means of the formulas, geared to legal concepts, of the Praetorian Edict.'[15]

Formal rationality and ethical values

Weber is sometimes understood to have treated formal legal rationality and ethical (or other) values as antithetical. One recent discussion of Weber's views in connection with traditional Chinese law – especially the Ch'ing Code, the last great imperial code, only abolished in 1910 – takes it for granted that legal formality and ethics must be segregated: 'Chinese legal decisions were rational because they were based on some general rules or principles, rather than being ad hoc, arbitrary rulings . . . But

---

[11] Borkowski and du Plessis, *Textbook on Roman Law*, 34.

[12] *Ibid.*; Wieacker, *Römische Rechtsgeschichte*, 452.

[13] Baker, *An Introduction to English Legal History*, 53.

[14] 'die alte Kunst der Isolierung der ausschlaggebenden juristischen Merkmale' (Wieacker, *Römische Rechtsgeschichte*, 453) – and see the whole passage beginning 'Die meisterliche Technik' and ending 'auf ähnliche Lagen' (*ibid.*).

[15] 'Die entscheidende Wendung des juristischen Denkens zum rationalen wurde zuerst durch die technische Art der Prozeßinstruktion an der Hand der auf Rechtsbegriffe abgestellten Formeln des prätorischen Ediktes vorbereitet' (Weber, *Wirtschaft und Gesellschaft*, vol. 2, p. 564).

the form of rationality was substantive, not formal. Instead of *separating* law and legal reasoning from Confucian ethics, the legal system melded the two together.'[16] Good examples of the influence of Confucian ethics on the Ch'ing Code are provided: for instance, the Confucian stress on hierarchy is reflected in statute 318, which laid down a far more severe penalty for intentional killing by a younger sibling of an elder sibling than for the reverse.[17]

It needs to be stressed again that the sharp conceptual dichotomy between values and formal rationality implied here is questionable, even if the concrete empirical findings are valid. Weber certainly underestimated the legal formality of Chinese imperial law, so the empirical correction was in order, but his critic probably does not do justice to the Weberian conceptual scheme: it seems unlikely that Weber thought of formal rationality as an ethics-free zone *tout court*; and whether or not he did, it may be urged that a definition of 'formal rationality' that excludes the influence of ethical and other values even on the formulation of the rules makes the term less serviceable for historical analysis, in fact an obstacle to it.[18]

It is not a matter of asking 'What is formal rationality?' but of shaping the concept into a useful aid to interpretation. If defined to exclude the influence of values on the rules themselves, formally rational law is in danger of becoming an empty set, for it is hard to find any body of rules the constitution of which was entirely unaffected by ethics, ideology or any other values. As Atiyah and Summers say: 'A formal reason usually incorporates or reflects substantive reasoning. Thus it is an admixture of certain formal attributes on the one hand, and substantive reasoning on the other.'[19] This substantive reasoning need not but can be a matter of values. They define a substantive reason as 'a moral, economic, political, institutional, or other social consideration'.[20] In short, moral considerations can be embodied in formal rationality. It can be strongly oriented towards values and convictions at the point when it is formulated. Once formulated, the rules take on a binding force of their own insofar as the law is formally rational, but commonly they are formulated with the idea of furthering – in the aggregate even if

---

[16] Marsh, 'Weber's Misunderstanding of Traditional Chinese Law', 296.
[17] *Ibid.*, 295. Cf. MacCormack, *The Spirit of Traditional Chinese Law*, 62–8.
[18] Marsh's attribution of his own usage to Weber does not strike me as an evident interpretation of the latter's mind, but this is an argument that can be left to one side, as peripheral to the purpose of this study, which is not to explicate Weber's concepts but to study rationalities using them when they can help, as they so often can.
[19] Atiyah and Summers, *Form and Substance*, 2.   [20] *Ibid.*, 5.

not in every individual case – certain explicit or unspoken values and convictions.

The concept of formal rationality, like the whole discipline of Rational Choice Theory which was discussed in Chapter 1, can work for the comparative historian so long as it is not left in a value vacuum. Values of one sort or another must frequently affect in one way or another the whole structure of formal rules, just as they tend to affect the character of rational choices. Instrumental reasoning usually takes place in a microclimate of conviction rationality, whether in modern Britain or in classical China.

Ethics and the formal rationality of traditional Chinese law

The influence of values on legal rules in traditional Chinese law had roots in the distant past. A Mongol-period commentary on a Sung-dynasty *Prose-Poem on the Penal Tradition*[21] (on which more in the next chapter) correlates the severity of punishments for crimes with a mourning relationship. Confucian-inspired ritual dictated different kinds of mourning for different kinds of deceased relatives. The penalties for crimes against those relatives corresponded to the amount of mourning. 'The sages instituted . . . mourning relationships in order to distinguish close relations from less close. The setting of the severity of punishments in accordance with the degree of relationships within the mourning system is the great purpose behind the instituting of law.'[22]

Even current secular legal systems like those[23] of modern Britain, which do not on the whole aim to promote virtue or prevent individual vices (so long as they do not harm other people's persons, property, or good name), are shaped among other things by the value attached to the right of individual freedom and a paternalistic attitude to people's physical well-being,[24] as well as 'values characteristically associated with the rule of law, such as uniformity, predictability, freedom from official arbitrariness in the administration of the law, and the like'.[25]

---

[21] Langlois, '"Living Law" in Sung and Yüan Jurisprudence', 175 (Yüan = Mongol). The work was written no later than 1339.

[22] Cited from the commentary (the *Hsing-t'ung fu shu*) *ibid.*, 179. As Langlois puts it: 'Law in the post-Ch'in empire is said to be "Confucianized" because it supported and reinforced the Confucian conventions and ideals of ritual propriety' (p. 178).

[23] The plural because the Scottish legal system is different from that of the rest of the UK.

[24] Cf. the views of Herbert Hart, who both reflected and affected the tendencies of English law in his time: see Lacey, *A Life of H. L. Hart*, 257–9.

[25] Atiyah and Summers, *Form and Substance*, 24.

The Congregation of the Council in a comparative perspective

As a case study of formal legality in its relation to ethics, it is worth looking at an example in greater detail, following up a hint by Weber. For one of his theses is that formal legal rationality is embodied to a degree quite exceptional, at least among religious legal systems, in the law of the Catholic Church. We will examine this system, or part of it, in the century after the French Revolution.[26] Weber traces this distinctive formal legality right back to the ancient world:

And finally, and above all, the character of ecclesiastical legislation was affected by the rational and bureaucratic official style of the Church's officials, a style which was characteristic of ecclesiastical organisation after the end of the charismatic period of the early Church, and which took on new life from the age of the Gregorian reform onwards, after the feudal interlude of the earlier Middle Ages, and which became absolutely dominant. It too was the result of continuity with the ancient world. In consequence, the Western Church, to an incomparably greater extent than any other religious community, followed the path of law-making by rational legislation ... Though ... in numerous individual cases canon law retained the specific characteristic of theocratic legal development – the mixing of substantive legislative motives, and substantive ethical aims, with the components of the legislation that were legally relevant from a formal point of view, with the loss of precision that followed from that – it was nevertheless more rigorously oriented towards formal legal technique than any other sacred law. We do not find here the growth of a tradition built up through the responses given by jurists, in the manner characteristic of Islamic and Jewish law; and the New Testament contains only such a bare minimum of formally binding norms of a ritual or legal character – a consequence of the focus on Last Things at the expense of interest in this world – that, for this very reason, the way was entirely clear for purely rational legislation. For anything analogous to the muftis, rabbis, and geonim one has to wait for the confessors and *directeurs de l'âme* of the Counter-Reformation and, in the early Protestant Churches, for the pastors, whose pastoral casuistry then too has some distant similarities, at least in Catholic lands, with the Talmudic products. Yet in the Catholic case everything was subject to the control of the central administrative bodies of the Curia, and the elaboration of binding ethical social norms could only take place via the highly flexible directives of these bodies. In this way a relationship between sacred and secular law found nowhere else grew up here: namely that canon law actually became one of the guides leading secular law along the path to rationality. And this was a result of the rational 'institutional' character of the Catholic Church, with which nothing comparable can be found in world history.[27]

[26] In the next chapter, on the other hand, the history of the Congregation of the Council (over a longer period) will be used to illustrate the interplay of formal and substantive rationality.

[27] Weber, *Wirtschaft und Gesellschaft*, 480–1, passage beginning: 'Und schließlich und vor allem wirkte' and ending 'infolge des rationalen "Anstalts"-Charakters der katholischen Kirche, der sonst sich nirgends wiederfindet'.

The import of this passage is hard to take in because Weber's prose is so compressed. The remark about 'flexible directives', for instance, is probably a parenthetical allusion to the handling of such things as the usury prohibition.[28] What is clear is that Weber recognised the importance of the post-Tridentine Congregations for the formally rational administrative execution of the law of the Catholic Church in the post-medieval period. He is above all drawing a contrast with both Jewish and Islamic law.

In both Islamic and Jewish law ethical and legal norms are not sharply separated. In Jewish law 'legally binding and ethical norms are not distinguished',[29] and Islamic law 'includes both ethical and legal commands'.[30] More formally rational legal systems will indeed also often, and probably usually, embody ethical norms, but once the legal rules have been formulated they take on a binding force of their own which has a different character from the hold of ethics on the individual's conscience. Canon law, on the other hand, is different from moral theology.

Canon law and Islamic law

Weber's remarks about the formal rationality of canon law should be contrasted with the following passage in his section on Islamic law:

The authoritative *responsa* obtained, in just the same way as with Roman law, from authorised legal experts, Muftis, with the *Sheikhu'-l islam* at the top, by a Qâdi or by the interested parties as the case might be, are to a remarkable degree the opportunistic products of particular situations, varying from person to person, are issued in the manner of oracles without any rational grounds being given, and have not in the least contributed to a rationalisation of law; on the contrary, in practice they have further increased the irrationality of the sacred law.[31]

---

[28] 'the rigorously rational hierarchical organisation of the Church made it easier for it to use general ordinances to treat rules that were economically impracticable, and therefore burdensome, as permanently or temporarily ... obsolete, as we saw in the case of the usury prohibition' ('die streng rationale hierarchische Organisation der Kirche erleichterte ihr ..., im Wege von allgemeinen Verfügungen ökonomisch undurchführbare und daher lästige Satzungen als dauernd oder zeitweilig ... obsolet zu behandeln, wie wir dies für das Wucherverbot sahen' (*ibid.*, 480).

[29] 'juristisch bindende und ethische Normen nicht geschieden' (*ibid.*, 479).

[30] 'Der fiqh umfaßt sittliche wie rechtliche Gebote' (*ibid.*, 474).

[31] *Ibid.*, 475–6, passage beginning 'Die gegebenenfalls vom Qâdî' and ending 'praktisch noch gesteigert'. My thanks to members of the Bloomsbury Sacred Law Group, above all Yossi Rappaport, Sami Zubaida and Werner Menski, for frank and comradely discussion about Weber's view of Islamic law. Caroline Humfress reminded me in a personal communication that 'Roman juristic *responsa* were also "tied to the specific situation to a remarkable extent"', though we see them in the context created by Justinian's legal commissioners.

This picture of Islamic law is not as negative as it sounds. Weber uses 'rational' and 'irrational' in remarkably value-free senses. It would be a crass misunderstanding of him to think that he approved of everything he called 'rational'. In *Wirtschaft und Gesellschaft* he tends to avoid the language of approval and disapproval altogether, but his strong reservations about modern rationalisation in the West are well known.[32] Even if one stays with Weber's own vocabulary there would be a case for calling the kind of judgements he has in mind substantively rational rather than irrational. They are one feature of a tradition full of rational debate about the will of God as expressed in the law – as is the very similar Jewish legal tradition.

Furthermore, the Islamic system of fatwas, to which he must be referring, has many practical advantages over the formally rational legal systems of modern Western countries.[33] In divorce settlements or property disputes the fatwa system makes it possible to obtain a judgement from an impartial and learned man at a fraction of the expense of a case in a modern court. In many respects it is a humane and cost-effective system, one which has a bad name in the West in recent times because of occasional fatwas urging bloodshed. These do highlight one of the informal characteristics of the system: to give a fatwa it is not necessary to hold an office in an institution, so there is nothing to stop the circulation of a plethora of mutually contradictory fatwas. Anyone can give one in principle. It is true that only those deemed learned in Islamic law are likely to be asked for a legal fatwa. As in academic life, however, the learned often disagree.

Weber's ideal-type needs to be corrected to some extent where the interesting Ottoman institution of the *Sheikhu'-l islam* is concerned. From the time of Ebu's-su'ud, *Sheikhu'-l islam* (1545–74),[34] we find a centralised organisation with a high level of legal rationality in certain respects: a real institutionalisation of the fatwa system. Ebu's-su'ud's new procedures

relied on a permanent staff, trained in the law and the art of legal formulation. In time, the system which Ebu's-su'ud had instituted became so sophisticated that the framing of the question in a fatwa usually presupposed the answer, and required the Mufti to add no more than a simple 'yes' or 'no' answer and his signature. When, after Ebu's-su'ud's time, rapid changes of *sheikhu'-l islam* became normal, it was the highly-trained permanent staff who effectively did all the work, ensuring continuity and maintaining legal standards in fatwas.[35]

---

[32] Mommsen, *The Age of Bureaucracy*, 99; Kronman, *Max Weber*, 183.
[33] On fatwas, see e.g. Masud, Messick, and Powers, *Islamic Legal Interpretation*.
[34] Imber, *Ebu's-su'ud*, 7.   [35] *Ibid.*, 14.

From Ebu's-su'ud's time until the end of the Ottoman empire the office of the *Sheikhu'-l islam* continued to be a rationalised legal bureaucracy,[36] with a notable concern for consistency at least in later periods.[37] There must have been limits to the amount of rational reflection that could be devoted to a given case, however, because the output of the office was extraordinarily large. A *Sheikhu'-l islam* writing at the beginning of the seventeenth century said that he had to do not far short of 200 *fatwas* on most days.[38] Ebu's-su'ud himself 'claimed to have once written 1,412 fetvas between the morning and the afternoon prayers and on another day 1,413 fetvas'.[39] Even allowing for a large office, there cannot have been too much time for careful scholarly analysis. The large output did, on the other hand, go with what looks like a very efficient working tempo: it would appear that 'two or three days were sometimes needed for the issuance of fetvas on less common questions', and that 'in later times the whole procedure of issuing a fetva took one week at the most'.[40] This tempo is much more rapid than that of a Catholic institution whose activity spanned much the same period (it lasted a little longer): the Congregation of the Council. Even more than the office of the *Sheikhu'-l islam* this bureaucracy shows formal legal rationality in action in the religious sphere.

The Congregation of the Council was established by the Counter-Reformation papacy at about the same time to interpret the decisions of the Council of Trent[41] and continued into modern times.[42] According to a nineteenth-century German priest who spent about four years dealing with this Congregation and went on to write an unusual book about the Curia, it was a central legal and governmental organ.[43] The archive of

---

[36] Cf. Imber, 'Eleven Fetvas', 141–2.

[37] 'There can . . . be little doubt that, at least in later periods, the Ottoman muftis and even the <u>Shaykh</u> al Islams generally ruled in conformity with the decisions of their great predecessors. The Ottoman fetva thus played a major role in the development and crystallisation of Muslim religious law in the last few centuries.' (Heyd, 'Some Aspects of the Ottoman Fetva', 56).

[38] *Ibid.*, 46.   [39] *Ibid.*   [40] *Ibid.*, 49.

[41] Prodi, 'Note sulla genesi del diritto nella Chiesa post-tridentina', esp. 198–9; P. Caiazza, 'L'archivio storico della Sacra Congregazione del Concilio'; and Blouin *et al.*, *Vatican Archives*, 21–7. For practical purposes a most useful guide is also *Vatican Secret Archives, Collection Index and Related Description and Research Resources*, 28. For a subset of this archive see W. Henkel, 'Das Inventar des "Fondo Concilii"'.

[42] Further bibliography on the history of the Congregation of the Council and of its archive is supplied at the end of the Appendix.

[43] Bangen, *Die Römische Curie*. On his personal acquaintance with the workings of the Congregation, p. v, passage beginning 'Ein beinahe vierjähriger Aufenthalt in Rom' and ending 'des reiflichen Studiums'; on his high opinion of the Congregation's efficacy in the realm of Church Law, *ibid.*, 146, sentence beginning 'Keine Congregation der Curie ist in unserer Zeit'; on its exemplary procedures, which stand out from and serve

the Congregation of the Council has survived and it is possible to see the careful rational legal argument that lay behind its answers, since the reasoning pro and contra which preceded its answers is preserved.[44] The final decision was taken by a committee of cardinals but behind it lay a process that exemplifies well both the concept of formal legal rationality and the way in which the latter can serve a value system.

As in the English common law tradition, the point of the final decision could have a 'charismatic' as well as a rational character. Max Weber observed that judges in the common law system could sometimes set by the personal authority of their judgements precedents that could not have been predicted,[45] an interpretation compatible with his view that the system could provide a highly rational resource for those who could afford it (an aspect of Weber's view of common law which gets too little attention). In the same way, even after the series of rational steps leading up to the final discussion and decision by the Cardinals of the Congregation, a 'charismatic' and unexpected solution might be reached, which our German observer attributed to the Holy Spirit as well as to their well-honed legal expertise.[46]

Furthermore, fully formal proceedings were not the only kind available through this Congregation. As will become clear later in the chapter, in some cases a full due-process approach was judged inappropriate.[47] This would not be an arbitrary judgement, but an instrumentally rational decision oriented towards the values the Congregation was supposed to serve. Even when the fully formal approach was discarded, the procedure was not so far from the ideal-type of legal formality, in that it made consistency with previous decisions a priority; and once the decision had been made to take the formal route the Congregation of the Council's proceedings fit the ideal-type of a formally rational legal system well.

as a model for those of the other curial Congregations, *ibid.* 164, sentence beginning 'Was... das Verfahren und den Geschäftsstil'. See also P. Hinschius, *Das Kirchenrecht der Katholiken und Protestanten in Deutschland*, 456–63, esp. 461–3 (this owes a lot to Bangen). For another account from a slightly earlier time see Zamboni, *Collectio declarationum* (Arras, 1860 edn), vol. 1, 'Introductio', especially sections VI, VII, VIII, XI, XII, XIV. Note too section IX, where Zamboni discusses the relation of the Congregation of the Councils to other Congregations, and expresses regret that the borders between their respective spheres were fluid (pp. xxviii–xxix, passage beginning 'At dolendum est, quod inter omnes sacras Congregationes' and ending 'Congregationes servare potuerunt'. This interesting passage pinpoints a major deviation from Weber's ideal-type of bureaucracy, with its clear division of functions: see Weber, *Wirtschaft und Gesellschaft*, vol. 2, p. 551.

[44] See Archivio Segreto Vaticano, *Congr. Concilio, Positiones*: an exciting fondo.
[45] d'Avray, 'Max Weber and Comparative Legal History', 195.
[46] Bangen, *Die Römische Curie*, 174 n. 1: passage beginning 'Man würde sehr irren, wenn' and ending 'oft in merkürdige Weise hervor'.
[47] Del Re, *La Curia Romana*, 166.

Legal rules governed procedure and substance once the formal route had been chosen.[48] This formal route ('iuris ordine servato') had to be chosen in cases where two parties were in dispute and one of them asked for it through an authorised lawyer (procurator) in the proper form: this was a request, called a 'Nihil transeat'; once it had been made both parties had to be heard.[49]

The rules demanded formal authentication of the 'acta' (documents, depositions, etc.) sent to the Congregation after the first stage of a contested case (which normally took place at the diocesan level).[50] The actual business of hearing the conflicting parties and recording evidence was normally entrusted to the local bishop, it being a general rule of the Congregation that he should almost never be bypassed.[51] When a case took this formal route the parties could be represented only by procurators qualified to appear before the Roman tribunals,[52] for the Congregation's formal legal activity belonged firmly in the great *ius commune* tradition of learned professional law.

Because they were administering legally formal procedures, the key personnel in the Congregation were academically trained and qualified in Roman and canon law. The cardinals who constituted the Congregation proper were those who stood out for their knowledge of canon law and Roman civil law. There was a tendency to choose some famous judge (Auditor) of the Rota (which unlike the Congregation of the Council was a legal tribunal – one whose judges were at the top of their profession) as Secretary of the Congregation. The Secretary was assisted by an Auditor, an ecclesiastical lawyer who was a doctor of both laws, i.e. formally qualified in both Roman civil and canon law. Anyone holding this post was well on the way to becoming a cardinal. Famous canon lawyers (and theologians) were nominated by the Pope as consultants.[53]

Attached to the Congregation was an interesting institution known as the *Studio*, which was both a training ground in ecclesiastical law for promising clerics and a legal labour force to assist the Congregation in reaching its decisions.[54] A talented young man could gain a place in the *Studio* through recommendations from his bishop and other referees.[55] Apparently Italians, French, Belgians, and (interestingly) Englishmen

---

[48] Bangen, *Die Römische Curie*, 148–9, sentence beginning 'Verfährt sie aber'.
[49] *Ibid.*, Anhang 14 (rules laid down by the Secretariat of the Congregation in 1847), 502–5, at 502: number 1, and note 1.
[50] *Ibid.*, Anhang 14, 502, number 4.   [51] *Ibid.*, 166–7 and 167 note 1.
[52] *Ibid.*, Anhang 14, 502, number 2.   [53] For the foregoing paragraph, *ibid.*, 162.
[54] In addition to Bangen, my main source for what follows, see Romita, 'Lo "Studio" della Sacra Congregazione del Concilio'.
[55] Bangen, *Die Römische Curie*, 163

had been prominent before the middle of the nineteenth century, after which Germans begin to be in evidence.[56] Demonstrable knowledge and ability in canon law was a requirement.[57] Bright young men from the *Studio* were entrusted with the task of drafting the analyses of the points of fact and law that would be put before the cardinals, the hardest cases going to the cleverest and most experienced aides.[58] Their analyses would be reviewed and if necessary revised by the Auditor and the Secretary: then a printed version would be produced.[59] Three days before the Cardinals of the Congregation met, the cases to be decided were discussed in the *Studio*. There was a verbal presentation of each case in Italian by a member of the *Studio* (presumably the one who had prepared the analysis of the case); this would involve a brief narrative, an account of the points at issue (the *dubia*), and an answer for each of these in the technical language of the Congregation, with legal grounds given. Discussion would follow. The Secretary, Under-Secretary and Auditor of the Congregation would be present. This would prepare their minds for the big meeting ahead.[60]

The hardest task for the apprentices in the *Studio* and the Congregation experts generally was to isolate these *dubia*: the doubtful points of law and fact. So far as the facts were concerned they had to pick out what was both relevant and proven (or common knowledge). So far as the law was concerned they had to assess the relevance and validity of the cases made by the parties in conflict and to form an independent judgement in line with previous decisions by the Congregation.[61] It is here that the formal legal rationality of the system is most clearly manifested.

A certain literal-minded rigour in following the rules is characteristic of formal legal rationality, and this is what we find with cases that went through the more formal of two possible routes, following what was called the *ordo iuris*, which one could roughly translate as 'due process'. As the Congregation's German admirer put it: 'When [the Congregation] operates by the rules of the *ordo iuris*, that is, following due process, it observes this strictly, in that it always pinpoints the decisive point at issue among the facts of the case in the form of a question (*dubium iuris*) and

[56] *Ibid.*, 163–4.
[57] For the foregoing, *ibid.*, 163–4 and Anhang 12. It appears to be unclear when the *Studio* was instituted: Del Re says it was 'Already in existence from a period which cannot be specified with any precision' ('Esistente già da epoca che non è possibile precisare con esattezza') (Del Re, *La Curia Romana*, 170).
[58] Bangen, *Die Römische Curie*, 170, passage beginning 'Die Abfassung dieser Referate' and ending 'einzuliefern haben'.
[59] *Ibid.*, 172.   [60] *Ibid.*, 173.   [61] *Ibid.*, 170–1.

answers it in a rigorously legal manner.'[62] The *Studio*'s legal eagles were expected to do research to ensure consistency with the previous practice of the Congregation. Internal consistency, which implies predictability, is a key feature of formal legal rationality.

It was mentioned above that even when the Congregation followed the less formal route, in a more streamlined procedure known as *per summaria precum*, it did not really desert the sphere of formal rationality: in fact decisions reached by this less formal route may have come even closer to the ideal of consistency with past decisions. This is not the paradox it seems to be: one reason for choosing the informal route would be that a case could be easily assimilated to multiple precedents.[63] A member of the *Studio* entrusted with a case had at his disposal the published past decisions of the Congregation and a large body of canon legal writings.[64]

Where some new point of law had arisen, however, or where the facts were complicated, or did not fall into a familiar pattern, it would be harder to make sure the system remained internally coherent – and this could be a reason for taking the more rigorous route. It was not enough to come up with an answer that worked for the case in hand. The concrete solution must not contradict previous practice. The crucial thing was to subsume it under legal principles that held good for the past and could hold good for the future also.

This brings one back to the relation between formal, instrumental and conviction rationality. To recapitulate, formal rationality, as most usefully defined, is frequently a subset of instrumental rationality of the sort that serves values and convictions, working within parameters set by conviction rationality. Ergo, legal formality is not an alternative to value/conviction rationality but tends to be its instrument. The formal rationality of the Congregation of the Council was essentially the same as that of the Roman law tradition in which Max Weber was formed and which clearly lies behind his ideal-type of formal legal rationality. It also served a set of values and convictions from which it can be distinguished conceptually, though the instrumental and value rationality merged in actual practice. Values and convictions permeate this formal rationality;

---

[62] 'Verfährt sie [the Congregation] . . . nach dem ordo iuris, d.h. processualisch, so führt sie dies strenge durch, in dem sie . . . aus dem Thatbestande jedesmal den zu entscheiden-den Punct in Form einer Frage (*dubium iuris*) aufstellt und streng juristisch beantwortet' (*ibid.*, 148–9).

[63] 'Durch *summaria precum* werden demnach resolvirt 1) die Fälle, welche *de stilo* d. h. durch öftere Entscheidung bereits normirt sind' (*ibid.*, 165); 'ein ganz kurzes, zumeist auf frühere analoge Entscheidungen der Congregation gestütztes Gutachten mit den förmlich ausgedrückten, aus jenen gewöhnlich entnommenen Antworten zu Grunde gelegt wird' (*ibid.*, 176).

[64] *Ibid.*, 171 and n. 1.

its 'colouring' by values makes the formal rationality seem at first sight more different from that of the modern state than it really is.

The legal formality of the Congregation's 'style' was directed in the first instance to religious reform as it had been understood at the Council of Trent. The Tridentine reforms were like any major legislative programme in that they generated many contentious cases and issues that the Council Fathers could hardly have envisaged. All such cases, whether real or (less often) in the form of abstract problems that might eventually turn up as real cases, were within the remit of the Congregation,[65] and in this sphere it automatically overrode any claims the better-known tribunal of the Rota might have to jurisdiction.[66] The Council had cognisance of cases involving the rights and duties of bishops and priests insofar as a legal decision was required and if a measure taken by the Council was relevant; the bishop's relation to his cathedral chapter would be an example:[67] it could be fraught. Canon law crimes such as simony came under the Congregation insofar as their legal consequences were at issue; it dealt with various kinds of disputes between religious orders and the secular clergy, notably in connection with parish churches.[68] Legal aspects of questions about the validity or invalidity of solemn vows were within its purview,[69] as were questions to do with betrothal and marriage when affected in some way by the Council of Trent's reform legislation.[70] The jurisdiction also extended to a wide range of cases and issues which did not necessarily fall under the rubric of Tridentine reform, including various kinds of marriage cases, so long as they were of an essentially spiritual character, monastic vows and the like, and oaths.[71] The formal and instrumental rationality employed in dealing with these cases is close to that of contemporary secular states, but its whole aspect is changed by the world-view which informed the Congregation's activity. It is a paradigm case of the relation between the different types of rationality analysed in this study. Values and convictions set the agenda. Sins of simony, monastic vows and the religious essence of marriage seem remote from the 'Modernity' which has so often been associated with formal rationality. Here the latter is an instrumental technique for implementing values that are, as they say, thoroughly medieval.[72] The technique is that of due legal process: a powerful instrument for achieving consistency

---

[65] *Ibid.*, 152, number 2.   [66] *Ibid.*, 156 n. 1.
[67] *Ibid.*, 156–7 (Bangen explains, p. 157, that not every kind of the bishop–chapter dispute came under the Congregation of the Council).
[68] *Ibid.*, 158.   [69] *Ibid.*   [70] *Ibid.*, 157.
[71] *Ibid.*, 160. Marriage cases that were primarily about property might go to another tribunal such as the Rota.
[72] See *Medieval Religious Rationalities*, chs. 5 and 6.

and avoiding the arbitrary, values which the Congregation shared with modern secular legal systems. As we shall see in the following chapter, it differs from them in formalising exceptions to legal formality, according to criteria still shaped by its value rationality.

Conclusion: formal rationality and value/conviction rationality

Two connected points should be emphasised in conclusion. On the one hand, formal legal rationality is commonly instrumental rationality, distinct from values and convictions. The Congregation of the Council was instituted to implement a law which was specifically and explicitly distinguished from dogma. The reforming decrees of the Council of Trent were the Congregation's remit, not its doctrinal pronouncements. The reforming decrees were positive law, a new canon law rather than an interpretation of the meaning of revelation. Moreover, the side of the Congregation's jurisdictional activity discussed above was conducted by lawyers qualified in civil and canon law, and it aimed at a consistent application of the ecclesiastical law, not at the development of theological doctrine. On the other hand, it should be stressed again that this formal legal rationality was a tool of the theological world-view that lay behind the reform legislation of the Council of Trent. Here, as with religious practice more generally, instrumental and value rationality are not antithetical but a symbiosis.

6   The formal–substantive interface

Formal/substantive and value/instrumental distinctions cross-cutting

The theme of the preceding pages was that legal formality, which is frequently a species[1] of instrumental rationality, tends in its specific social and historical contexts to be coloured and shaped by the values and convictions that lie behind instrumental rationality. In the present chapter the interface between formally and materially rational law will be explored. To anticipate the conclusion: both can serve values and convictions instrumentally, with the value system working out rules for suspending the rules.

From now on 'substantive'[2] and 'material' will be used as synonyms. Some conceptual clarification is required here. 'Substantive' or 'material' rationality is often more or less equated with value rationality,[3] just as 'formal rationality' is with instrumental rationality. Words are free but

---

[1] Similarly, because formal rationality can sometimes be elevated to the status of a value, and because there are many other sorts of instrumental rationality in addition to formal rationality, I think it unhelpful absolutely to equate formal with instrumental rationality as Stanley Tambiah seems to do (Tambiah, *Magic, Science, Religion*, 144–5). The 'formal–substantive' and 'value–instrumental' distinctions are best treated as cross-cutting if confusion is to be avoided.

[2] Discussion of legal formality is complicated by two meanings of the 'substantive': see above, p. 147, for the sense used in this book. To elaborate a little on the semantics: here 'substance' is contrasted with the formal rule and means any consideration which would deserve consideration even if the rule did not exist. As noted above, 'substantive' can also be contrasted with 'procedural'. Substantive law would include such matters as the speed limit and grievous bodily harm. Procedural law includes such matters as admissibility of evidence and how to bring a case. Procedural law, like substantive law in this second sense, can be very formal, when strict rules govern the conduct of the case from beginning to end, say by ruling out decisive evidence illegally acquired; or it can make concessions to considerations outside the formal law, as for instance if a DNA sample which should not have been kept is allowed as evidence to convict a rapist.

[3] 'Communism, feudalism, hedonism, egalitarianism, Calvinism, socialism, Buddhism, Hinduism, and the Renaissance view of life, no less than all aesthetic notions of "the beautiful", are also examples of substantive rationalities' (Kalberg, 'Max Weber's Types of Rationality', 1155).

this equation is an obstacle to analysis. It leaves us without the language to cover a common kind of case, viz., the suspension of formal legal rules for instrumental reasons of convenience (policemen allowing each other to drink and drive), utility (dropping a minor prosecution in return for information leading to a major one), or personal advantage (a favour to a possible patron). More on this below. The 'formal v. substantive' and the 'instrumental v. value' distinctions are most usefully regarded as cross-cutting:

1. Formal Value Rationality	2. Substantive Value Rationality
3. Formal Instrumental Rationality	4. Substantive Instrumental Rationality

The use of the terms 'substantively legal' and 'formally legal' proposed here would incidentally seem to be truer to Weber's usage, which is inexplicit but not opaque. If the following passage about administration is read attentively it maps on to the table above, as the numbers added in square brackets should make clear.[4]

One must distinguish above all between the material [= substantive] rationalisation of *administration* and provision of justice by a patrimonial prince, who makes his subjects happy in the same *utilitarian [4.]* and socially ethical *[2.]* way as the head of a great household makes its members happy, and formal rationalisation through the imposition by trained jurists on all 'citizens' of the rule of universally binding legal norms *[3.or 1.]* ... And the birth of the modern Western 'State', *as also of the Western 'Churches' [3. in the service of values]*, is in its essential core the work of jurists.[5]

It is worth reflecting on the words I have italicised. He is talking about *administration*. Even the most ethical administration involves a host of practical decisions which cannot be read off from moral maxims. This is certainly true of the running of a large household, with which Weber compares patrimonial state administrations. He uses the word *utilitarian*,

---

[4] I cannot recall an explicit statement by Weber to the effect that legal formality can be a value per se as well as an instrument of values, but such a statement would be entirely consistent with his thinking.
[5] 'Vor allem ist zwischen der materialen Rationalisierung der Verwaltung und Rechtspflege durch einen Patrimonialfürsten, der seine Untertanen utilitarisch und sozialethisch beglückt so, wie ein großer Hausherr seine Hausangehörigen, und der formalen Rationalisierung durch die von geschulten Juristen geschaffene Durchführung der Herrschaft allgemeinverbindlicher Rechtsnormen für alle "Staatsbürger" zu scheiden.' (Weber, 'Die Wirtschaftsethik der Weltreligionen. Einleitung', in *Gesammelte Aufsätze zur Religionssoziologie*, vol. 1, p. 272.)

showing ethical imperatives are not the only alternative to formal legality: practical case-by-case common sense without any high-level moral norm involved is typical of 'household' administration that is untrammelled by formal rules. There is a value framework, but the same is true, as we saw above, of legal formality. And this is clearly Weber's sense also because he associates formal rationalisation by jurists with the Catholic Church as well as with the modern State. Weber needs to be reread without a preconceived schema in mind. Then he explains himself well and the confusion disappears.[6]

Even if the foregoing restoration of Weber's meaning were mistaken, however, there would be a strong case for adopting the terms as defined here, because they are less confusing than the version of Weber in circulation in some scholarly quarters. For if the reading of Weber just criticised above were correct, his terminology would indeed be unsatisfactory and the words would require definition. In other words, there is not much point in getting too far into an exegetical argument about Weber's true intentions, as if that could rule out the usage of 'formal' and 'substantive/material' adopted here. It is used not *because* it is Weber's, but because it works.

Practically speaking, 'material/substantive rationality' is most lucidly used as a 'parasite' concept dependent on 'formal rationality': material or substantive rationality is any kind of rational consideration that overrides, replaces, or operates freely within the formal rules. Such considerations may be values or convictions but they do not have to be: they could equally be pragmatic economic or political considerations, or simple convenience.[7]

The formal–substantive interface in traditional Chinese law

How to draw the line between formal and substantive reasoning is a problem which usually involves instrumental calculation informed by values. As is normal with such calculations there is room for disagreement

---

[6] The confusion that excellent scholars have seen in Weber is not apparent to me; their reading of him may be flawed, not from any lack of acuity but, probably, by preconceived schemata. See e.g. Eisen, 'The Meanings and Confusions of Weberian "Rationality"', 57: 'the distinction between formal and substantive rationality is . . . judged [by Eisen] to be . . . theoretically confused'. Read carefully, in the original, and without preconceptions, Weber's concepts of formal and substantive rationality are entirely coherent, even if the relation between them is not always fully spelled out.

[7] Atiyah and Summers, *Form and Substance*, 8, imagine a statute prohibiting the driving of vehicles in a park, and a man who ignores the law because he needs to get to an important meeting in time. This substantive reason of breaking the law is instrumentally rational and need have no proximate connection with values and convictions.

within the same general framework. A study by John Langlois of traditional Chinese law and jurisprudence of the Sung and Yüan periods (roughly corresponding with the central Middle Ages in the West) brings this out particularly well.[8] The views he studies are all those of the *litterati*, the Chinese elite who achieved their status by passing public examinations, and from whom the governing civil service was recruited. His analyses show us a legal culture with a broad consensus about values: belief in a moral order and the reinforcement of it by what we would call positive law; differences in emphasis on priorities within the system of convictions; instrumentally rational debate about how rigidly the letter of the law should be interpreted, if it was to serve its purpose; and a preponderance of opinion for the view that formal legality needed to be tempered in particular cases by substantive considerations, the precise balance being a matter for instrumental calculation.

A disagreement between two senior officials about the application of legal formality to a particular case is one of Langlois's main topics. The Emperor had told these two officials, Wang An-shih and Ssu-Ma Kuang, to come up with an answer.[9] There were conflicting approaches. To quote Langlois:

Ssu-Ma Kuang subordinated law to the Tao, a higher morality, one that was unwritten yet accessible to learned scholars. Wang, however, held that the law that had been written down under the auspices of the Emperor and promulgated throughout the empire had to be faithfully interpreted and exercised. He argued that it was the duty of an official to see that the law was applied consistently, fully, and truthfully, for only in that way would the people know how to conduct themselves. Ssu-Ma's position implied that the people did not have to refer to a code of laws to know how to behave. The law, in effect, was an expression of morality but not its definitive formulation.[10]

Behind this disagreement there was a good deal of consensus. Both thought that the law should 'deter people from committing wrongs'.[11] Ssu-Ma Kuang, on the 'substantive rationality' wing, was not ignoring the written code or suggesting that judges had a free hand.[12] Ssu-Ma

---

[8] Langlois, '"Living Law" in Sung and Yüan Jurisprudence'. For background on law under the Sung, see McKnight, *Law and Order in Sung China*, 61–6; for a fascinating body of source material in English translation, see McKnight and Liu, *The Enlightened Judgements*.
[9] Langlois, '"Living Law"', 205.   [10] *Ibid.*, 206.   [11] *Ibid.*, 217.
[12] Freedom of judges to decide case by case what seems to them fair – the opposite of legal formality – was sometimes called 'Qâdi-Justice' (from *Qâdi*, an Islamic judge) by Weber and others. It is worth noting here that Weber at least made it clear that he used the phrase as a shorthand expression, not a historical description of Islamic justice: see Weber, *Wirtschaft und Gesellschaft*, vol. 3, p. 657, passage beginning 'im sprichwörtlichen, nicht im historischen Sinn' and ending 'wo jene Erkenntnismittel versagen'.

seems to have emphasised the deterrent effect of the law, while Wang emphasised the aim of making criminals confess and reform, and the law 'was susceptible to their conflicting approaches because both values – the high esteem for the deterrent effect of the law and the high esteem for the reform of criminals – were firmly embedded in traditional Chinese jurisprudence'.[13]

Furthermore, the issue was not whether one should apply the law but: how literally. The argument centred on technicalities. There was a rule that some crimes could be analysed into two elements. If you committed a robbery and wounded someone in the course of it, the two elements would be the wounding and the robbery. Furthermore, if you confessed before the start of the investigation, you could gain immunity from punishment for the first of the two elements, the 'antecedent causal act'.[14]

So the question was whether these technical rules applied in the case at issue.[15] The accused was a woman who was unwillingly betrothed to a man she strongly disliked. She attacked him when he was sleeping, wounding him but not killing him. Wang, on the 'legal formality' wing of the argument, thought he could see two crimes here, and since she had confessed to premeditation, peeled off that first crime and left only the second one, the act itself.[16] For him, the 'antecedent causal act' was the premeditation of murder (or injury). If confessing could gain her immunity for that crime, the punishment would be for intentional injury only. Ssu-Ma's counter-argument came down to the absurdity of treating the intention and the act as two separate crimes in circumstances like this. In fact his line seems a defensible reading of the written code, but he seems to have chosen to defend it partly by stressing the limits of legal formality.

Most scholars in the Chinese mandarin tradition, according to Langlois, 'have supported Ssu-Ma Kuang's view that the Tao transcended the law, that justice should not be the rigid captive of the law codes'.[17] This is not because Chinese *litterati* were all amateur generalists, ignorant of the law. Max Weber, who seems to have thought something of the kind, appears to have been unaware also of the legal expertise of

---

[13] Langlois, '"Living Law"', 216.

[14] *Ibid.*, 201, 203. Not quite predictably, the advocate of confession and reform was the protagonist of strong legal formality, and the advocate of deterrence of a more flexible and common-sense exegesis of the law code.

[15] The simplified summary that follows is based on *ibid.*, 201–17.

[16] There was room for debate about that too, but it was an aspect of the case that was apparently put on a back burner.

[17] *Ibid.*, 208.

civil servants in 'medieval' China.[18] Modern scholarship has corrected Weber on this point: 'In T'ang and Sung times one could compete in the civil service recruitment examinations in the field of legal studies', and 'Beyond the realm of legal specialisation... all scholars sitting for the *chin-shih*... examination were expected to have a knowledge of legal matters.'[19] The contrast clearly in Weber's mind between imperial Chinese civil servants and the legally qualified civil servants of modern Germany was an empirical mistake. Nonetheless, the legal system that Chinese scholar-civil servants enforced and the philosophy behind it allowed substantive considerations to override the formal rules. The extent to which that could happen was open to debate between scholars who were nevertheless writing within the same framework. This space for individual judgement left open by the value system can be observed in practice too, incidentally, to judge from the fascinating compilation known as 'The Enlightened Judgements' (*Ch'ing-ming chi*).[20]

As well as presenting the interesting debate between Ssu-Ma Kuang and Wang about the appropriate degree of legal formality, Langlois analyses a prose poem about the Sung legal code and a set of commentaries on the poem, where the same interplay of formal and substantive considerations is in the forefront. Here the element of controversy seems to be lacking, and the emphasis seems to be on the need to temper formality with substantive reasoning. Langlois sees these texts as representative of a more general pattern in the history of imperial China: 'Each era in Chinese history produced efforts by intellectuals and leaders in society to readjust the balance between printed, limited, yet essential formal law on the one hand, and unprinted, abstract, and transcendent demands of justice on the other hand.'[21]

[18] Ringer, *Max Weber*, 162; Weber, *Gesammelte Aufsätze zur Religionssoziologie*, vol. 1, pp. 409, 422.
[19] Langlois, '"Living Law"', 172.
[20] McKnight and Liu, *The Enlightened Judgements*, introduction, 4–5: 'Some magistrates usually applied the law as written. Others threatened the participants in cases with the literal enforcement of the law and then offered them the opportunity to resolve issues in less injurious ways. Occasionally judges seem torn between a clear understanding of the law and their own beliefs. They might feel deeply that their approach was the morally correct one and yet feel constrained to hand down decisions shaped at least in part by views with which they as individuals were not wholly in agreement. Finally, those more driven by their deeply felt doctrinal views sometimes simply ignored the clear provisions of the laws as these applied to certain central social problems. We should be careful, however, not to overestimate how commonly Sung judges tried to reshape the law to fit their own prejudices. There are far more cases in the *Ch'ing-ming chi* in which judges either follow the law closely or set it aside not with any intention of shaping future law but merely from a felt need to settle specific problems in a socially acceptable fashion.'
[21] Langlois, '"Living Law"', 168–9.

It was noted above that in Sung law there was a correlation between the ritual mourning obligation towards a given class of persons on the one hand, and the punishment for a crime against the same class of persons on the other. There was a formal system for this. The code specified the punishment for a crime where there was no special status or ritual relationship between perpetrator and victim. Where there was a relationship the punishment should be increased by 'degrees', ranging from 'light stick' to death.[22] The closer the ritual or status relationship of criminal to the victim, the higher the degree of punishment. So far, we are still in the realm of legal formality, though it is not the 'equal before the law' formality claimed by modern Western legal systems.

But the formal system could be overridden by considerations not covered by the rules. The commentary on the *Prose-Poem on the Penal Tradition* briefly discussed in the previous chapter sets limits to formal legality:

In a case in which the mourning relationship is slight but the moral obligation... is deep and weighty, overpowering the mourning relationship, then the [prescribed] punishment will not fit the circumstances [of the criminal act]. In such cases [the judge] must ignore the mourning relationship and sentence according to the principles of moral obligation.[23]

The 1339 preface to the same commentary[24] says that 'The circumstances of crimes range from light to grave. With regard to the law on increasing and reducing punishments, if one does not take into account the purpose behind the statutes, then penal sanctions will not hit the mark and the people will get panicky.'[25] The last phrase is an allusion to words by Confucius. We have already looked at a counterpart of this approach in one of the few thinkers of equal stature in the Western tradition.

Equity again

The foregoing passage is reminiscent of the theory of *epieikeia* or equity, discussed above in Chapter 4: Aristotle's famous argument that the laws of the city state might be good in general yet not good in all circumstances,[26] and its heirs or analogues in other systems, such as England's in the late medieval and early modern periods.[27] We must return to *epieikeia* and equity now because they label an important sort of substantive rationality in law. Here they will be understood broadly to take in not only decisions that actually go against the letter of the law but

[22] *Ibid.*, 192–3.   [23] *Hsing-t'ung fu shu*, cited *ibid.*, 179; cf. *ibid.*, 197.   [24] *Ibid.*, 175.
[25] Cited *ibid.*. 193.   [26] See Chapter 4, pp. 138–40 above.
[27] Baker, *An Introduction to English Legal History*, 106.

also judgements in matters where the letter of the law simply provides no remedy.

In the later Middle Ages the Court of Chancery developed as a forum with cases where the common law could not find a way for justice to be done. The rationale and workings of the court have been well summarised by Sir John Baker. The origin of the jurisdiction was the possibility of appealing to the King for justice:[28]

Decrees were at first made in the name of the King in council, and then by the 'court', sometimes reciting the presence of judges and king's serjeants, councillors, and advisers; but during the fifteenth century the chancellor came to issue decrees in his own name. In making such decrees, medieval councillors or chancellors did not regard themselves as administering a system of law different from the law of England. They were reinforcing the law by making sure that justice was done in cases where shortcomings in the regular procedure, or human failings, were hindering its attainment by due process. They came not to destroy the law but to fulfil it . . . The stock example was that of the debtor who gave his creditor a sealed bond, but did not ensure that it was cancelled when he paid up. The law regarded the bond as incontrovertible evidence of the debt, and so payment was no defence . . . Again, if someone granted land to others on trust to carry out his wishes, he would find that at law the grantees were absolute owners . . . those were the results which followed from observing strict rules of evidence, . . . which could not be relaxed without destroying certainty . . . The Chancery worked differently. The chancellor was free from the rigid procedures under which such injustices sheltered. His court was a court of conscience.[29]

In 1615 a Chancellor eloquently stated the rationale for his courts: 'men's actions are so divers and infinite that it is impossible to make a general law which may aptly meet with every particular and not fail in some circumstances'.[30] This is reminiscent of the following remarks in a commentary on Fu Lin's *Prose-Poem* on the Sung code (the *Penal Tradition*): 'the circumstances of human beings are without limits, while the purposes of law are limited. If unlimited circumstances are controlled by means of limited laws, then the circumstances of people will be out of the reach of the law.'[31]

Even before the sixteenth century legal formality was beginning to stiffen Chancery justice. The volume of cases meant that it was impossible to treat each one as unique. Inevitably both procedure and substantive decisions began to be stereotyped.[32] Reporting of cases was symptomatic

---

28 *Ibid.*, 101.
29 *Ibid.*, 102–3; cf. Haskett, 'The Medieval Court of Chancery', notably 267–8.
30 Cited by Baker, *Introduction*, 106.
31 Cited by Langlois, '"Living Law"', 168. The solution proposed in the commentary is to cite law by analogy.
32 Baker, *Introduction*, 110.

of the drift towards legal formality:[33] it presupposes that precedent itself is an argument, by contrast with the case-by-case-fairness justice of the earlier period. Eventually the Court of Chancery became almost the opposite of the original ideal of a court of conscience righting the wrongs done by an over-formalised law.

Clearly, however, there were problems with both extremes. An early sixteenth-century critic, from the common law side, said: 'divers men, divers consciences'.[34] It was the old debate between certainty and fairness: the precise balance being a matter of instrumental calculation.

The kind of flexibility which the Court of Chancery originally aimed to provide is not immediately apparent in the modern common and Roman law traditions. (The role of the Ombudsman in modern Britain is too modest to delay us.) But the role of material rationality may have been larger than at first appears. Weber alluded to the habit of French juries in his day of disregarding formal law and acquitting husbands who had caught their wives *in flagrante delicto* with a lover and killed him.[35]

One could cite other examples of unofficial *epieikeia* in modern systems. Traffic policeman turn a blind eye to motorists who exceed the speed limit by a few miles per hour, if they are otherwise driving safely. More systematically, something akin to *epieikeia* may be exercised when it comes to sentencing. Probation in a criminal case, or token damages in a civil suit, may come close to suspension of the law. Then again: sometimes a jury may acquit someone who is clearly guilty according to the law, because they think he did right to break the law. This happened in a famous British case after the Falklands War in the 1980s. The civil servant Clive Ponting had made known facts in conflict with government statements about the sinking of an Argentinian ship. The jury decided that he was in the right, whatever the law might say (he had certainly broken it), and he was acquitted.[36] This was a dramatic clash between a jury's idea of what was fair and the exigencies of the formal system, but where facts or law are less clear-cut one can assume that juries often exercise a degree of *epieikeia*. That is still rather different from *epieikeia* built into the system's conceptual structure.

Formal and substantive rationality in the common law tradition: England and the USA

The interplay of formal and substantive rationality has been particularly well studied for modern England and the USA (by P. S. Atiyah and

[33] *Ibid.* [34] *Ibid.*, 107. [35] Weber, *Wirtschaft und Gesellschaft*, 471.
[36] Ponting, '*R. v. Ponting*'.

R. S. Summers, whose conceptual scheme has been largely followed in this chapter[37]). On the one hand, in the USA there seems to be a stronger tradition of legal formality when it comes to the rigorous enforcement of rules of evidence. The 'fruit of the poisoned tree' doctrine, which excludes evidence which would not have come to light but for an illegal act (such as a search without a warrant), is apparently more powerful in the USA than in England.[38] This can rule out evidence that would decisively convict someone known for certain to be guilty of a crime. The instrumental calculation that may lie behind this apparently paradoxical approach may be that the police cannot be trusted so that drastic measures are required. On the other hand, when it comes to the non-procedural content[39] of the law there seems to be a higher degree of legal formality in England.[40]

Atiyah and Summers analyse the unhappy late nineteenth-century (1884) case of the British ship *Mignonette*.[41] A sailor from that ship had been killed and eaten by shipmates when they were in a desperate state after a shipwreck. The authorities wanted and got a conviction of murder (softened, as they also intended by a very light sentence). In a rather similar American case (where passengers had been thrown out of an overloaded lifeboat, admittedly a somewhat different type of action), the result had been acquittal.[42]

The result of the *Mignonette* case seems so typical of the English approach to such problem cases that it is worth a moment's reflection to ask why it should seem appropriate to the authorities to seek a conviction for murder in circumstances in which no one would expect or want the punishment for murder to be carried out. It seems clear to us that the answer lies partly in the more formal approach the English judges take to law. They believe in law having a high degree of mandatory formality, and are especially unwilling to carve out substantively grounded exceptions to general liability in what appear to be marginal cases.[43]

Again, an instrumental explanation is at hand: 'Elitist judges are worried about the effect which famous cases may have on the general public; they believe, rightly or wrongly, that people will misinterpret the results of such cases if they show a wavering from the strict application of formal law.'[44] These differences between two branches of the common law

---

37 See above, pp. 148–9.
38 Atiyah and Summers, *Form and Substance*, 179; Cf. Cross, 'Confessions and Cognate Matters', esp. 86.
39 I avoid the word 'substantive' because of its ambiguity in the present context.
40 The foregoing generalisations may already be out of date, but should be taken as a description of the situation in the second half of the twentieth century.
41 For details see Simpson, *Cannibalism and the Common Law*.
42 Atiyah and Summers, *Form and Substance*, 181.   43 *Ibid.*, 181–2.
44 *Ibid.*, 182.

tradition are not grounds for inferring any fundamental divergence of values. More probably, they represent different collective calculations of how the law can best serve a set of values shared by judges in both jurisdictions: the protection of life, property, etc. The fact that the USA tends more to legal formality in matters of procedure and England more in matters of legal content is hard to explain in terms of any fundamental value and more probably correlates with other empirical attitudes.[45]

Dispensations

Neither in England nor in the USA does the common law tradition allow for explicit dispensations from the law. Judges allow formal to give way to substantive considerations but this will usually be in cases where statutes and precedent give them at least some room for manoeuvre. Occasionally a judge like Lord Denning may be prepared to override the meaning of the law as others have understood it.[46] In principle, though, the law once established does not admit of exceptions.

Other systems, however, explicitly allow for dispensations, which may be defined as suspensions of the law in particular cases. Roman law had a place for what were in effect dispensations,[47] but they went under different names: *Venia, Liberatio, Indulgentia, Beneficium, Licentia, In integrum restitutio.*[48] Thus *Beneficium* was a 'legal benefit or remedy of an exceptional character, granted in certain legal situations or to a specific category of persons by a statute, the praetorian edict, a senatusconsult or by the emperor (imperial constitutions)'.[49] Here is an example from the second century AD:

We are moved both by the length of time during which, in ignorance of the law, you have been married to your uncle, and the fact that you were placed in matrimony by your grandmother, and by the number of your children. So, as all these considerations come together, we confirm that the status of your children who result from this marriage, which was contracted forty years ago, shall be as if they had been conceived legitimately.[50]

---

[45] Cf. *ibid.*, 39: 'English judges tend to trust the rest of the legal-political "establishment" – government, legislatures, officials, police – and, in elitist fashion, to distrust the public at large and their representative, the jury. American judges, by contrast, distrust the "establishment" and trust the people and the jury. We believe this difference leads to – or anyhow is related to – other major differences. English judges are more likely to use formal reasoning in many sorts of cases where this means the substantive issues are left to others in the legal-political "establishment". American judges, on the other hand, are more likely to use formal reasoning where they are laying down rules of conduct for other officials whom they do not trust, such as the police.'
[46] Goff, 'Denning, Alfred Thompson', 812–13. Denning's not negligible influence probably tended to diminish the formalism of the English common law.
[47] Stiegler, *Dispensation*, 13–14.   [48] *Ibid.*, 14.
[49] Berger, *Encyclopedic Dictionary of Roman Law*, 372.
[50] Quoted by Millar, *The Emperor in the Roman World*, 548.

'This is a clear instance where what the emperors granted was a *beneficium* as against the strict provisions of the law.'[51]

Dispensations play a large part in a peculiar 'law' enforced in university departments: the law of assessment. Deadlines for course work and rules for final classification are a kind of legal system, though not a state system. Departmental tutors and examination chairs often dispense from these rules on medical or compassionate grounds. For almost any rule, a dispensation may be obtained if the substantive grounds are solid and if faculty members are prepared to go high enough in the committee structure.

The Congregation of the Council and dispensations

It is perhaps surprising that a system of dispensations is not found more often in legal history. The most rational form is probably the one that developed within the positive law of the Catholic Church. (Here 'rational' is used, as always in this book, in a value-neutral sense.) It is worth freezing the camera to show the system at work in the nineteenth century, the period for which the Congregation of the Council's formal rationality was analysed above. For in this period the same Congregation had extensive dispensing powers. It is a perfect instance of the interplay of formal and material rationality, guided by a value-saturated instrumental rationality.

One manifestation of the system's rationality is the clear articulation of general rules that should govern the granting of dispensations: a formally rational hedge around the exercise of material rationality. Notably, the Congregation ruled that they must be construed strictly, to the letter rather than broadly: the assumption would be that a dispensation meant exactly what it said and no more, so that it should be interpreted almost legalistically.[52] In the same spirit of formal legality, they should not be extended to other similar cases by analogy.[53]

---

[51] So Millar, *ibid.*

[52] 'Furthermore it is a feature and strength of a papal dispensation and grace that it is to be construed strictly, and cannot be extended beyond the limits set to it by the same pope who granted the dispensation and conceded the grace [reference to a decision of the Congregation follows] ('Ea porro indoles ac vis est Pontificiae dispensationis et gratiae, ut stricte interpretari debeat, nec ultra limites, quibus ab eodem Pontifice dispensante et gratiam concedente coercita fuit, extendi possit *in Alatrina die 26 Augusti 1820 # Ea (2)*') (Pallottini, *Collectio omnium conclusionum*, vol. 7, Dispensatio, # I. Dispensatio in genere, 2, p. 243).

[53] 'Nec imo ex tritissima iuris regula dispensatio tam facile ad alios casus, licet fortassis consimiles, est protrahenda, cum privilegii instar haberi debeat *in Bononien. Montis Pietatis die 23 Iunii 1838 #. Habent*' (*ibid.*, #. I. Dispensatio in genere, 5, p. 243); '6. Dispensationes enim ita inter res odiosas referuntur, ut dispensatus in uno non intelligatur dispensatus in alio, nisi verba dispensationis claris verbis alium casum comprehendant

Formal procedures are notably strict for a particularly interesting class of dispensations: those that dissolved marriages that had not been consummated. (As will become clear, such cases were conceptually quite distinct from annulments on grounds of impotence, though the two issues could become intertwined in actual practice.) Proving the impotence was likely to involve a system called the 'oath of the seventh hand', by which each partner produced oath helpers.[54]

A formal procedure for dealing with such cases at Rome was included in the 1741 constitution *Dei miseratione* of Benedict XIV[55] – a procedure designed to ensure a maximum of rational consideration.[56] Normally the first stage was the preparation of the dossier by the Congregation of the Council. When everything was in order, it was passed to the Pope, so that he could make his own mind up about the case. After careful deliberation he could either reject it or pass it back to the Congregation of the Council (or another Congregation) for further consideration. They were then expected to come up with a recommendation, but 'the Pope reserved for himself the possibility of examining it again',[57] after which he would either approve it or redirect it to another Congregation or to one of the tribunals at the Curia ('tribunals' like the 'Rota' were distinguished from Congregations).

This again highlights the close interaction of formal and substantive rationality. The substantive rationality of the Pope's personal intervention is achieved by formal procedures that were designed to ensure that each case was rigorously considered and the arguments debated and weighed, rather than settled arbitrarily. In 1840 the Congregation of the Council issued an instruction through which still more rigour was brought to the non-consummation cases.[58]

There are also more general principles, very interesting for the application of the typologies or rationality developed here. In a nutshell, a

[p. 244] *in Praenestina Pensionis die 13 Ianuarii 1844 #. Ad rem'* (*ibid.*, #. I. Dispensatio in genere 6, pp. 243–4).

[54] Plöchl, *Geschichte des Kirchenrechts*, vol. 4, p. 406: 'Selbstverständlich war es nicht notwendig, daß tatsächlich sieben Zeugen beigebracht wurden, doch mußte ihre Qualität besonders hoch anzuschlagen sein, um ihrem Zeugnis erhöhtes Gewicht beizumessen.' Cf. Oesterlé, 'Consummation'; Gratian, *Decretum*, Pars II, C. 33. q. 1, c. 2, Friedberg, *Corpus Iuris Canonici*, vol. 1, col. 1149; Richter and von Schulte, *Canones et decreta Concilii Tridentini*, Sessio XXIV, no. 147, p. 284.

[55] This reform constitution was a general revision of marriage law, of which the regulation of *ratum non consummatum* procedure was only one part: see Plöchl, *Geschichte des Kirchenrechts*, vol. 4, pp. 399–403.

[56] *Ibid.*, 402–3.

[57] 'Der Papst behielt sich eine neuerliche Prüfung vor' (*ibid.*, 403).

[58] '*Cum moneat Glossa*, which introduced stricter controls into the procedure for impotence and non-consummation cases' ('*Cum moneat Glossa*, worin das Verfahren bei Impotenz- und Inkonsumationsprozessen einer genaueren Regelung unterzogen wurde') (*ibid.*, 406).

dispensation should only be granted when there were strong instrumental reasons for doing so. An 1836 statement by the Congregation puts it thus, invoking Aquinas: 'The legitimate grounds for a dispensation, as St Thomas teaches [references follow], may be reduced to three: so, first to public or private utility, secondly to common or individual necessity, thirdly to piety [or: mercy].'[59] 'Necessity' and 'utility': this is the language of instrumental reasoning. But 'necessary', or 'useful', according to what criteria? Evidently, the criteria are assumed to be those of Roman Catholicism, its value rationality.

Unconsummated marriage and dispensations

To illustrate instrumental rationality's role as mediator between formal legality and substantive considerations there is no better class of examples than 'non-consummation' cases at the papal court, as they were played out from the fifteenth century onwards. On the one hand we see a formal rule: a valid marriage should be permanent even though unconsummated. On the other hand, we see substantive reasons for dissolving it. Only in exceptional cases would these outweigh the importance of maintaining the formal rule. This formal rule should be sharply distinguished from the principle that a consummated marriage between Christians could never be dissolved, and the exceptions to it should be no less sharply distinguished from annulments on grounds of impotence.

In the last analysis the indissolubility of an unconsummated marriage had come to be viewed as positive ecclesiastical law rather than a fundamental value.[60] The rule was inferred remotely rather than proximately from the principles of natural law and contained an element of human as opposed to divine regulation.[61] The consummated marriage is a quite different case, at least where the couple had been baptised: it could not be dissolved however powerful the contrary considerations.[62] Still, the formal rule was so strong even with unconsummated marriages that only the Pope dissolved them. As we have seen, from 1741 on an elaborate sequence of stages ensured that both the Congregation of the Council

---

59 'Unde legitimae dispensationis causae, ut docet S. Thomas 2 quaest. 63 art. 2 et quaest 67 art. 4, ad tria rediguntur; nimirum primo ad publicam sive privatam utilitatem, secundo ad communem sive particularem necessitatem, tertio ad pietatem *in Nullius Dispensationis die 16 Iulii 1836 #. Legitimae*' (Pallottini, *Collectio*, vol. 7, #. I. Dispensatio in genere, 19, p. 244).

60 For the whole development see d'Avray, *Medieval Marriage*, ch. 4, with further references.

61 *Ibid.*, 194.   62 Ibid., ch. 2, with further references.

(occasionally another Congregation) and the Pope weighed the pros and cons very carefully.

The contrast between dissolutions of unconsummated marriages and annulments on grounds of impotence, in the sense of the physical incapacity to consummate the marriage, cannot be stressed too strongly (if only because they are easily confused). The former were instrumental decisions, while the latter belong to the sphere of value rationality, it being a matter of absolute principle that the marriage be found null once it had become clear that one of the partners was permanently incapable of consummating it.

Paradoxically, cases where impotence was a possibility but difficult to prove might be the occasion for the instrumental calculation that a 'non-consummation' dissolution (a real divorce in the modern sense) was the safest outcome. The calculation would be this: we think that one of the partners is impotent. An annulment on those grounds might well go through; that would leave the other partner free to remarry; but suppose subsequent events prove the original judgement mistaken? The 'impotent' partner might turn out to be able to have sex after all. If so, the annulment would be revealed as a judicial error and it would have to be reversed. Then the remarried partner would turn out to have been unconsciously living in sin. The second marriage would be the invalid one and he or she (perhaps usually she) would have to return to the original partner, probably the last thing that anyone wanted by that stage, especially if the formally impotent partner wanted to marry the person with whom he (perhaps usually 'he') had overcome his problem.

Just such a case came to the Congregation of the Council from Bologna in 1836. The couple had lived together for three years without consummating the marriage: because of the man's impotence, they claimed. Sworn midwives testified to the wife's virginity, but that of course did not prove that the man was permanently impotent, the condition for an annulment. Oath helpers (in effect) for both husband and wife supported their claim. They were 'propinqui', relatives or just possibly neighbours. (The 'oath of the seventh hand' system used for for non-consummation cases has already been mentioned.[63]) The question was, should the Congregation declare an annulment or should they take the 'ratum non consummatum' route? The Pope was consulted and he sent the matter back to the Congregation for further discussion. The outcome was that they should ask the Pope to grant a 'ratum non consummatum' dispensation, but require the man to consult the Congregation before contracting another marriage. (This last provision was because of the evidence for

---

[63] See above, p. 175.

his impotence, which if absolute would be a bar to a new marriage.) This was the outcome in 1836. It was not the end of the story. Unsurprisingly, the woman married someone else. Then the man asked permission to get married, claiming that he had got over his problem. After a physical examination he received permission, in 1842.[64] So the instrumental calculation which lay behind the decision – to dissolve the marriage, if it was a marriage – rather than declaring that it was not and never had been a marriage – proved to be absolutely correct.

A similar line of instrumental reasoning could lead to a non-consummation dissolution where the marriage's validity was questionable for some reason other than impotence. In one case a 13-year-old girl's father died and her mother entrusted her to the care of a priest, for whatever reason – it looks as if he was a relative. This priest wanted the girl to marry his brother. He obtained the mother's assent by threats, though the girl resisted the idea. Using his clerical connections, no doubt, but without telling the girl, he obtained a dispensation for the affinity that linked her to his brother. (This is the reason for supposing that he was a relative of the girl.) He also got the vicar general of the diocese to dispense from the reading of the banns. Finally, he got the parish priest to agree to the celebration of the marriage at home, apparently with himself as officiant. Then the priest, with his brother the would-be bridegroom and some others, went to the house and intimidated the girl into consenting to the marriage. The mother was not present. At least she, the priest and the bridegroom had made an agreement before the marriage that it should not be consummated immediately, because of the girl's youth. The girl brought suit to have the marriage annulled on grounds of defective consent. Finally the husband backed up her story. So the Congregation judged an annulment to be justified. Nevertheless, it also granted a provisional 'ratum non consummatum' dispensation.[65]

It is worth dwelling for a moment on this decision. No one thought that annulments were infallible decisions, any more than we think the judgements of secular courts are infallible. Nor were they 'performative': for in this value system, annulling a marriage did not *make* it invalid, it merely declared it to be invalid – just as convicting a criminal does not make him guilty, but merely declares him to be guilty with all the legal

---

[64] Richter and von Schulte, *Canones*, Sessio XXIV. De Reform. Matrimonii, no. 147, p. 284: passage beginning 'N. et N. post celebratas nuptias per triennium' and ending 'inspectione, S. C. rescr. "licere eidem inire matrimonium *cum vidua*." 23. Apr. 1842'.

[65] *Ibid.*, no. 146, pp. 283–4, passage beginning '146. T. puella tredecim annorum' and ending 'et *ad cautelam* saltem esse dispensandum super matrimonio rato et non consummato. *Lunen. Sarzanen.* 22. Ian. 1833'.

consequences that follow. In both cases further evidence can in principle overturn the verdict.

That was unlikely to happen in this case, but the Congregation must have felt a degree of doubt about the annulment. The priest had taken great care to make sure that the formal law laid down since Trent for contracting a valid marriage was observed to the letter. Defective consent by the girl was the only ground for annulment. On the facts as we and the Congregation have them, there was probably enough proof, beyond reasonable doubt, that she had been bullied into consenting. Still a qualm of uncertainty remains. We read that the putative husband too eventually backed up the coercion story. That must raise at least a question about the possibility of collusion: often a danger in annulments. Suppose the girl had given a sufficient consent at the time but then changed her mind, and suppose that the husband decided in the end that he did not want to be tied to her for life against her will? If so, there was a danger of granting a mistaken annulment, which would mean in turn that any subsequent marriage by the girl and/or her husband would be invalid. That danger was avoided by the provisional 'non-consummation' dissolution – which was in effect a safety-net for the annulment: if what the annulment claimed to declare was not the case, the non-consummation brought it about. The declarative judgement was backed up by a performative judgement, averting in advance any danger of subsequent invalid marriages.

The instrumental calculation in this and the other cases was saturated with values that shaped the whole course of the Congregation's reasoning. The values informing their calculations about marriage had been originally formed in a long development going back to Roman times, in which a crucial role was played by a symbol, one so strong as to be a social force.[66] Christian marriage represented the marriage of Christ to his Church. The symbolic correspondence was deemed to be incomplete until the marriage had been consummated – real sex was crucial in the Catholic marriage symbolism. All consummated marriages between Christians were deemed to be absolutely indissoluble (making Catholicism the only value system in a literate civilisation to impose monogamy and indissolubility at the same time[67]). An unconsummated marriage was still a valid marriage, provided that it was capable of being consummated, but the defect in the symbolism had a large implication: that the

---

[66] I recapitulate some of the main conclusions of d'Avray, *Medieval Marriage*.

[67] I try this generalisation out on colleagues with appropriate expertise whenever possible, and no one has yet produced a counter-example, though I see no reason why there should not be one.

marriage was not indissoluble. Its permanence was not an absolute value. Ultimately, it was guaranteed by a formal legality with a very high but not absolute degree of generality. Granted these values, the instrumental reasoning of the Congregation of the Council makes sense: the values and convictions gave criteria for deciding between legal formality and concrete substantive considerations.

The Doisnel case

The relationships between fundamental values, formal rationality and instrumental rationality are encapsulated in a memorable case from the diocese of Lisieux which the Congregation of the Council dealt with in the late seventeenth century (the crucial stages at least took place in 1674). This is worth dwelling on because the value framework behind the instrumental decision between formal and material considerations is set out explicitly.

The facts around which the Congregation reasoned were extremely unhappy. The story as told by the petitioner Nicolas Peauger was as follows. When he was about 20 he married a girl called Catharine Doisnel to please his father. He was still under his father's authority. She was the illegitimate daughter of Nicolas Doisnel. He says that the latter had already 'abused' his daughter incestuously (the Latin does not necessarily imply compulsion). It was a proper church wedding. He lived under the same roof as Catharine and her father for three days but she did not like the marriage or her husband and refused to sleep with him, and told people as much – people who were able to bear witness. After three days she got him out of the house and seven months later she had a child, whose father was her father. Perhaps the marriage had been arranged to cover up her pregnancy from incestuous sex. Later on Catharine and her father had other children together. In the end it came before the secular court. The couple were condemned to be burned. Their ashes were to be scattered to the winds. They escaped, however, and left France. Some sixteen years later Nicolas wanted to marry someone else, but of course he was still married to Catharine Doisnel. He petitioned the Congregation of the Council to get the Bishop of Lisieux to confirm the facts of the case. Then he hoped that the Congregation would declare that his first marriage 'did not hold', and allow him to remarry.[68] In the dossier this petition is followed by a letter dated 1674 from the Archdeacon of Lisieux, who was also the 'Official' (entitled to

---

[68] Archivio Secreto Vaticano, Congr. Conc. Positiones (carte sciote) 4 (not foliated): see Appendix, Doc. 1.

act legally and administratively vice the bishop), supporting Peauger's request.

The Congregation, a powerful committee of cardinals, met on Saturday, 16 February 1675.[69] They did not give the go-ahead for an enquiry that might have lead to the dissolution of the marriage.[70] We do not know the reasons, though we can guess at the arguments on either side. On the one hand, there was Peauger's unhappy situation. On the other hand, there was the formal rationality of the indissolubility rule, binding normally even with unconsummated marriages. To the committee this may have looked like one of those cases that, in Aristotle's words, 'do not fall under any art or set of precepts', where 'the agents themselves must in each case consider what is appropriate to the occasion'.[71]

No general rule could settle this case. It had to come down to weighing the concrete facts and probabilities and the likely consequences of a 'yes' or a 'no' in this particular instance. Against the sympathy that one hopes the committee felt for Peauger, they may have considered the following questions: How much probative force should be attributed to Catharine Doisnel's reported assertions, sixteen years before, that she had not slept with Peauger, when it was known that the couple had lived under the same roof for a few days? How great was the danger that Peauger's neighbours would take the decision as a straightforward divorce, without awareness of the crucial theological difference made by non-consummation? Or that they would take it as an annulment on grounds of impotence, where the

[69] 'Saturday 16 Feb. 1675. The Congregation of the Council of Trent held a meeting in the Quirinal Apostolic Palace, at which the most eminent and reverend lord Cardinals [names follow – see below for identifications] were present' ('Die sabathi 16. Februarii 1675. Habita fuit Congregatio Concilii Tridentini in Palatio Apostolico Quirinali in qua interfuerunt eminentissimi et reverendissimi domini cardinales Pius, Carrafa, Ninius, Portocarrero, de Carpineo, S.ti Sixti Praef.', Foelix Rospiliosus, Facchenettus, et Albitius.') (ASV Congr. Concilii Libri Decret. 29, fo. 11r-v). On the basis of P. Gauchat, *Hierarchia Catholica Medii et Recentioris Aevi*, vol. 4, and Ritzler and Sefrin, *Hierachia Catholica Medii et Recentioris Aevi*, vol. 5, they can be identified as the following cardinals: Carolus Pius de Sabaudia (Pio di Savoia): Gauchat, p. 31, no. 38; Carolus Carafa/Caraffa: Gauchat, p. 34, no. 22; Iacobus Philippus Nin(i)us (Nini): Gauchat, p. 35, no. 30; Ludovicus Emmanuel Fernández de Portocarrero: Ritzler and Sefrin, pp. 4–5, no. 5; Gaspar Carpineus seu de Carpineo (Carpegna): Ritzler and Sefrin, p. 7, no. 3 (probably, rather than Uldericus Carpineus al. de Carpinea (di Carpegna): Gauchat, p. 24, no. 41); 'Vincentius Maria Ursinus de Gravina (Orsini)...tt. S. Sixti 16 Maii 1672': Ritzler and Sefrin, p. 7, no. 5; Felix Rospilios(i)us (Rospigliosi): Ritzler and Sefrin, p. 8, no. 9; Caesar Fachinettus (Facchinetti): Gauchat, p. 25, no. 62; Franciscus Albitius (Albizzi): Gauchat, p. 31, no. 36.
[70] See Appendix, Doc. 4.
[71] Aristotle, *Nicomachean Ethics*, 2.2, Bekker 1104a; *The Complete Works of Aristotle*, ed. Barnes, vol. 2, p. 1744: see above, p. 181.

impotence had not been proved (and when Peauger hoped to remarry)? Would Peauger's neighbours in Lisieux begin to understand the subtleties of non-consummation theology?

The subtleties were, however, set out with clarity for the benefit of the committee, which can have been left with no doubt that there was no absolute value at stake and that it was up to them to decide whether to stick to the formal law or to be swayed by the sad substantive circumstances of the case. For together with the legal and administrative documents the dossier contains a theoretical essay on the values, rules and considerations justifying suspension of the rules: not the kind of thing one usually finds in an archival series – but then the archive of the Congregation of the Council is no ordinary archive. It is not clear in the present state of research on the archive who wrote the memorandum. It looks like an expert opinion, but whether it was produced 'in house', or at the request of the Congregation, or on behalf of the petitioner, is unclear to me. The document is certainly relevant enough to the core arguments of this book. It begins by recapitulating the facts of the case and then proceeds as if addressing a scholastic 'quaestio', starting with arguments which would seem to show that the marriage between Nicolas Peauger and Catharine Doisnel could not be dissolved.

Powerful linked arguments are advanced. Indissolubility is of the essence of marriage. The Pope cannot change the essence of marriage. But there can be a true marriage even without consummation.

To solve the problem thus presented, the author of the memorandum breaks it up into smaller questions – a classic technique of scholasticism, still the most powerful intellectual tool in the service of Catholic doctrine and law a century and a half after the Reformation. There are five:

1. From what does marriage derive its indissolubility?
2. Can a genuine but unconsummated marriage be dissolved by the Pope?
3. In what kinds of cases can this be done?
4. Can it be done in cases which are not explicitly stated in the law (*expressa in iure*)?
5. Is this particular case such as to justify dissolving the marriage, so that Nicolas can remarry even without Catharine's consent?

In answer to the first, he argues that indissolubility derives not from marriage's sacramentality but by reason of its signification: for a ratified marriage signifies only the union between Christ and the soul in a state of grace, whereas a consummated marriage signifies the indissoluble union of Christ and the Church through the mystery of the Incarnation. In the middle of a legal dossier, we meet head on the theme that had come to penetrate and saturate marriage doctrine by the end of the Middle Ages, no mere image or symbol or metaphor but a value and conviction with far-reaching practical consequences.[72]

So on to the second question. The link between indissolubility and consummation established, the memorandum is able to develop reasons why the Pope can dissolve a marriage that is ratified but not consummated. There is the logic of the symbolism: the soul's union with Christ through grace can be dissolved by mortal sin, so the corresponding union between man and wife can also be dissolved for a legitimate reason; for just as the indissolubility of Christ's marriage to the Church is implied by his taking flesh, so too the dissolubility of a marriage arises from the absence of consummation. Then again, the Pope can dispense people from solemn vows, which are made to God, whereas marriage is merely between humans. The fact that marriage is a sacrament, while a vow is not, is irrelevant because indissolubility does not derive from marriage's sacramentality. (One notes the typical scholastic nimbleness in disposing of secondary objections with a rapid sidestroke.) Finally, there are plenty of precedents for papal dispensations from unconsummated marriages.

The third question, about the kinds of cases which admit of this drastic dispensation, is dealt with quite succinctly. (References to the most important canon law compilation[73] and to the standard work on marriage by the Jesuit Thomas Sanchez would have enabled the reader to pursue the matter further.) There are two categories: entry by one partner into a religious order, and 'other just causes'.

The relation between different kinds of rationality is encapsulated in the reply to the fourth question, though the assumptions are partly implicit. Underlying thoughts seem to be these. The indissolubility of an unconsummated marriage is not divine law but positive law made by the Church.[74] The Pope has the power to make positive law about marriage, even to the point of creating new man-made impediments which would invalidate marriages subsequently contracted in defiance of them. Here we seem to be in the realm of formal legality. Insofar as the law of marriage is created by the positive law of the Church, it admits of dispensation by the Pope.

---

[72] d'Avray, *Medieval Marriage*, ch. 4 *passim*.

[73] Friedberg, *Corpus Iuris Canonici*: see Appendix, Doc. 3 for references.

[74] See Appendix for the canon law sources. A key passage in the decretals he cites would seem to be: 'Indeed, the Lord's statement in the Gospel that a man is not allowed to send away his wife except on account of fornication should be understood according to the interpretation of the sacred text to apply to those whose marriage has been consummated by the union of the flesh' ('Sane, quod Dominus in evangelio dicit, non licere viro, nisi ob causam fornicationis, uxorem suam dimittere, intelligendum est secundum interpretationem sacri eloquii de his, quorum matrimonium carnali copula est consummatum') (X. 3.32.7; Friedberg, *Corpus Iuris Canonici*, vol. 2, p. 581).

That established, it is not difficult to show in answer to the fifth question that this particular case warrants the dispensation. The crime is atrocious and there could be no graver reason for a husband to feel hatred. The flight of a wife who will never return, and who is dead morally speaking because of the secular court's sentence, makes procreation impossible just as physical impotence would.[75] Nicolas has just cause and the Pope has the power so Catharine does not have to consent. Here we have substantive or material rationality overriding formal legality because of the circumstances of the case and the nature of the value framework. Though the committee in the end decided otherwise, their value rationality had not presented them with that decision as a categorical imperative, so they had been left with instrumental calculation.

Conclusion

In this still disturbing case the argument of the book is embodied in microcosm. The Congregation of the Council was there to implement a system of convictions where marriage was connected metonymically and by symbolism with the whole idea of the Church and its union with Christ. Where unconsummated marriages were concerned, no absolute rule dictated how this value system be applied to each case. The field was open for instrumental reasoning, and a choice between staying within the formal legality that normally governed valid but unconsummated marriages, and suspending it in an act of substantive justice. In this case the choice was for legal formality.

[75] A loose paraphrase, but the Latin is not meant to be taken literally here.

Conclusions

The apparently antithetical theories of a universal rationality and of multiple specific rationalities can be brought together within the framework of Weber's value rationality/instrumental rationality distinction. Instrumental rationality is defined here simply as the matching of causes and consequences on a practical and logical level – putting two and two together when values do not deliver definitive answers. Values can shape it: and this is not simply because values are ends or objectives that instrumental rationality serves. Values can also take the form of premises and of side-constraints.

Religious values and other values can be studied together: they seem to work in the same way, insofar as both are resistant to attack on any one front without thereby losing their rational character. This is because the different parts of value systems are mutually supporting, so that the prior probability of any one being right is greatly enhanced by its connection with all the others. Thus an attack on one element flies in the face of antecedent probability – so far as the people whose value is attacked are concerned. The phenomenology of belief in reincarnation is in this respect much the same as that of belief in human rights. Immunity to refutation turns out to be (paradoxically enough) a feature shared by some Enlightenment thought and by Azande magic – it is a very general characteristic of conviction systems. The durability of values is further secured by their concrete character, deriving from experiences or at least from strong mental images. Again this is true of both religious values as generally understood and of, say, patriotic convictions.

Nevertheless, values and value systems advance and retreat, by recruiting well or failing to, and even come and go altogether. Charismatic leaders can create or at least launch new values: Muhammad, Lenin. Experiences, individual and collective, can be crucial in the crystallisation of values and convictions: the idea of racial equality in the second half of the twentieth century gaining strength by reaction against the Holocaust. Oral cultures may modify values more easily because they have not been fixed in texts: thus the religions of non-literate African societies put up less resistance to Christianity and Islam than did (for example) Confucianism and Buddhism in China. Changes in values are more likely to occur when independent developments converge towards a single point, as nineteenth-century biblical criticism and science seemed to do in undermining Christianity. Sometimes changes are deceptive, because people may shop around for the church or movement that most closely embodies values that they hold from start to finish – as a biblical fundamentalist may change churches as he looks for a preacher who understands the Bible as she or he does. On a charitable view, there was an underlying continuity behind Winston Churchill's changes of political party. Sometimes value systems may themselves generate crises of conviction, even without attacks from outside: the Catholic Apostolic Church being an extreme case. Then the system may or may not develop answers to the problems that it has, so to speak, posed to itself.

Without reducing the 'dynamics' to a single formula, it was suggested that the 'symbiosis' of values and instrumental rationality should never be far from the attention of historians and social scientists. The relationship is reciprocal. Systems of values and convictions have to use instrumental technique to attract followers and to retain those already committed – or at least, since real commitment can be very durable, to retain the children of the committed. Hence rituals, processions and pledges of allegiance to the Flag. So far, so extrinsic: but our ideal-type of value rationality included the concreteness of the images which hold convictions in the mind, and those concrete and vivid convictions may have been saved from abstraction and a merely verbal, notional and propositional existence by instrumental techniques such as those just listed.

The instrumental/value rationality distinction cuts across the substantive/formal rationality distinction. The tendency in the scholarly literature to equate formal rationality with instrumental rationality and substantive rationality with value rationality is potentially a source of great confusion, sufficient to rule out these identifications from the set of useful conceptual schemes. On the one hand, substantive rationality need not have anything to do with values: as when formal rules for making fair appointments or allocating contracts are ignored for reasons of personal or power-political advantage. On the other hand, formal rationality commonly works within a value framework, even if the values are as general as even-handedness and consistency. Formal legality can indeed be a tool of value systems that go far beyond that, as was the case with the formal procedures and rules of the Congregation of the Council, which served the values embodied in the

Council of Trent. Cases decided by the Congregation were given a good deal of space in the body of the book as a reminder that formal rationality, defined in any useful way, has no necessary association with modernity or secularisation.

The symbiosis of value rationality and legal formality extends to a symbiosis of the latter and substantive rationality. 'Interface values' regulate the boundary between formal rules and considerations that are extrinsic to them but which may sometimes override them. Value systems allow this kind of deviation from strict legal formality in varying degrees, from mass pardons by Chinese emperors to the blind eye turned to minor infractions of the speed limit. Formally legal systems can even embody formal rules for suspending the rules, though this is not common in modern common law or Roman law areas. Such value-driven rules for suspending the rules were, however, integral to the workings of the Congregation of the Council, which emerges as an institution hard to parallel in Western or even world history.

Weber's comparative Sociology or History – for in his synthesis the difference narrows to a vanishing point – always had the double agenda of bringing out generalities and identifying particularities. Thus he generalises that the development of the money economy is a precondition for the modern bureaucratic office ('Amt'), but then reels off a list of the six quantitatively greatest examples of bureaucracy – 'Burökratismus' – in world history (Egypt in the age of the new kingdom, the Roman empire after Diocletian, the Roman Catholic Church, classical China, the modern European state, and the great capitalist firm), and points out that under the first four of them the payment of officials in kind rather than money was a significant element of the system, and that for particular reasons the historical prototype of bureaucracies, New Kingdom Egypt, was at the same time one of the most extraordinary examples in world history of a natural economy.[1] Because he looked so hard for common patterns in different societies he was well placed to recognise developments that were unusual or unique in world history. The present investigation has concentrated on aspects of rationalities that transcend particular societies, but one unusual body above has nevertheless commanded attention: the Congregation of the Council, established in the sixteenth century and lasting into the twentieth. Weber can have known little of this remarkable institution, though (as noted above) his sure instinct led him to comment on 'the rational "institutional" character of the Catholic Church, with which nothing comparable can be found

---

[1] Weber, *Wirtschaft und Gesellschaft*, vol. 2, p. 556.

188 Rationalities in History

in world history'.[2] In the final chapter the intimate connection between the different rationalities distinguished in this study were analysed via a case brought before the Congregation in the later seventeenth century. Weber's very general ideal-types thus elucidate very specific and individual historical situations and events.

[2] 'des rationalen "Anstalts"-Charakters der katholischen Kirche, der sonst sich nirgends wiederfindet'. *Ibid.*, vol. 2, pp. 480–1.

Appendix: rationalities in a case before the Congregation of the Council

In Chapters 5 and 6 the Congregation of the Council had a prominent place as exemplifying the interplay of different kinds of rationality. Its archive is rich and the *Positiones* fondo in particular has been very little explored. A bibliography is supplied at the end of the appendix: though too long for a footnote, it is tiny in relation to the importance of the Congregation's archive, which is now part of the Archivio Segreto Vaticano.

The following documents are explained and analysed at the end of Chapter 6. In them we see a value rationality which provides guidelines for a difficult and distressing case, without imposing a decision either way, the dilemma being whether to adhere to the formal law or suspend it in this particular case. The reasoning is a classic illustration of how convictions shape instrumental rationality.

DOC. 1

Archivio Segreto Vaticano, Congr. Conc. Positiones (carte sciolte) 4 (not foliated)

Beatissime Pater

Exponitur humiliter S.V. pro parte devoti illius oratoris Nicolai Peauger laici Lexoviensis diocesis ex | loco de Bertonville oriundi quod alias ipse orator tunc in vicesimo circiter sue etatis anno ac sub | potestate patris sui nunc adhuc viventis constituti ut voluntati eiusdem patris satisfaceret matrimonium | cum quadam Catharina Doisnel muliere illarum partium filia naturali [1]Nicolai Doisnel laici | dicte diocesis, qua secundo dictus Nicolaus prius incestuose abusus fuerat, in facie ecclesie, servatis | alias servandis, contraxit, quod quidem matrimonium dicta Catharina gratum non habens, virum aversata, | licet cum ipso in domo eiusdem secundo dicti Nicolai per triduum [2]remasisset, illud nunquam consummari permisit, | prout ipsa coram fide dignis testibus pluries publicavit, sed eum e

---

[1] Nicolai] *MS.* Nicolai e *followed by what seem to be deleted letters: perhaps read:* Nicolai etiam.
[2] remasisset] *sic: read* remansisset.

dicta domo post tres dies eiici procuravit, | et lapsis septem circiter
mensibus dicta Catharina prolem ex dicti Nicolai patris sui operibus
incestuose | procreatam peperit, ac postmodum plures alios liberos edidit,
de cuius incestus gravitate et horrore | competens iudex illarum partium
admonitus, processu desuper fabricato ac ex illo criminis veritate | et
atrocitate comperta, diffinitiva sententia secundo dictum Nicolaum et
[3]Catrarinam eius filiam predictam | ab igne comburendos et eorum
cineres ad ventum proiiciendos damnavit, sed ipsi ad huiusmodi sup-
plicium | evitandum extra Regnum Francie [4]in fugam versi sunt. Cum
autem dictus orator qui nunc in xxxvi° | circiter sue etatis anno consti-
tutus existit ac matrimonium huiusmodi nunquam consummavit, quam-
primum | premissorum conscius fuerit dictum matrimonium ratum nec
gratum habuerit, sed semper ab eo | reclamaverit ac ipse cum quadam alia
muliere nullo alias iure sibi prohibito matrimonialiter copulari | desideret,
supplicat igitur humiliter S.V. dictus orator quatenus episcopo Lexoviensi
sive eius officiali qui vocatis qui | fuerint evocandi si inquisita super pre-
missis diligentius veritate rem ipsam ita esse repererit | prout superius
enarratur, dictum oratorem matrimonio huiusmodi non teneri sed cum
aliqua alia muliere | nullo alias sibi iure prohibita matrimonium contra-
here illudque in facie ecclesie solemnizare ac | in eo postmodum remanere
libere et licite [5]valeat prolemque [6]suscipiendam exinde legitimam esse
declaret | prout de iure fuerit declarandum committere et mandare digne-
mini de gratia speciali non obstantibus premissis | ac constitutionibus et
ordinibus apostolicis ceterisque contrariis quibuscumque cum clausulis
opportunis.

DOC. 2

ASV Congr. Conc. Positiones (carte sciolte) 4 (not foliated)[7]
    Gaspardus de Nossy presbiter, Licentiatus | utriusque Iuris, canonicus
magnus cathedralis | ecclesiae Lexoviensis archidiaconus, nec non Iudex |
ordinarius et officialis dictae dioecesis Lexoviensis, | notum facimus
et testamur sanctissimo domino | nostro papae Clementi decimo rev-
erendissimo | domino eius vicecancellario aut alteri ad id | potestatem
habenti Nicolaum Peauger de | parrochia de Batonville et Catharinam
Doisnel | filiam naturalem Nicolai utrosque dictae | dioecesis inter se
matrimonium legitime | contraxisse, quod quidem ob dictae mulieris |

---

[3] Catrarinam] *sic MS, with otiose stroke on second* r.   [4] in] *a deletion follows in MS.*
[5] valeat] *sic, though* valere *would fit the syntax better.*   [6] suscipiendam] suscipiend' *MS.*
[7] Here I have to thank Prof. Marc Smith of the École des chartes for checking my tran-
scription of this document (which is in a script unfamiliar to me), and correcting more
errors than I would care to mention.

repugnantiam inter partes non potuit consommari, | nihilominus tamen praedicta Catharina | plurimos filios et filias de coitu incestuoso | praedicti Nicolai patris sui peperit et in lucem | condidit; cuius incesti gravitate et horrore iudex | regius ita commotus est ut praedictos | patrem et filiam ab igne comburendos et | eorum cineribus ad ventum proiiciendos damnaverit. | Haec autem sententia propter praedictorum Doismel [*sic*] | fugam et absentiam suum non potuit sortiri | effectum, ita ut si cum praedicto Peauger super | dissolutione et nullitate praedicti matrimonii | per sanctitatem domini nostri papae iudicetur, eo | fine ut aliam possit ducere coniugem, nullus | inde pravus exitus aut scandalum oriri possit. | Testamurque praeterea eundem Peauger quae ad sui | vitam necessaria sunt nisi cum studio, industria | et labore sibi comparare non posse. In quorum | fidem praesentibus litteris manu nostra et | magistri Francisci Armenoult ordinarii scribae | nostri subsignatis sigillum dicti episcopatus | Lexoviensis duximus apponendum die sexta Augusti | anni domini millesimi sexcentesimi septuagesimi quarti. |

De Nossy Armenoult

DOC. 3

ASV Congr. Conc. Positiones (carte sciolte) 4 (not foliated)

Nicolaus Peauger orator laicus Lexoviensis diocesis alias in vigesimo suae[8] | etatis anno, matrimonium per verba de presenti cum Catharina | Doisnel canonice contraxit et post tridui cohabitationem, illo (ut | ipsa Catharina publicavit) minime consummato, ab illius consortio | eiectus fuit, quia dicta Catharina post aliquot menses prolem operibus | sui patris procreatam peperit, et deinde plures alios liberos ex | eodem incestuoso concubitu edidit, et iudicis competentis sententiam | qua pater et filia ad ignis supplicium damnati fuerant, fuga | extra regnum Francie arrepta, evasit, orator iusto tanti criminis | horrore commotus, ac spe recuperandae uxoris, et fine matrimonii | perpetuo privatus, supplicat committi ordinario, qui constito de | narratis et vocatis vocandis matrimonium predictum dissolvat, et | cum oratore dispenset, ut cum alia muliere nullo iure prohibita | contrahere possit. |

Quamvis propositus casus cuiusvis dispensationis causa sufficiens | videatur, nihilominus, quia matrimonii essentia in unione | indissolubili consistit, D. Tho. 4. d. 27. q. 1 art. 2 questiunc. 1 | ad 2,[9] Victoria Sum. de

---

[8] Here and below 'e caudata' rendered as 'ae'.

[9] Thomas Aquinas, *In 4 Sententiarum*, Dist. 27, q. 1, a. 2: *S. Tommaso d'Aquino: Commento alle Sentenze di Pietro Lombardo*, 232: possibly an error, as Dist. 27, q.1 a.1, Solutio II, *S. Tommaso d'Aquino: Commento*, p. 228 might be thought a better fit.

matrim. q. 44 art. 3. concl. 1,[10] et Summus | Pontifex essentiam auferre nequit, Sanch. De matrim. Lib. 2 De | essentia et consens. matrim. disp. 14. n. 1.,[11] et matrimonium ratum | est verum matrimonium, idem ibidem disp. 1. n. 4:[12] |

pro maiori presentis petitionis enodatione examinandum est, 1° a quo | proveniat indissolubilitas matrimonii; 2° an matrimonium | ratum possit dissolvi a papa; 3° in quibus casibus possit | dissolvi a papa; 4° utrum possit dissolvi in casibus non expres|sis in Iure, ac denique, utrum casus adductus sit causa sufficiens | dissolutionis matrimonii rati, ita ut Nicolaus matrimonium cum | alia muliere etiam invita seu inaudita Catharina contrahere | possit. |

Et quo ad primum, indissolubilitas matrimonii non provenit ex [*verso folio*] ratione sacramenti, cum, ut supra dixi, matrimonium ratum sit vere | sacramentum, et a consummato differat tantum accidentaliter. | Idem Sanch. ibi. Disp. 14. n. 1.[13] Sed dicta indissolubilitas provenit | ex ratione significationis per quam inter ratum et consummatum | infertur differentia, cum ratum significet unionem dissolubilem | Christi cum anima existente in gratia; consummatum vero | indissolubilem unionem Christi cum [14]Ecclesia per incarnationis | mysterium. Idem Sanch. ibi disp. 13. n. 1.[15] |

Ex quo resultat resolutio secundi Dubii, videlicet quod matrimonium ratum | potest dissolvi a papa, nam sicuti unio Christi cum anima | existenti in gratia est dissolubilis per peccatum lethale, ita | unio maritalis in hoc statu sacramenti est quoque dissolubilis | ex causa legitima ante con-summationem, quia sicut indissolu|bilitas Christi ab Ecclesia infertur ab

---

[10] This reference does not match the numbering systems in relevant published works of Francisco de Victoria [or Vittoria]: I have looked at the *Summa Sacramentorum Ecclesiae ex doctrina Francisci a Victoria... cui adiecimus conclusiones in singulis quaestionibus* (Venice, 1586) [British Library call number 3832 a.34], and *Summa Sacramentorum* [etc.] *per... Thomam a Chaues illius discipulum... Huic ex tertia Authoris recognitione, nunc denuo multo plures quam antea quaestiones accesserunt* (Salamanca, 1570) [British Library call number Cup. 408.nn.14], and *Relectiones Theologicae* [etc.] (Lyons, 1587) [British Library call number 4374.aaa.18]. The Congregatio document may, however, refer to his commentary on the *Summa Theologica* of Thomas Aquinas. Apparently only the *Secunda Secundae* commentary has been published: see *Comentarios a la Secunda secundae de Santo Tomás*, ed. V. Beltrán de Heredia; Beltrán de Heredia, *Los Manuscritos del Maestro Fray Francisco de Vitoria*; and Hurter, *Nomenclator Litterarius Theologiae Catholicae*, vol. 2 (1906), cols. 1367–70, at 1370: 'Inedita reliquit commentaria in summam s. Thomae'. The content of Supplementum q. 44 a. 3, Respondeo section would seem to fit: see *Sancti Thomae Aquinatis... opera omnia, iussu... Leonis XIII P. M. edita*, vol. 12, p. 86.

[11] Thomas Sanchez, *De sancto matrimonii sacramento disputationum tomi tres*, i, Lib. 2. Disputatio 14.1; Avignon, 1689 edn, BL call number 1240.k.1, p. 132.

[12] *Ibid.*, Disputatio 1.4, p. 119 [by the 4 in margin, sentence beginning 'Ergo matrimonii consummatio'].

[13] *Ibid.*, Disputatio 14.1, p. 132.   [14] Ecclesia] Eeclesia *MS*.

[15] Sanchez, *Disp.*, i, Lib. 2. Disputatio 13.1, p. 130.

assumptione carnis, ita | matrimonii rati dissolubilitas oritur ex defectu consummationis. | 2° probatur quia Papa potest dispensare in Voto solemni re|ligionis, ergo et in matrimonio rato; nam Votum solemne | religionis est fortius vinculum cum dissolvat matrimonium | ratum, et utrobique sit traditio imo minor in matrimonio in | quo fit soli homini, in Voto autem Deo et homini Sanch. disp. | 14. n. 2,[16] nec obstat disparitas quod matrimonium ratum | sit sacramentum, Votum autem nequaquam, nam, ut supra | dixi, indissolubilitas matrimonii non provenit ex ratione sa|cramenti, sed ex ratione significationis per quam infertur | dissolubilitas in rato, et indissolubilitas in consummato. |

3° probatur ab exemplis, quia multi summi pontifices super | huiusmodi matrimonio rato dispensarunt, ut refert idem Sanch. dicta | disp. 14 n. 2.[17] cum multis quos ibi citat. |

Ad tertium dubium: matrimonium ratum potest dissolvi per religionis | ingressum cap. 2[18] et cap. Ex publico De convers. coniug.,[19] et propter | alias iustas causas Sanch. ibidem. Disp. 16 n. i,[20] inter quas [21]adducit [new folio] adducit Odium, ibi n. 4[22] et impotentiam n. 6.[23] |

4[um] Certum est videlicet quod matrimonium ratum possit dissolvi a papa | in casibus non expressis in iure, quia matrimonium ratum | sortitur naturam ex constitutione Ecclesiae, ut declarant [24]D. D. in | dicto capitulo Ex publico De convers. coniug.,[25] in cap. Gaudemus,[26] et in | cap. 4. De divortiis,[27] cum constet ex multis impedimentis dirimen | tibus que per constitutiones SS. pontificum inducta sunt, ex | quo concluditur quod papa in matrimonio rato potest statuere | quod placet et inducere novum impedimentum, Fagnan. in 4 | lib. Decretal. De clandest. despons. c. Quod nobis[28] n. 23 et 24.[29] | – quae conclusio est de fide ex Concil. Trid. Sess. 24. de matrim. | can. 4.[30]|

[16] Ibid., 2. Disputatio 14. 2, p. 133.   [17] Ibid.
[18] X.3.32.2 (Friedberg, Corpus Iuris Canonici, vol. 2, p. 579).
[19] X.3.32.7 (Friedberg, Corpus, vol. 2, pp. 580–1).
[20] Sanchez, Disp., i, Lib. 2. Disputatio 16.1, p. 136.
[21] adducit] lower margin, as catchword.
[22] Sanchez, Disp., i, Lib. 2. Disputatio 16.4, p. 136.
[23] Ibid., Disputatio 16.6, pp. 136–7.
[24] D.D.].
[25] X.3.32.7 (Friedberg, Corpus, ii, 580–81).
[26] Probably X.3.32.19 (Friedberg, Corpus, ii. 586), rather than X.4.19.8 (Friedberg, Corpus, 723–4).
[27] X.4.19.4 (Friedberg, Corpus, ii, 721).
[28] X.4.3.2 (Friedberg, Corpus, ii, 679).
[29] Prosper Fagnanus, P. F. Commentaria (super quinque libros Decretalium), 3 pts. (Rome, 1661) [British Library call number RB.31.C.276: note that at least in this copy the commentary on book 4 of the Decretals is bound in vol. 1], 'in IV. Librum Decretal., De Clandest. desponsat. c. Quod nobis' marginal numbers 23 and 24, p. 29.
[30] Tanner, Alberigo, et al., Decrees of the Ecumenical Councils, vol. 2, p. 757.

Quibus probatis certo concluditur allegatam causam esse sufficientem |
pro dissolutione matrimonii inter Nicolaum et Catharinam, cum | non
possit dari causa gravior odii in viro, quam atrocitas tanti | criminis, nul-
laque maior impotentia quam uxoris numquam | [31]rediturae, et propter
dictam sententiam moraliter mortuae | fuga, propter quas omnino cessat
matrimonii finis, scilicet | procreatio prolis. |

Nec ad hoc requiritur consensus Catharine quia ipsius repugnantia
| nequit impedire pontificis potestatem, ne consulat Nicolao ha|benti
iustam dissolvendi causam et petenti Dispensationem. – |

Gozadinus Cons. 2. n.14. Ant. Gabr. to. 2 com. lib. 11(?), verbo *matrimonium*. Metina(?) lib. 5 de Sacr. hominum contin. 89.[32]

Quare etc

Among other notes on the back of the dossier is the date 'Die 16 Feb.
1675'.

DOC. 4

ASV Congr. Concilii Libri Decret. 29, fol. 11^{r-v}. At head of both pages
is written '16 Februarii 1675'.

In left-hand margin: c. 1. Ses. 24 | De Reformatione Matrimonii

Lexovien. Dispensationis. Nicolaus [33]Pauger orator laicus | alias in
vigesimo suae aetatis anno matrimonium per | verba de presenti cum
Catherina Doisnel canonice contraxit | propter cuius repugnantiam con-
sumatum non fuit, licet | orator per tres dies in illius domo remansisset,
ut ipsa | Catharina publicavit. Oratore igitur e domo eiecto Catharina
| inde ad septem menses filium et successive plures | alios ex incestu
proprii genitoris peperit, ex qua enor|mitate per iudicem ad ignis suppli-
cium pater et filia | damnati fuere, sed, cum fugam arripuissent, poenam
| evasere. Exinde orator ab illa semper abhorruit, | et extra spem coniugii
nunc in 36. aetatis anno supplex | instat apud Sanctissimum pro com-
missione ad ordinarium | ut constito sibi de narratis, et vocatis vocandis,
matri|monium predictum dissolvat et cum oratore dispenset ut | cum alia
muliere contrahere possit. |

Instantiam huiusmodi Sanctitas sua ad hanc Sacram Congregationem
remisit | et pro facti comprobatione procurator exhibuit fidem officialis
| Lexoviensis qui de praemissis testatur et subdit ex | tali dispensatione
nullum pravum exitum aut scandalum [*fol. 11^v*] oriri posse. Quibus stan-
tibus quaeritur |

---

[31] rediture] *preceded by* reddit (?), *deleted.*
[32] I have failed to identify these last three writers and their works.
[33] Pauger] *sic for* Peauger.

An petita commissio sit signanda?|
Sacra Congregatio Concilii respondit negative.

BIBLIOGRAPHY ON THE CONGREGATION
OF THE COUNCIL

For a survey of its whole history up to and including its transmutation
into the 'Congregazione per il Clero' see N. Del Re, *La Curia Romana:
Lineamenti storico-giuridici*, 4th edn (Vatican City, 1998), 161–73. Cf. also
R. Parayre, *La Sacrée Congregation du Concile: Son histoire – sa procédure –
son autorité* (Paris, 1897); N. Hilling, *Procedure at the Roman Curia:
A Concise and Practical Handbook* (New York, 1907), 61–8, 177–82;
G. Le Bras and J. Gaudemet (eds.), *Histoire du droit et des institutions de
l'Église en Occident*, vol. 15/1: C. Lefebvre, M. Pacaut and L. Chevailler,
*L'Époque moderne 1563–1789: Les sources du droit et la seconde centralisation
romaine* (Paris, 1976), 160–2; 'Prof. Dr. Sägmüller' [*sic*], 'Die Geschichte
der Congregatio Concilii vor dem Motu-proprio "Alias nos nonullas"
vom 2. August 1564', *Archiv für katholisches Kirchenrecht*, 80/3rd ser.,
4 (1900), 3–17; *La Sacra Congregazione del Concilio: Quarto centenario
dalla fondazione (1564–1964)* (Vatican City, 1989). The archive has not
been used much by historians of the Counter-Reformation Church. Cf.
G. Zarri, 'Il matrimonio tridentino', in P. Prodi and W. Reinhard (eds), *Il
Concilio di Trento e il moderno* (Annali dall'Istituto storico italo-germanico,
45; Bologna, 1996), 437–83, at 465 n. 85. She herself makes use of a
three-volume manuscript synopsis of decisions of the Congregation of
the Council, compiled in the eighteenth century: BUB [Bibliotheca Uni-
versitaria Bologna] 537: see *ibid.*, 465–6, 470, 477–8. Pioneering work
has been done by A. J. Schutte: see 'La Congregazione del Concilio e
lo scioglimento dei voti religiosi: Rapporti tra fratelli e sorelle', *Rivista
storica italiana*, 118 (2006), 51–79. A book is to follow. The archive is one
of the sources for the important thesis of Benedetta Albani, 'Sposarsi nel
Nuovo Mondo: Politica, dottrina et pratiche della concessione di dispense
matrimoniali tra la Nuova Spagna e la Santa Sede (1585–1670)' (Uni-
versità degli Studi di Roma 'Tor Vergata', Facoltà di Lettere e Filosofia:
Dottorato in 'Storia politica e sociale dell'Europa Moderna e Contem-
poranea', XXI ciclo; Anno Accademico, 2008–9), notably section II.4.1.
John Noonan and his then research assistant Richard Helmholz managed
to consult the archive, *before* it was deposited in the Vatican Archives, for
Noonan's *Power to Dissolve: Lawyers and Marriages in the Courts of the
Roman Curia* (Cambridge, Mass., 1972).

For collections of the Congregation's decisions see notably *Novae Declarationes Congregationis S.R.E. Cardinalium ad Decreta Sacros. Concil.*

Tridentini, iisdem Declarationibus conserta (Lyons, 1633) [British Library call no. 1600/181]; A. [Aemilius = Emil] L. Richter and F. von Schulte, *Canones et decreta Concilii Tridentini ex editione Romana A. MDCC-CXXXIV. repetiti. Accedunt S. Congr. Card. Conc. Trid. interpretum declarationes ac resolutiones ex ipso resolutionum thesauro, bullario romano et Benedicti XIV. S. P. operibus...* (Leipzig, 1853); J. F. Zamboni, *Collectio declarationum Sacrae Congregationis Cardinalium Sacri Concilii Tridentini interpretum*, 8 vols. (Vienna, 1812–16), and 4 vols. (Arras, 1860–8) (on the chronological scope of Zamboni's work, see *ibid.*, pp. xlvii and xlviii); S. Pallottini, *Collectio Omnium Conclusionum et resolutionum quae in causis propositis apud Sacram Congregationem Cardinalium S. Concilii Tridentini Interpretum Prodierunt ab eius Institutione anno MDLXIV ad annum MCCCCLX*, 17 vols. (1868–93). Cf. also S. Tromp, 'De duabus editionibus Concilii Tridentini: Commentario vario et declarationibus Cardinalium Concilii Interpretum desumptis e bibliothecis Prosperi Farinacci et Roberti Card. Bellarmini illustratis', *Gregorianum*, 38 (1957), 51–96, and Tromp, 'De manuscriptis acta et declarationes antiquas S. Congregationis Con. Trid. continentibus', *Gregorianum*, 39 (1958), 93–129; for letters sent by the Congregation early in its history see *J. Pogiani... Epistolae et Orationes... Accessere Cardinalium Tridentini interpretum nomine scriptae annis 1564–1568*, ed. G. Lagomarsini [= Ieronymus Lagomarsinius], 4 vols. (Rome, 1762), vol. 1, pp. 335–496, on which edition see Tromp, 'De manuscriptis', *Gregorianum*, 39 (1958), 104–5.

Bibliography

Ainslie, G., *Breakdown of Will* (Cambridge, 2001).

Aitken, R., 'Formal Practice: Buddhist or Christian', *Buddhist–Christian Studies*, 22 (2002), 63–76.

Althoff, G., 'Zur Bedeutung symbolischer Kommunikation für das Verständnis des Mittelalters', *Frühmittelalterliche Studien*, 31 (1997), 370–89.

Anderson, E., *Value in Ethics and Economics* (Cambridge, Mass., 1993).

Antoun, R. J., *Muslim Preacher in the Modern World: A Jordanian Case Study in Comparative Perspective* (Princeton, 1989).

Aquinas, *see* Thomas Aquinas.

Ariely, D., *Predictably Irrational: The Hidden Forces that Shape Our Decisions* (New York, 2008).

Aristotle, *The Complete Works of Aristotle*, ed. J. Barnes, 2 vols. (Princeton, 1984). *Nicomachean Ethics*, trans. H. Rackham (Cambridge, Mass., 1982).

Arnold, J. H., *Belief and Unbelief in Medieval Europe* (London, 2005).

Atiyah, P. S., and Summers, R. S., *Form and Substance in Anglo-American Law: A Comparative Study of Legal Reasoning, Legal Theory, and Legal Institutions* (Oxford, 1987).

Austin-Broos, D., 'The Anthropology of Conversion: An Introduction', in A. Buckser and S. D. Glazier (eds.), *The Anthropology of Religious Conversion* (Lanham, Md., 2003), 1–12.

Bailey, G., and Mabbett, I., *The Sociology of Early Buddhism* (Cambridge, 2003).

Baker, J. H., *An Introduction to English Legal History*, 4th edn (Bath, 2002).

Bangen, J. H., *Die Römische Curie, ihre gegenwärtige Zusammensetzung und ihr Geschäftsgang, nach mehrjähriger eigener Anschauung dargestellt* (Münster, 1854).

Barbalet, J., *Weber, Passion and Profits: 'The Protestant Ethic and the Spirit of Capitalism' in Context* (Cambridge, 2008).

Bartlett, R., 'Reflections on Paganism and Christianity in Medieval Europe', *Proceedings of the British Academy: 1998 Lectures and Memoirs*, 101 (1999), 55–76.

Bataillon, L.-J., *La Prédication au XIIIe siècle en France et Italie: Études et documents* (Aldershot, 1993).

Becker, G. S., *Accounting for Tastes* (Cambridge, Mass., 1996).

Beckford, J. A., *Social Theory and Religion* (Cambridge, 2003).

Beltrán de Heredia, V., *Los Manuscritos del Maestro Fray Francisco de Vitoria . . . Estudio crítico de introducción a sus Lecturas y Relecciones* (Biblioteca de Teólogos Espanoles, 2–6; Madrid, 1928).

Berend, N. (ed.), *Christianization and the Rise of Christian Monarchy: Scandinavia, Central Europe and Rus' c. 900–1200* (Cambridge, 2007).

Berg, A. van den, review of I. Wallerstein, *The End of the World as We Know It: Social Science for the Twenty-First Century*, in *Canadian Journal of Sociology*, 29 (2004), 324–8.

Berger, A., *Encyclopedic Dictionary of Roman Law* (Transactions of the American Philosophical Society, 43, part 2; Philadelphia, 1953).

Bériou, N., *L'Avènement des maîtres de la parole: La prédication à Paris au XIIIe siècle*, 2 vols. Collection des Études Augustiniennes, Série Moyen Âge et Temps Modernes, 31–2 (Paris, 1998).

Biale, R., *Women and Jewish Law* (New York, 1984).

Binmore, K., *Just Playing: Game Theory and the Social Contract II* (Cambridge, Mass., 1998).

Natural Justice (Oxford, 2005).

Playing for Real: A Text on Game Theory (Oxford, 2007).

Rational Decisions (Princeton, 2009).

Blackman, W. S., 'The Rosary in Magic and Religion', *Folklore*, 29 (1918), 255–80.

Blouin, F. X., *et al.*, *Vatican Archives: An Inventory and Guide to the Historical Documents of the Holy See* (New York, 1998).

Borkowski, A., and du Plessis, P., *Textbook on Roman Law*, 3rd edn (Oxford, 2005).

Borofsky, R., Kane, H. K., Obeyesekere, G., and Sahlins, M., 'CA Forum on Theory in Anthropology: Cook, Lono, Obeyesekere, and Sahlins [and Comments and Reply]', *Current Anthropology*, 38 (1997), 255–82.

Boucock, C., *In the Grip of Freedom: Law and Modernity in Max Weber* (Toronto, 2000).

Boudon, R., 'A propos du relativisme des valeurs: Retour sur quelques intuitions majeures de Tocqueville, Durkheim et Weber', *Revue française de sociologie*, 47 (2006), 877–97.

Bouglé, C., *Leçons de sociologie sur l'évolution des valeurs* (Paris, 1922).

Bovens, L., and Hartmann, S., *Bayesian Epistemology* (Oxford, 2003).

Boyer, P., 'Functional Origins of Religious Concepts: Ontological and Strategic Selection in Evolved Minds', *Journal of the Royal Anthropological Institute*, 6 (2000), 195–214.

Brentano, R., *Two Churches: England and Italy in the Thirteenth Century* (Princeton, 1968).

Breuer, S. *Bürokratie und Charisma: Zur politischen Soziologie Max Webers* (Darmstadt, 1994).

Brubaker, R., *The Limits of Rationality: An Essay on the Social and Moral Thought of Max Weber* (London, 1984).

Bruce, S., *Choice and Religion: A Critique of Rational Choice Theory* (Oxford, 1999).

Buckser, A., and Glazier, S. D. (eds.), *The Anthropology of Religious Conversion* (Lanham, Md., 2003).

Caiazza, P., 'L'archivio storico della Sacra Congregazione del Consilio (primi appunti per un problema di riordinamento)', *Ricerche di storia sociale e religiosa*, NS 42 (1992), 7–24.

Callinicos, A., *Making History: Agency, Structure and Change in Social Theory*, 2nd edn (Leiden, 2004).

Carroll, A. J., SJ, *Protestant Modernity: Weber, Secularisation and Protestantism* (Scranton, Pa., 2007).

Chadwick, O., *The Early Reformation on the Continent* (Oxford, 2001).

The Reformation (Harmondsworth, 1972).

The Victorian Church, vol. 1: 1829–1859 (London, 1971).

Chalcraft, D. J., and Harrington, A., see *The Protestant Ethic Debate*.

Chong, D., *Rational Lives: Norms and Values in Politics and Society* (Chicago, 2000).

Clark, S., *Thinking with Demons: The Idea of Witchcraft in Early Modern Europe* (Oxford, 1997).

Cohen, G. A., *If You're an Egalitarian, How Come You're So Rich?* (Cambridge, Mass., 2001).

Karl Marx's Theory of History: A Defence (Oxford, 2000).

Coleman, J. S., *Foundations of Social Theory* (Cambridge, Mass., 1990).

Crook, J. A., 'The Development of Roman Private Law', in J. A. Crook *et al.* (eds.), *The Cambridge Ancient History*, 2nd edn, ix: *The Last Age of the Roman Republic, 146–43 B.C.* (Cambridge, 1994), 531–59.

Law and Life of Rome (London, 1967).

Cross, R., 'Confessions and Cognate Matters: An English View', *Columbia Law Review*, 66 (1966), 79–93.

Dahan, G., *L'Exégèse chrétienne de la Bible en Occident medieval, XIIe–XIVe siècle* (Paris, 1999).

Davidson, D., *Essays on Actions and Events* (Oxford, 2001).

'Incoherence and Irrationality', in his *Problems of Rationality*, 189–98.

'The Objectivity of Values', in his *Problems of Rationality*, 39–57.

'Paradoxes of Irrationality', in his *Problems of Rationality*, 169–87 (originally published in 1982).

'Problems in the Explanation of Action', in his *Problems of Rationality*, 101–16 (originally published in 1987).

Problems of Rationality (Oxford, 2004).

Davis, J., *Exchange* (Minneapolis, 1992).

d'Avray, D. L., 'Comparative History of Memorial Preaching', *Transactions of the Royal Historical Society*, 5th ser., 40 (1990), 25–42.

Death and the Prince: Memorial Preaching before 1350 (Oxford, 1994).

'Max Weber and Comparative Legal History', in A. Lewis and M. Lobban (eds.), *Law and History* (Current Legal Issues, 6; Oxford, 2004), 189–99.

Medieval Marriage: Symbolism and Society (Oxford, 2005).

Medieval Religious Rationalities (Cambridge, 2010).

'Papal Authority and Religious Sentiment in the Late Middle Ages', in D. Wood (ed.), *The Church and Sovereignty, c.590–1918: Essays in Honour of Michael Wilks* (Studies in Church History Subsidia, 9; Oxford, 1991), 393–408.

The Preaching of the Friars: Sermons Diffused from Paris before 1300 (Oxford, 1985).

'Printing, Mass Communication, and Religious Reformation: The Middle Ages and After', in Julia Crick and Alexandra Walsham (eds.), *The Uses of Script and Print, 1300–1700* (Cambridge, 2004), 50–70.

Deegalle, M., *Popularising Buddhism: Preaching as Performance in Sri Lanka* (Albany, NY, 2006).

Del Re, N., *La Curia Romana: Lineamenti storico-giuridici*, 4th edn (Vatican City, 1998).

De Victoria, Francisco, *see* Vittoria.

Dokumente zu Luthers Entwicklung (bis 1519), ed. O. Scheel (Sammlung ausgewählter kirche- und dogmengeschichtlicher Quellenschriften, Zweite Reihe, 9; Tübingen, 1911).

Douglas, M., *Evans-Pritchard* (Fontana, 1980).

A Feeling for Hierarchy (Marianist Award Lecture; University of Dayton, 2002).

How Institutions Think (Syracuse, NY, 1986).

Natural Symbols (London, 1996).

Purity and Danger: An Analysis of the Concepts of Pollution and Taboo (London, 2002).

'Rightness of Categories', in Douglas and Hull (eds.), *How Classification Works*, 239–71.

and Hull, D. (eds.), *How Classification Works: Nelson Goodman among the Social Sciences* (Edinburgh, 1992).

Dowding, K., 'Choice: Its increase and its Value', *British Journal of Political Science*, 22 (1992), 301–14.

Duncan, C. R., 'Untangling Conversion: Religious Change and Identity among the Forest Tobelo of Indonesia', *Ethnology*, 42 (2003), 307–22.

Earman, J., *Bayes or Bust? A Critical Examination of Bayesian Confirmation Theory* (Cambridge, Mass., 1992).

Hume's Abject Failure: The Argument against Miracles (Oxford, 2000).

Eisen, A., 'The Meanings and Confusions of Weberian "Rationality"', *British Journal of Sociology*, 29 (1978), 57–70.

Elman, B. A., *A Cultural History of Civil Examinations in Late Imperial China* (Berkeley, 2000).

Elster, J., *Sour Grapes: Studies in the Subversion of Rationality* (Cambridge, 1983).

Evans-Pritchard, E. E., *Nuer Religion* (Oxford, 1956).

Witchcraft, Oracles and Magic among the Azande, abridged with an introduction by E. Gillies (Oxford, 1976).

Fagnanus, Prosper, *P. F. Commentaria (super quinque libros Decretalium)*, 3 pts. (Rome, 1661; British Library call number RB.31.C.276)

Favereau, O., 'The Missing Piece in Rational Choice Theory', *Revue française de sociologie*, 46 (2005), supplement, 103–22.

Feyerabend, P., *Farewell to Reason* (London, 1987).

Fogelin, R. J., *A Defence of Hume on Miracles* (Princeton, 2003).

Foxhall, L., and Lewis, A. D. E. (eds.), *Greek Law in its Political Setting: Justifications not Justice* (Oxford and New York, 1996).

Francisco de Victoria, *see* Vittoria.

Freiberger, O., *Der Orden in der Lehre: Zur religiösen Deutung des Sangha im frühen Buddhismus* (Studies in Oriental Religions, 47; Wiesbaden, 2000).

Friedberg, E., *Corpus Iuris Canonici*, 2 vols. (Leipzig, 1879–81; repr. Leipzig, 1922 and Graz, 1959).

Friedman, J., 'Introduction: Economic Approaches to Politics', in Friedman (ed.), *The Rational Choice Controversy: Economic Modes of Politics Reconsidered* (New Haven and London, 1996), 1–24.

Friedrich-Silber, I., *Virtuosity, Charisma, and Social Order: A Comparative Sociological Study of Monasticism in Theravada Buddhism and Medieval Catholicism* (Cambridge, 1995).

Galland, O., and Lemel, Y., 'Présentation', in *Revue française de sociologie*, 47/4 (2006), 683–5.

Gauchat, P., *Hierarchia Catholica Medii et Recentioris Aevi*, vol. 4: *A Pontificatu Clementis PP. VIII (1592) usque ad Pontificatum Alexandri PP. VII (1667)* (Monasterii, 1935).

Geertz, C., 'Thick Description: Toward an Interpretive Theory of Culture', in id., *The Interpretation of Cultures: Selected Essays* (London, 1973; repr. 1993).

Gernet, J., *Les Aspects économiques du bouddhisme dans la société chinoise du Vᵉ au Xᵉ siècle* (Publications de l'École Française d'Extrême-Orient, 39; Saigon, 1956).

A History of Chinese Civilisation (Cambridge, 1996).

Giddens, A., 'Jürgen Habermas', in Q. Skinner (ed.), *The Return of Grand Theory to the Human Sciences* (Cambridge, 1985), 121–39.

New Rules of Sociological Method: A Positive Critique of Interpretative Ideologies, 2nd edn (Stanford, 1993).

Gigerenzer, G., and Selten, R., 'Rethinking Rationality', in Gigerenzer and Selten, *Bounded Rationality: The Adaptive Toolbox* (Cambridge, Mass., 2001), 1–12.

Gildea, R., *Education in Provincial France, 1800–1914: A Study of Three Departments* (Oxford, 1983).

Godelier, M., *Rationalité et irrationalité en économie* (Économie et socialisme, 5; Paris, 1966).

Rationality and Irrationality in Economics, trans. B. Pearce (London, 1972).

Goff, R., 'Denning, Alfred Thompson', in *Oxford Dictionary of National Biography*, xv. 812–13.

Gombrich, R., *Theravada Buddhism: A Social History from Ancient Benares to Modern Colombo* (London, 1988).

Goulde, J., review of R. E. Buswell, *The Zen Monastic Experience* (Princeton, 1992), in *History of Religions*, 35 (1995), 187–8.

Graeber, D., *Toward an Anthropological Theory of Value* (New York, 2001).

Gray, J., *Black Mass: Apocalyptic Religion and the Death of Utopia* (London, 2007).

Green, P., and Shapiro, I., 'Pathologies Revisited: Reflections on our Critics', in Friedman (ed.), *The Rational Choice Controversy*, 235–76.

Pathologies of Rational Choice Theory: A Critique of Applications in Political Science (New Haven, 1994).

Guitton, J., *Écrire comme on se souvient* (Paris, 1974).

Gunawardana, R. A. L. H., *Robe and Plough: Monasticism and Economic Interest in Early Medieval Sri Lanka* (Tucson, Ariz., 1979).

Harrell, D. E., 'Oral Roberts: Religious Media Pioneer', in Sweet (ed.), *Communication*, 320–34.

Hart, H. L. A., *The Concept of Law*, 2nd edn (Oxford, 1994).

Harvey, P., *An Introduction to Buddhism: Teachings, History and Practices* (Cambridge, 1990).

Haskett, T. H., 'The Medieval Court of Chancery', *Law and History Review*, 14 (1996), 245–313.

Heath, J., *Communicative Action and Rational Choice* (Cambridge, Mass., 2001).

Heisenberg, W., *Physics and Beyond: Encounters and Conversation*, trans. A. J. Pomerans (London, 1971).

Henkel, W., 'Das Inventar des "Fondo Concilii" im Archiv der Konzilskongregation', *Annuarium Historiae Conciliorum*, 15 (1983), 430–51.

Heyd, U., 'Some Aspects of the Ottoman Fetva', *Bulletin of the School of Oriental and African Studies*, 32 (1969), 35–56.

Hilling, N., *Procedure at the Roman Curia: A Concise and Practical Handbook* (New York, 1907).

Hinschius, P., *Das Kirchenrecht der Katholiken und Protestanten in Deutschland*, vol. 1: *System des katholischen Kirchenrechts mit besonderen Rücksicht auf Deutschland* (Berlin, 1869).

Holden, L., *Hindu Divorce: A Legal Anthropology* (Aldershot, 2008).

Hollis, M., *The Philosophy of Social Science: An Introduction* (Cambridge, 2002).

and Lukes, S., *Rationality and Relativism* (Cambridge, Mass., 1982).

Hsiang-Ling Hsu, E., 'Visualisation Meditation and the Siwei Icon in Chinese Buddhist Sculpture', *Artibus Asiae*, 62 (2002), 5–32.

Hume, D., *An Enquiry Concerning Human Understanding*, ed. T. L. Beauchamp (Oxford, 2000).

Humphrey, C., and Laidlaw, J., *The Archetypal Actions of Ritual: A Theory of Ritual Illustrated by the Jain Rite of Worship* (Oxford, 1994).

Hurter, H., *Nomenclator Litterarius Theologiae Catholicae, theologos exhibens aetate, natione, disciplinis distinctos*, 3rd edn (Vienna, 1903–13), ii (1906).

Huyler, S. P., *Meeting God: Elements of Hindu Devotion* (New Haven, 1999).

Ignatius of Loyola, *The Spiritual Exercises*, trans. T. Corbishley (Wheathampstead, 1973).

Imber, C., *Ebu's-su'ud: The Islamic Legal Tradition* (Edinburgh, 1997).

'Eleven Fetvas of the Ottoman Sheikh ul-Islam 'Abdurrahim', in Masud *et al.* (eds.), *Islamic Legal Interpretation*, ch. 11.

Israel, J., *Radical Enlightenment: Philosophy and the Making of Modernity 1650–1750* (Oxford, 2001).

Jansen, M. B., *China in the Tokugawa World* (Cambridge, Mass., 1992).

Jasper, D., and Fuhrmann, H., *Papal Letters in the Early Middle Ages* (Washington, DC, 2001).

Jerolmack, C., and Porpora, D., 'Religion, Rationality and Experience: A Response to the New Rational Choice Theory of Religion', *Sociological Theory*, 22 (2004), 140–60.

Jha, M., 'The Origin, Type, Spread and Nature of Hindu Pilgrimage', in id. (ed.), *Dimensions of Pilgrimage* (New Delhi, 1985), 11–16.

Joas, H.. *The Genesis of Values* (Cambridge, 2000).

Johansen, B., *Contingency in a Sacred Law: Legal and Ethical Norms in Muslim Fiqh* (Leiden, 1999).

Jones, J. W., *The Law and Legal Theory of the Greeks: An Introduction* (Oxford, 1956).

Jones, W. R., 'The English Church and Royal Propaganda during the Hundred Years War', *Journal of British Studies*, 19/1 (Autumn 1979), 18–30.

Kaelber, L., *The Protestant Ethic Turns 100: Essays on the Centenary of the Weber Thesis* (Boulder, Colo.: 2005).

Kalberg, S., 'Max Weber's Types of Rationality: Cornerstones for the Analysis of Rationalisation Processes in History', *American Journal of Sociology*, 85 (1980), 1145–79.

Kant, I., *Grundlegung zur Metaphysik der Sitten*, ed. T. Valentiner (Stuttgart, 1984).

Die Metaphysik der Sitten, ed. H. Ebeling (Stuttgart, 1990).

Kennedy, D., 'Legal Formality', *Journal of Legal Studies*, 2 (1973), 351–98.

Khalid Masud, *see* Masud.

Kienzle, B. (ed.), *The Sermon* (Typologie des Sources du Moyen Âge Occidental, 81–3; Turnhout, 2000).

King, U., 'Some Reflections on Sociological Approaches to the Study of Modern Hinduism', *Numen*, 36 (1989), 72–97.

Kippenberg, H. G., and Riesebrodt, M. (eds.), *Max Webers 'Religionssystematik'* (Tübingen, 2001).

Kirsch, T. G., 'Restaging the Will to Believe: Religious Pluralism, Anti-Syncretism, and the Problem of Belief', *American Anthropologist*, 106 (2004), 699–709.

Knoke, D., 'Incentives in Collective Action Organisations', *American Sociological Review*, 53 (1988), 311–29.

Körner, A., 'Antiklerikale Ideen und religiöse Formen: Arbeiterkultur in Frankreich und Deutschland, 1830–1890', in B. Unfried (ed.), *Riten, Mythen und Symbole: Die Arbeiterbewegung zwischen 'Zivilreligion' und Volkskultur* (Leipzig, 1999), 60–89.

Das Lied von einer anderen Welt: Kulturelle Praxis im französischen und deutschen Arbeitermilieu, 1840–1890 (Frankfurt, 1997).

Kronman, A. T., *Max Weber* (London, 1983).

Kuhn, T. S., *The Structure of Scientific Revolutions* (Chicago, 1962).

Lacey, N., *A Life of H. L. Hart: The Nightmare and the Noble Dream* (Oxford, 2004).

Langlois, J. D., Jr., '"Living Law" in Sung and Yüan Jurisprudence', *Harvard Journal of Asiatic Studies*, 41 (1981), 165–217.

Larsen, T., *Contested Christianity: The Political and Social Contexts of Victorian Theology* (Waco, Tex., 2004).

Levenson, J. R., *Confucian China and its Modern Fate*, 3 vols. (London, 1958–65).

Lewis, P. S., 'War Propaganda and Historiography in Fifteenth-Century France and England', *Transactions of the Royal Historical Society*, 15 (1965), 1–21.

'Lire Max Weber': issue of the *Revue française de sociologie*, 46/4 (2005).

Lobrichon, G., *La Bible au Moyen Age*, Les Médiévistes français, 3 (Paris, 2003).

Longère, J., *La Prédication médiévale* (Études Augustiniennes; Paris, 1983).

Luce, R. D., and Raiffa, H., *Games and Decisions: Introduction and Critical Survey* (New York, 1957).

Lukes, S., 'Some Problems about Rationality', in Wilson (ed.), *Rationality*, 195–213.

MacCormack, G., *The Spirit of Traditional Chinese Law* (Athens, Ga., 1996).

MacIntyre, A., *After Virtue: A Study in Moral Theory* (London, 1981).

—— *Whose Justice? Which Rationality?* (London, 1988).

McKnight, B. E., *Law and Order in Sung China* (Cambridge, 1992).

—— and Liu, J. T. C., *The Enlightened Judgements, Ch'ing-ming Chi: The Sung Dynasty Collection* (Albany, NY, 1999).

Makdisi, J., 'Legal Logic and Equity in Islamic Law', *American Journal of Comparative Law*, 33 (1985), 63–92.

Marsh, R. M., 'Weber's Misunderstanding of Traditional Chinese Law', *American Journal of Sociology*, 106 (2000), 281–302.

Martin, M., *Verstehen: The Uses of Understanding in Social Science* (New Brunswick, NJ, 2000).

Masud, M. Khalid, Messick, B., and Powers, D. S., *Islamic Legal Interpretation: Muftis and their Fatwas* (Cambridge, Mass., 1996).

Meiland, J. W., 'Bernard Williams' Relativism', *Mind*, NS 88 (1979), 258–62.

Melchert, C., *The Formation of the Sunni Schools of Law, 9th–10th Centuries C.E.* (Leiden, 1997).

Mele, A. R., and Rawling, P., *The Oxford Handbook of Rationality* (Oxford, 2004).

Menski, W., *Comparative Law in a Global Context: The Legal Systems of Asia and Africa*, 2nd edn (Cambridge, 2006).

Merryman, J. H., *The Civil Law Tradition: An Introduction to the Legal Systems of Western Europe and Latin America*, 2nd edn (Stanford, 1985).

Michaels, A., *Der Hinduismus: Geschichte und Gegenwart* (Munich, 1998).

Mihelic, J. L., 'The Influence of Form Criticism on the Study of the Old Testament', *Journal of Bible and Religion*, 19 (1951), 120–9.

Millar, A., *Understanding People: Normativity and Rationalizing Explanation* (Oxford, 2004).

Millar, F., *The Emperor in the Roman World* (London, 1977).

Mommsen, W. J., *The Age of Bureaucracy: Perspectives on the Political Sociology of Max Weber* (Oxford, 1974).

—— *Max Weber and German Politics, 1890–1920*, trans. Michael S. Steinberg (Chicago, 1984).

Murray, A., 'Piety and Impiety in Thirteenth-Century Italy', in G. J. Cuming and D. Baker (eds.), *Popular Belief and Practice* (Studies in Church History, 8; Cambridge, 1972), 83–106.

Newman, J. H., *An Essay in Aid of a Grammar of Assent* (New York, 1955).

Norris, R. S., 'Converting to What? Embodied Culture and the Adoption of New Beliefs', in Buckser and Glazier (eds.), *The Anthropology of Religious Conversion*, 171–81.

Novae Declarationes Congregationis S.R.E. Cardinalium ad Decreta Sacros. Concil. Tridentini, iisdem Declarationibus conserta (Lyons, 1633) (British Library call no. 1600/181).

Novak, D., 'The Structure of Halakhah', in R. M. Seltzer (ed.), *Judaism: A People and its History* (New York and London, 1989), 221–34.

Nozick, R., *The Nature of Rationality* (Princeton, 1993).

Oberman, H. A., *Luther: Man between God and the Devil* (New York, 1992).

Obeyesekere, G., *The Apotheosis of Captain Cook: European Mythmaking in the Pacific* (Princeton, 1992, 1997).

O'Brien, P., 'Historiographical Traditions and Modern Imperatives for the Restoration of Global History', *Journal of Global History*, 1 (2006), 3–39.

Oesterlé, G., 'Consummation', in *Dictionnaire de droit canonique*, vol. 4 (Paris, 1947), cols. 381–2.

Ostrom, E., 'Rational Choice Theory and Institutional Analysis: Toward Complementarity', *American Political Science Review*, 85 (1991), 237–43.

Oxford Dictionary of National Biography, ed. H. C. G. Matthew and Brian Harrison (Oxford, 2004).

Oxford Dictionary of the Christian Church, ed. F. L. Cross and E. A. Livingstone, 3rd edn (Oxford, 1997).

Oxford Dictionary of World Religions, ed. J. Bowker (Oxford, 1997).

Ozment, S., *The Age of Reform, 1250–1550: An Intellectual and Religious History of Late Medieval and Reformation Europe* (New Haven, 1980)

Pallottini, S., *Collectio omnium conclusionum et resolutionum quae in causis propositis apud Sacram Congregationem Cardinalium S. Concilii Tridentini interpretum prodierunt ab eius institutione anno MDLXIV ad annum MCCCCLX*, 17 vols. (1868–93).

Papineau, D., 'The Evolution of Means–Ends Reasoning', in his *The Roots of Reason: Philosophical Essays on Rationality, Evolution, and Probability* (Oxford, 2003), 83–129.

Parayre, R., *La Sacrée Congregation du Concile: Son histoire, sa procédure, son autorité* (Paris, 1897).

Pelikan, J., *The Christian Tradition: A History of the Development of Doctrine*, vol. 4: *Reformation of Church and Dogma (1300–1700)* (Chicago, 1984).

Peter, F., and Schmid, H. B. (eds.), *Rationality and Commitment* (Oxford, 2007).

Pettegree, A., *The Reformation and the Culture of Persuasion* (Cambridge, 2005).

Plöchl, W. M., *Geschichte des Kirchenrechts*, iv (Munich, 1966).

Ponting, C., 'R. v. Ponting', *Journal of Law and Society*, 14 (1987), 366–72.

Prodi, P., 'Note sulla genesi del diritto nella Chiesa post-tridentina', in *Legge e vangelo: discussione su una legge fondamentale per la Chiesa* (Testi e Ricerche di Scienze Religiose, 8; Brescia, 1972), 190–223.

Prosper Fagnanus, *see* Fagnanus.

The Protestant Ethic Debate: Max Weber's Replies to his Critics, 1907–1910, ed. D. J. Chalcraft and A. Harrington, trans. A. Harrington and M. Shields (Liverpool, 2001).

Radkau, J., *Max Weber: Die Leidenschaft des Denkens* (Munich, 2005).

Ranger, T. O., 'Connexions between "Primary Resistance" Movements and Modern Mass Nationalism in East and Central Africa', *Journal of African History*, 9 (1968), 437–53.

Rawls, J., *A Theory of Justice*, rev. edn (Oxford, 1999).

Rébelliau, A., *Bossuet, historien du Protestantisme: Étude sur l'Histoire des variations et sur la controverse entre les Protestants et les Catholiques au dix-septième siècle* (Paris, 1891).

Revue française de sociologie, 47/4 (2006) (issue devoted to the sociology of values, with special reference to Europe).

Reynolds, S., 'Social Mentalities and the Case of Medieval Scepticism', *Transactions of the Royal Historical Society*, 6th ser. 1 (1991), 21–41.

Richter, E. L., and von Schulte, F., *Canones et decreta Concilii Tridentini ex editione Romana A. MDCCCXXXIV. repetiti. Accedunt S. Congr. Card. Conc. Trid. interpretum declarationes ac resolutiones ex ipso resolutionum thesauro, bullario romano et benedicti XIV. S. P. operibus*... (Leipzig, 1853).

Ringer, F., *Max Weber: An Intellectual Biography* (Chicago, 2004).

Ritzler, R. and Sefrin, P., *Hierarchia Catholica Medii et Recentioris Aevi*, v (Padua, 1952).

Roberts, J. M., *The New Penguin History of the World*, 4th edn (London, 2002).

Romita, F., 'Lo "Studio" della Sacra Congregazione del Concilio e gli "Studi" della Curia Romana', in *La Sacra Congregazione del Concilio: Quarto Centenario dalla Fondazione (1564–1964)* (Vatican City, 1964), 633–77.

Rosen, F., 'The Political Context of Aristotle's Categories of Justice', *Phronesis*, 20 (1975), 228–40.

Rosen, L., *The Justice of Islam* (Oxford, 2000).

Roth, A. E., 'Introduction to Experimental Economics', in J. H. Kagel and A. E. Roth, *Handbook of Experimental Economics* (Princeton, 1995).

Roth, G., and Wittich, C., *Economy and Society: An Outline of Interpretative Sociology*, 2 vols. (Berkeley, 1978).

Rubin, M., *Corpus Christi: The Eucharist in Late Medieval Culture* (Cambridge, 1991).

Rubinstein, A., *Modeling Bounded Rationality* (Cambridge, Mass., 1998).

Runciman, W. G., *A Critique of Max Weber's Philosophy of Social Science* (Cambridge, 1972).

A Treatise on Social Theory, vol. 1: *The Methodology of Social Theory* (Cambridge, 1983).

A Treatise on Social Theory, vol. 2: *Substantive Social Theory* (Cambridge, 1989).

Ruotsila, M., 'The Catholic Apostolic Church in British Politics', *Journal of Ecclesiastical History*, 56 (2005), 75–91.

La Sacra Congregazione del Concilio: Quarto centenario dalla fondazione (1564–1964) (Vatican City, 1989).

Sahlins, M., *How 'Natives' Think: About Captain Cook, for Example* (Chicago, 1995).

Sanchez, Thomas, *De sancto matrimonii sacramento disputationum tomi tres*, i, Lib. 2 (Avignon, 1689) (British Library call number 1240.k.1).

Satris, S. A., 'The Theory of Value and the Rise of Ethical Emotivism', *Journal of the History of Ideas*, 43 (1982), 109–28.

Saussure, F., *Cours de linguistique générale*, ed. Charles Bally, Albert Sechehaye, and Riedlinger (Lausanne, 1916).

Schluchter, W., *The Rise of Western Rationalism: Max Weber's Developmental History*, trans. and introd. Guenther Roth (Berkeley, 1981).

Schutte, A. J., 'La Congregazione del Concilio e lo scioglimento dei voti religiosi: Rapporti tra fratelli e sorelle', *Rivista storica italiana*, 118 (2006), 51–79.

Sen, A., *Rationality and Freedom* (Cambridge, Mass., 2002).

Sharot, S., *A Comparative Sociology of World Religions: Virtuosos, Priests and Popular Religion* (New York, 2001).

Shepsle, K. A., and Bonchek, M. S., *Analyzing Politics: Rationality, Behaviour and Institutions* (New York, 1997).

Silber, I. F., *Virtuosity, Charisma, and Social Order: A Comparative Sociological Study of Monasticism in Theravada Buddhism and Medieval Catholicism* (Cambridge, 1995).

Simpson, A. W. B., *Cannibalism and the Common Law: The Story of the Last Tragic Voyage of the Mignonette and the Strange Legal Proceedings to which It Gave Rise* (Chicago, 1984).

Skinner, Q., 'Interpretation, Rationality and Truth', in id., *Visions of Politics*, vol. 1: *Regarding Method* (Cambridge, 2002), 27–56.

Smalley, B., *Study of the Bible in the Middle Ages* (Oxford, 1983).

Smart, J. J. C., 'Ruth Anna Putnam and the Fact–Value Distinction', *Philosophy*, 74 (1999), 431–7.

Spiro, M. E., *Buddhism and Society: A Great Tradition and its Burmese Vicissitudes* (London, 1971).

Stark, R., and Bainbridge, W. S., *A Theory of Religion* (New Brunswick, NJ, 1996).

Stiegler, M. A., *Dispensation, Dispensationswesen und Dispensationsrecht im Kirchenrecht* (Mainz, 1901).

Stone, L., 'The Revival of Narrative: Reflections on a New Old History', *Past and Present*, 85 (1979), 3–24.

Stout, H. S., 'Religion, Communications, and the Career of George Whitefield', in Sweet (ed.), *Communication and Change*, 108–25.

Stroud, S., and Tappolet, C. (eds.), *Weakness of Will and Practical Irrationality* (Oxford, 2003).

Swartz, M. L., 'The Rules of the [*sic*] Popular Preaching in Twelfth-Century Baghdad, According to Ibn al-Jawzî', in *Prédication et propagande au Moyen Âge: Islam, Byzance, Occident: Penn–Paris–Dumbarton Oaks Colloquia, iii*, organized by G. Makdisi *et al.* (Paris, 1983), 223–39.

Swatos, W. H., Jr., and Kaelber, L., *The Protestant Ethic Turns 100: Essays on the Centenary of the Weber Thesis* (Boulder, Col., 2005).

Sweet, I. (ed.), *Communication and Change in American Religious History* (Grand Rapids, Mich., 1993).

Swinburne, R. (ed.), *Bayes's Theorem* (Proceedings of the British Academy, 113; Oxford, 2002).

Tambiah, S. J., *Magic, Science, Religion, and the Scope of Rationality* (Cambridge, 1990).

Tanner, N. P., Alberigo, G., et al., Decrees of the Ecumenical Councils, vol. 2: Trent to Vatican II (London, 1990).

Taylor, C., 'Rationality', in Hollis and Lukes (eds.), Rationality and Relativism, 87–105.

Thomas Aquinas, Comentarios a la Secunda secundae de Santo Tomás, ed. V. Beltrán de Heredia, 5 vols. (Salamanca, 1932).

Commento alle Sentenze di Pietro Lombardo e testo integrale di Pietro Lombardo. Libro quarto. Distinzioni 24–42. L'Ordine, il Matrimonio, trans. and ed. 'Redazione delle Edizioni Studio Domenicano' (Bologna, 2001).

Compendium theologiae (Sancti Thomae de Aquino Opera omnia iussu Leonis XIII P.M. edita, 42; Rome, 1979).

Sancti Thomae Aquinatis... opera omnia... Leonis XIII P.M. edita (Rome, 1882–).

Triantaphyllopoulos, J., Das Rechtsdenken der Griechen (Münchener Beiträge zur Papyrusforschung und antiken Rechtsgeschichte, 78; Munich, 1985).

Uecker, S., Die Rationalisierung des Rechts: Max Weber's Rechtssoziologie (Berlin, 2005).

Vatican Secret Archives, Collection Index and Related Description and Research Resources (Vatican City, 2006).

Vinaya Texts, Part I: The Pâtimokkha. The Mahâvagga, I–IV, trans. T. W. Rhys Davids and H. Oldenberg (The Sacred Books of the East, 13; Oxford, 1881; repr. Delhi, 1968).

Vittoria [Francisco de Victoria], Relectiones Theologicae [etc.] (Lyons, 1587) (British Library call number 4374.aaa.18).

Summa Sacramentorum Ecclesiae ex doctrina Francisci a Victoria... cui adiecimus conclusiones in singulis quaestionibus (Venice, 1586) (British Library call number 3832 a.34).

Summa Sacramentorum [etc.] per... Thomam a Chaues illius discipulum... Huic ex tertia Authoris recognitione, nunc denuo multo plures quam antea quaestiones accesserunt (Salamanca, 1570) (British Library call number Cup. 408.nn.14).

Walker, D., The Oxford Companion to Law (Oxford, 1980).

Walker, R. C. S., The Coherence Theory of Truth: Realism, Anti-Realism, Idealism (London, 1988).

Wallerstein, I., 'Liberalism and Democracy: Frères Ennemis?', in id., The End of the World as We Know It: Social Science for the Twenty-First Century (Minneapolis, 1999), 87–103.

Webb, D., Medieval European Pilgrimage, c. 700–c.1500 (Basingstoke, 2002).

Weber, M., Gesammelte Aufsätze zur Religionssoziologie, 2 vols. (Tübingen, 1988).

Gesammelte Aufsätze zur Wissenschaftslehre, ed. J. Winckelmann, 7th edn (Tübingen, 1988).

'Die protestantische Ethik und der Geist des Kapitalismus', in his Gesammelte Aufsätze zur Religionssoziologie, vol. 1 (Tübingen, 1988), 17–206.

Wirtschaft und Gesellschaft, 5th edn, ed. J. Winckelmann, 3 vols. (Tübingen, 1976).

Weber, Marianne, Max Weber: Ein Lebensbild (Tübingen, 1984).

Whimster, S., Understanding Max Weber (London, 2007).

White, S. A., Sovereign Virtue: Aristotle on the Relation between Happiness and Prosperity (Stanford Series in Philosophy; Stanford, 1992).

Wickham, C., *Framing the Middle Ages: Europe and the Mediterranean 400–800* (Oxford, 2005).

Problems in Doing Comparative History (Reuter Lecture; Southampton, 2005).

Wieacker, F., *Römische Rechtsgeschichte: Quellenkunde, Rechtsbildung, Jurisprudenz und Rechtsliteratur*, vol. 1: *Einleitung, Quellenkunde, Frühzeit und Republic* (Rechtsgeschichte des Altertums im Rahmen des Handbuchs der Altertumswissenschaft, 3.1.1; Munich, 1988).

Wigger, J. H., *Taking Heaven by Storm: Methodism and the Rise of Popular Christianity in America* (New York, 1998).

Wijayaratna, M., *Buddhist Monastic Life according to the Texts of the Theravada Tradition*, trans. C. Grangier and S. Collins, introd. S. Collins (Cambridge, 1990).

Williams, B., *Morality: An Introduction to Ethics* (Cambridge, 1976).

Wilson, B. R. (ed.), *Rationality* (Oxford, 1970).

Winch, P., *The Idea of a Social Science and its Relation to Philosophy* (2nd edn, London, 1990).

'Understanding a Primitive Society' (1964), repr. in Wilson (ed.), *Rationality*, 78–111.

Winckelmann, J., *see* Weber, M.

Winston-Allen, A., *Stories of the Rose: The Making of the Rosary in the Middle Ages* (University Park, Pa., 1997).

Wittgenstein, Ludwig, *On Certainty*, ed. G. E. M. Anscombe and G. H. von Wright, trans. D. Paul and G. E. M. Anscombe (Oxford, 1974).

Wood, A. W., *Kantian Ethics* (Cambridge, 2008).

Zamboni, J. F., *Collectio declarationum Sacrae Congregationis Cardinalium Sacri Concilii Tridentini interpretum*, 8 vols. (Vienna and Rome, 1812–1816); 4 vols. (Arras, 1860–8).

Zarri, H., 'Il matrimonio tridentino', in P. Prodi and W. Reinhard (eds), *Il Concilio di Trento e il moderno* (Annali dall'Istituto storico italo-germanico, 45; Bologna, 1996), 437–83.

Index

administration, Weber on, 164; *see also* bureaucracy
affect, *see* emotion
Ainslie, G., 17n.56, 40n.34
akrasia, 17
Althoff, G., 20
anarchy, 40
animals, difference from humans, 16n.52
Annales School, 11
anthropology, 13, 14, 79
  children as hermeneutic anthropologists, 121
  see also Azande; Evans-Pritchard; Obeyesekere; Sahlins
apologetics, 107, 122–3
Aquinas, *see* Thomas Aquinas
Aristotle, 63n.88, 138–40, 145, 147, 181
asceticism
  Hindu, the most rationalised, 126–7
  this-worldly, 125–6
assent, real, 90
Atiyah, P. S., and Summers, R. S., 143n.100, 146n.3, 148–9, 151–2, 165n.7, 171–3
Awakening, *see* Great Awakenings
Azande, 53–7, 79–81, 83, 89, 136

Baker, Sir John, 150, 169–71
Bangen, J. H., on the Congregation of the Council, 156–61
Bayes, 76–7
beliefs, as understood in Rational Choice Theory, 30–1
Benedict XIV, Pope, 175
Benthamism, 137
Bible, and the Reformation, 107–8
biblical criticism, German, 13, 103
Binmore, K., 29n.3, 30n.6, 31n.11, 34n.18, 40n.33, 41n.36, 43n.41, 45n.44
blood libel, 18
Boucock, C., 19

Boudon, R., 21n.75
Bouglé, C., 120–1, 122n.24
Bounded Rationality, 17, 31–2
Breuer, S., 20
Brubaker, R., 19, 20nn.71–2
Buddhist monasticism, 5, 22–4, 27, 128–30; *see also under* preaching
bureaucracy, 187
bureaucratic rationalisation, 104n.34

Callinicos, A., 36n.24, 38n.27
canon law, 9
Carroll, A. J., 9n.32
casuistry, 43–4
Catholic Apostolic Church, 100–1, 186
Catholic Church, Weber on, 187–8
Chadwick, O., 103n.30
Chalcraft, D. J., 10n.35
charisma 104–6, 108, 118–19, 157
China, Confucian, 98; *see also* Chinese law; Ch'ing Code
Chinese law, classical, 150–2, 165–9
Ch'ing Code, 150–1
Chong, D., 57
city, the Western, 7
civil (Roman) law tradition, 141–2, 147, 187; *see also* Roman law
civil wars, 39–40
Clark, S., 78–9
Cohen, G. A., 2n.3, 36, 66, 73, 95
Cold War, monogamy valued on both sides during, 74, 102
Coleman, J., 3n.4, 29n.3, 30, 42
common law, 157
comparative history, 5, 8
computers, difference from humans, 16n.52
concepts, and need for distinctions, 44
concrete thought, 89–92, 94, 108–10, 113–14
Confucian-imperial system, 98–100; *see also* Chinese law, classical

210

values, 49; *see also* value rationality
Verstehen, see hermeneutic explanation
visualisation, 134–5

war, and national identity, 98
Weber, Marianne, 7
Weber, Max, 3–8, 57–9, and *passim*
  his personal psychology, 9
  his politics, 9
  his religious convictions, 9
Wertrationalität, see value rationality
West, the, and Weber, 20
Whimster, S., 9n.29

Whitefield, George, 116–17
Wickham, C., 5nn.10, 14
Wilson, B., 3n.4
Winch, P., 15, 52–6, 75n.19,
  77n.22
witchcraft, 78–81; *see also* poison oracles
Wittgenstein, 52, 75n.19, 91
Wood, A. W., 66, 137–8
world history, analytical, 5–8, 20
  metanarratives of, 5–6

Zweckrationalität, see instrumental
  rationality